WORKING PAPERS

Managerial Accounting
Tools for Business Decision Making

5TH Edition

Jerry J. Weygandt, Ph.D., C.P.A.
Arthur Andersen Alumni Professor of Accounting
University of Wisconsin - Madison
Madison, Wisconsin

Paul D. Kimmel, Ph.D., C.P.A.
Associate Professor of Accounting
University of Wisconsin - Milwaukee
Milwaukee, Wisconsin

Donald E. Kieso, Ph.D., C.P.A.
KPMG Peat Marwick Emeritus Professor of Accountancy
Northern Illinois University
DeKalb, Illinois

Prepared By
Dick D. Wasson, M.B.A., C.P.A.
Southwestern College
San Diego State University
University of Phoenix

WILEY

John Wiley & Sons, Inc.

Cover photo credit: John Feingersh / Stone / Getty Images

To order books or for customer service call 1-800-CALL-WILEY (225-5945).

ISBN-13 978-0-470-50696-7

Printed in the United States of America

10 9 8 7 6 5 4 3 2 1

Printed and bound by Courier Westford, Inc.
Covers printed at Courier Westford Inc.

CONTENTS

Working Paper templates are provided for end-of-chapter brief exercises, Do It! exercises, exercises, problems, and broadening your perspective problems. Working Paper templates are not provided for solutions that are textual in nature.

BE1-7

	Product Costs		
	Direct Materials	Direct Labor	Factory Overhead
(a)			
(b)			
(c)			
(d)			

BE1-8

			Factory Overhead
(a)			
(b)			

BE1-9

	Diaz Company
	Balance Sheet
	December 31, 2011

1	Current assets			
2				
3				
4				
5				
6				
7				
8				
9				
10				
11				
12				
13				
14				
15				

BE1-10

	Direct Materials Used	Direct Labor Used	Factory Overhead	Total Manufacturing Costs
(1)	$ 25000	$ 61000	$ 5000	
(2)		$ 75000	$ 14000	$ 296000
(3)	$ 55000		$ 11000	$ 310000

BE1-11

	Total Manufacturing Costs	Work in Process (January 1)	Work in Process (December 31)	Cost of Goods Manufactured
(1)		$ 120000	$ 82000	
(2)	$ 296000		$ 98000	$ 321000
(3)	$ 310000	$ 463000		$ 715000

Rolen Manufacturing Company			
Cost of Goods Manufactured Schedule			
For the Month Ended April 30			

1	(a)			1
2				2
3				3
4				4
5				5
6				6
7				7
8				8
9				9
10	(b)			10
11				11
12				12
13				13
14				14
15	(c)			15
16				16
17				17
18				18
19				19
20				20
21				21
22				22
23				23
24				24
25				25
26				26
27				27
28				28
29				29
30				30
31				31
32				32
33				33
34				34
35				35
36				36
37				37
38				38
39				39
40				40

E1-7

1	(a) Delivery service (product) costs:	
2		
3		
4		
5		
6		
7		
8		
9		
10	(b) Period costs:	
11		
12		
13		
14		
15		
16		
17		
18		
19	**E1-8**	
20	(a) Cost of goods manufactured:	
21		
22		
23		
24		
25		
26		
27		
28		
29		
30		
31		
32		
33		
34	(b) Cost of goods sold:	
35		
36		
37		
38		
39		
40		

E1-9

Garcia Manufacturing Company		
Cost of Goods Manufactured Schedule		
For the Year Ended December 31, 2011		
1 Work in process (1/1)		$ 21,000
2 Direct materials:		
3 Raw materials inventory (1/1)		
4 Add: Raw materials purchases	158,000	
5 Total raw materials available for use		
6 Less: Raw materials inventory (12/31)	12,500	
7 Direct materials used	$ 190,000	
8 Direct labor		
9 Manufacturing overhead:		
10 Indirect labor	18,000	
11 Factory depreciation	36,000	
12 Factory utilities	68,000	
13 Total overhead	122,000	
14 Total manufacturing costs		
15 Total cost of work in process		
16 Less: Work in process (12/31)		81,000
17 Cost of goods manufactured		$ 510,000

E1-10

	Case A	Case B	Case C
21 Direct materials used		$ 58,400	$ 130,000
22 Direct labor	57,000	86,000	
23 Manufacturing overhead	46,500	81,600	102,000
24 Total manufacturing costs	185,650		253,700
25 Work in process 1/1/11		16,500	
26 Total cost of work in process	221,500		337,000
27 Work in process 12/31/11		11,000	70,000
28 Cost of goods manufactured	185,275		

Alternative Approach to Solving for Missing Data									
1	**CASE A:**								1
2	(a)								2
3									3
4									4
5									5
6									6
7	(b)								7
8									8
9									9
10									10
11	(c)								11
12									12
13									13
14	**CASE B:**								14
15	(d)								15
16									16
17									17
18									18
19									19
20	(e)								20
21									21
22									22
23									23
24	(f)								24
25									25
26									26
27	**CASE C:**								27
28	(g)								28
29									29
30									30
31									31
32									32
33	(h)								33
34									34
35									35
36									36
37	(i)								37
38									38
39									39
40									40

(a)

	Direct Materials Used	Direct Labor Used	Manufacturing Overhead	Total Manufacturing Costs	Work in Process 1/1	Work in Process 12/31	Cost of Goods Manufactured
(1)	$127000	$140000	$77000		$33000		$360000
(2)		200000	132000	450000		40000	470000
(3)	80000	100000		245000	60000	80000	
(4)	70000		75000	288000	45000		270000

(b)

Mabry Company

Cost of Goods Manufactured Schedule

For the Year Ended December 31, 2011

(a)

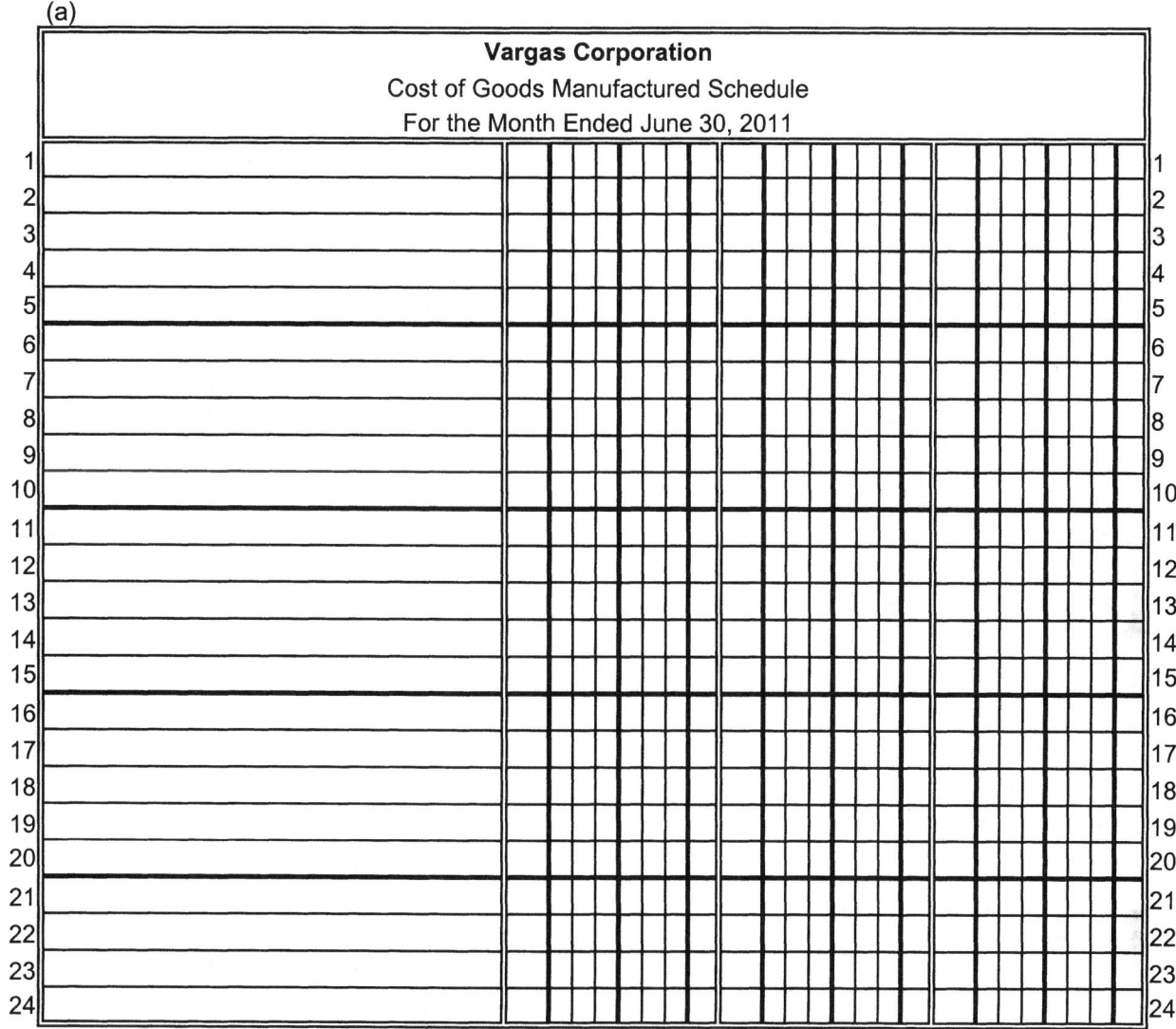

Vargas Corporation

Cost of Goods Manufactured Schedule

For the Month Ended June 30, 2011

(b)

Vargas Corporation

Income Statement (Partial)

For the Month Ended June 30, 2011

Net sales	$	87100

E1-13 (a)

	Woyak Consulting		
	Schedule of Cost of Contract Services Provided		
	For the Month Ended August 31, 2011		
1			
2			
3			
4			
5			
6			
7			
8			
9			
10			

(b)

11	
12	
13	

E1-14

(a)

1				
2				
3				
4				
5				
6				
7				
8				
9				
10				
11				
12				
13				
14				

(b)

15			
16			
17			
18			
19			
20			
21			
22			

E1-14 (Continued)

1	(c) Current assets:		1
2			2
3			3
4			4
5			5
6			6
7	(d)		7
8			8
9			9
10			10
11			11
12			12
13			13

(a)

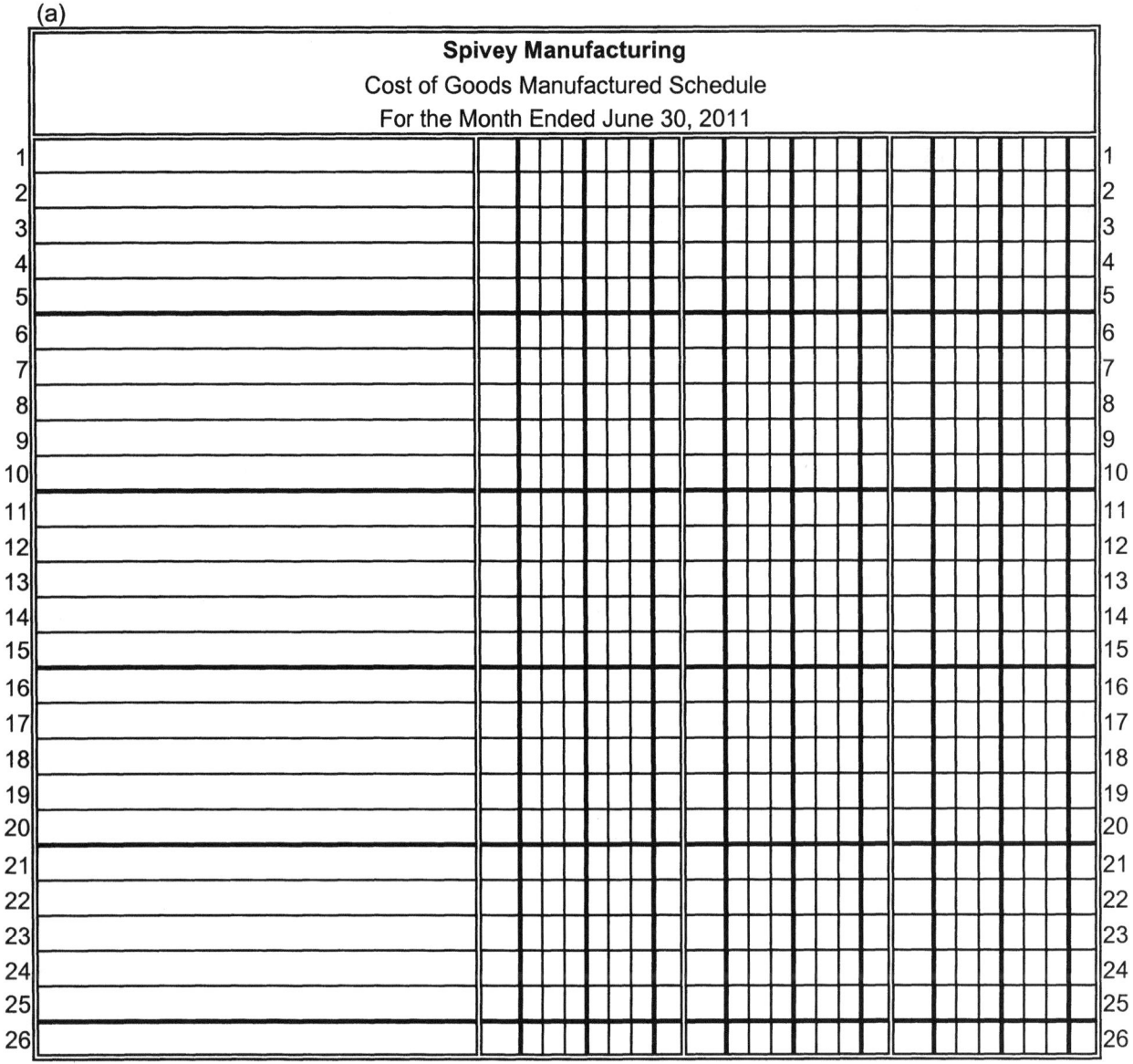

Spivey Manufacturing
Cost of Goods Manufactured Schedule
For the Month Ended June 30, 2011

(b)

Spivey Manufacturing
(Partial) Balance Sheet
June 30, 2011

You will find this working paper at the end of this booklet.

(a)

Cost Item	Product Costs			Period Costs
	Direct Materials	Direct Labor	Manufacturing Overhead	
1 Rent on factory equipment				
2 Insurance on factory building				
3 Raw materials				
4 Utility costs for factory				
5 Supplies for general office				
6 Wages for assembly line workers				
7 Depreciation on office equipment				
8 Miscellaneous materials				
9 Factory manager's salary				
10 Property taxes on factory building				
11 Advertising for helmets				
12 Sales commissions				
13 Depreciation on factory building				
14 Totals				
15				
16				
17				
18 (b)				
19 Total production costs:				
20				
21				
22				
23				
24				
25 Production cost per helmet:				

(a)

Cost Item	Product Costs			Period Costs
	Direct Materials	Direct Labor	Manufacturing Overhead	
1 Raw materials				
2 Wages for workers				
3 Rent on equipment				
4 Indirect materials				
5 Factory supervisor's salary				
6 Janitorial costs				
7 Advertising				
8 Depreciation on factory building				
9 Property taxes on factory building				
10 Totals				
11				
12				
13				
14				
15				
16				
17				

(b)

18 Total production costs:		
19		
20		
21		
22		
23		
24 Production cost per system:		
25		

(a)

	CASE 1	
1		1
2		2
3		3
4		4
5		5
6		6
7		7
8		8
9		9
10		10
11		11
12		12
13		13
14		14
15		15
16		16
17		17
18		18
19		19
20		20
21	CASE 2	21
22		22
23		23
24		24
25		25
26		26
27		27
28		28
29		29
30		30
31		31
32		32
33		33
34		34
35		35
36		36
37		37
38		38
39		39
40		40

(b)

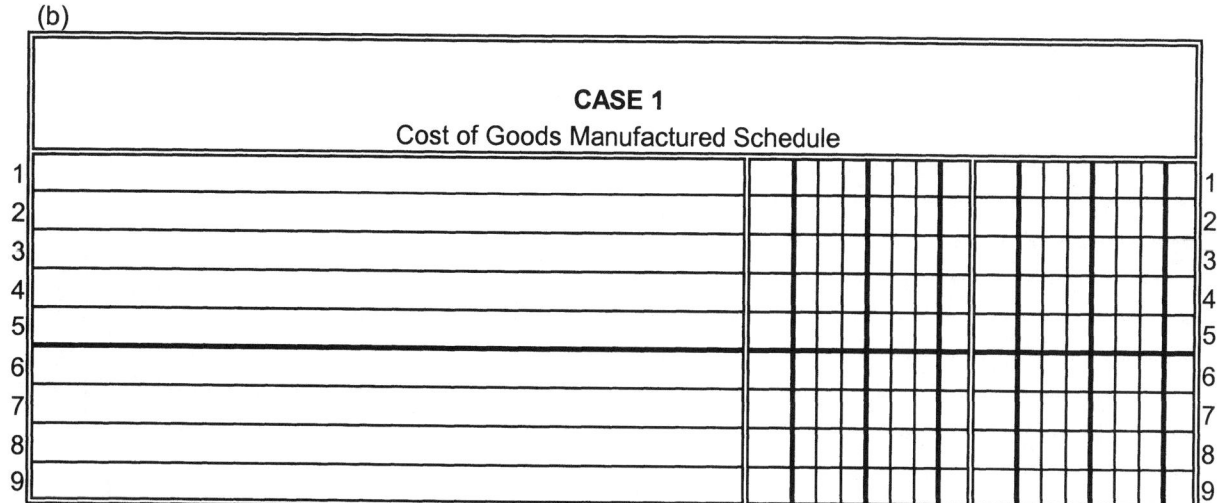

CASE 1

Cost of Goods Manufactured Schedule

(c)

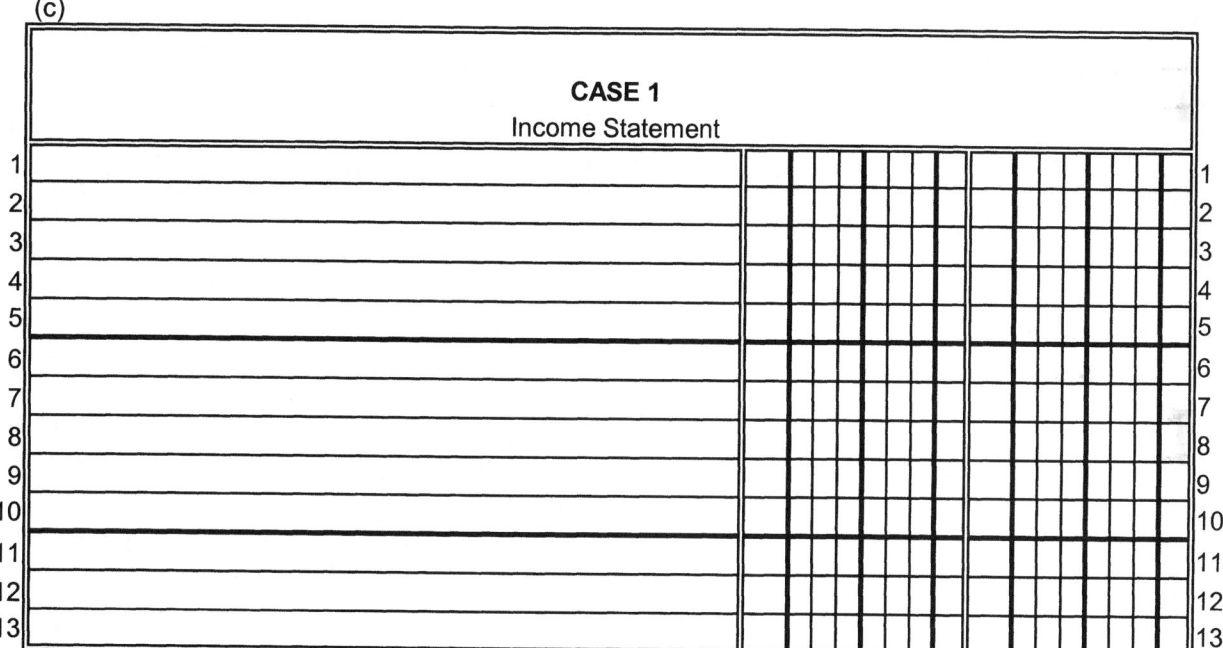

CASE 1

Income Statement

CASE 1

(Partial) Balance Sheet

Current assets:

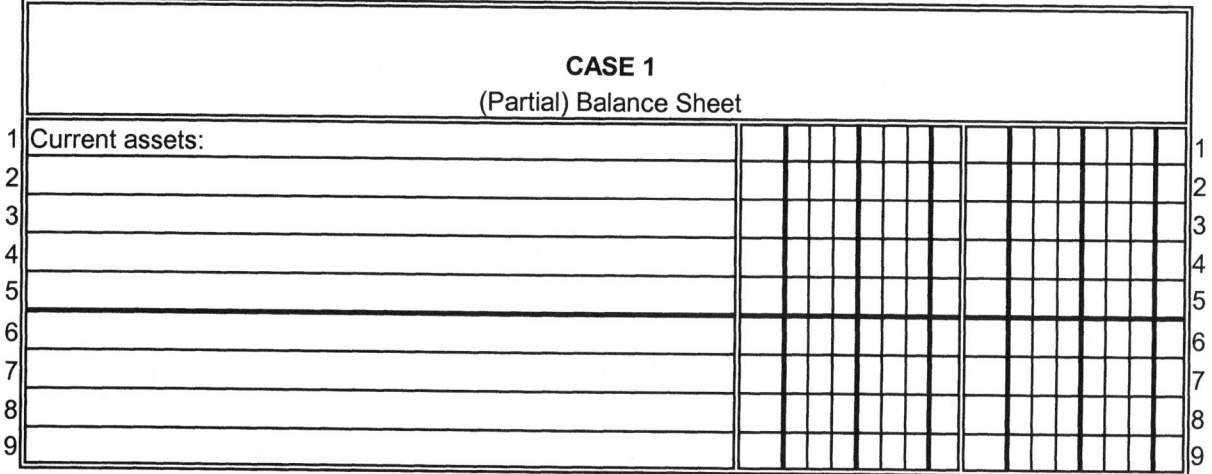

(a)

Stellar Manufacturing Company
Cost of Goods Manufactured Schedule
For the Year Ended June 30, 2011

	1	2	3	4
1				
2				
3				
4				
5				
6				
7				
8				
9				
10				
11				
12				
13				
14				
15				
16				
17				
18				
19				
20				
21				
22				
23				
24				
25				
26				
27				
28				
29				
30				
31				
32				
33				
34				
35				
36				
37				
38				
39				
40				

(b)

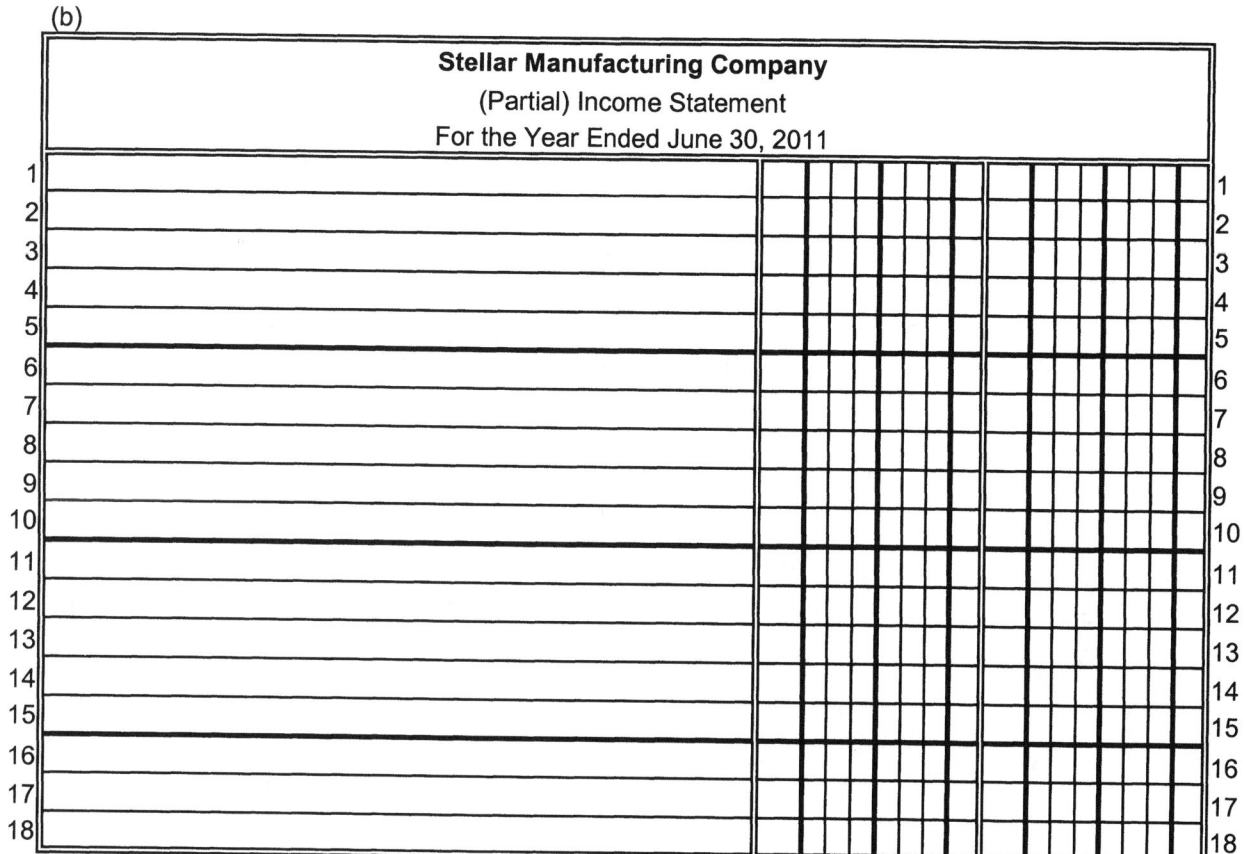

Stellar Manufacturing Company

(Partial) Income Statement

For the Year Ended June 30, 2011

(c)

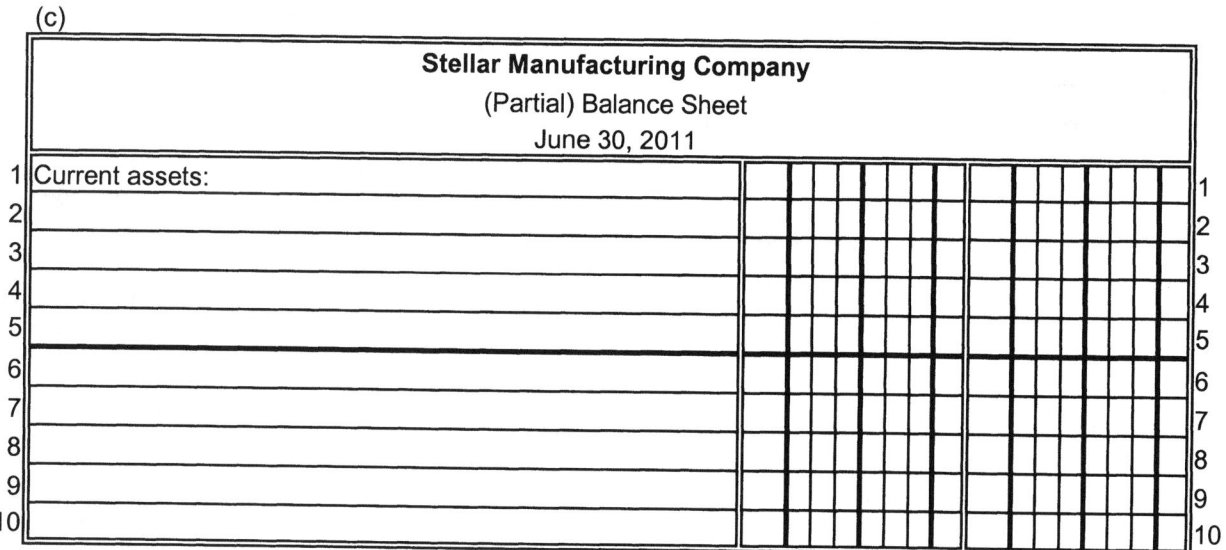

Stellar Manufacturing Company

(Partial) Balance Sheet

June 30, 2011

Current assets:

(a)

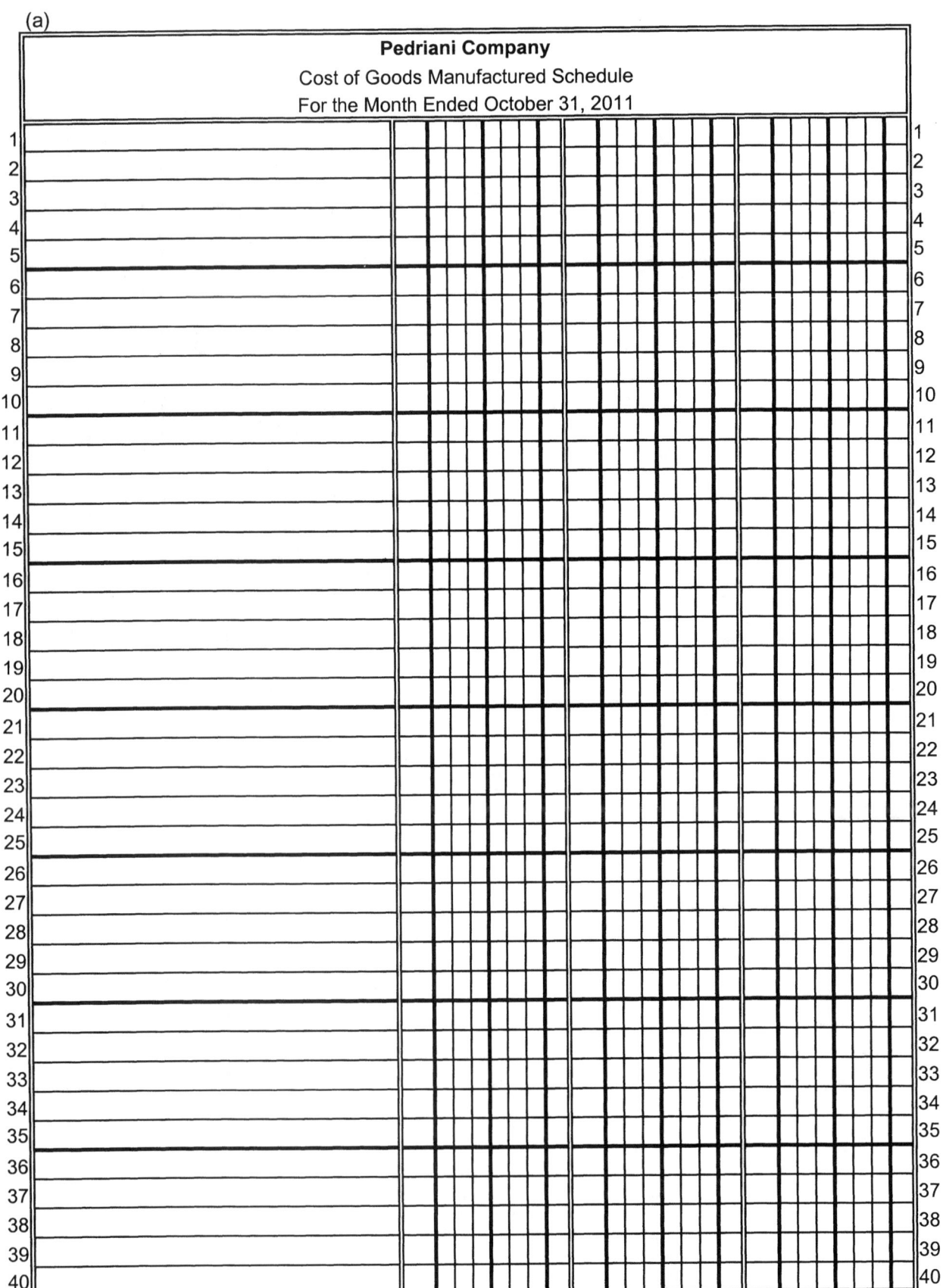

Pedriani Company

Cost of Goods Manufactured Schedule

For the Month Ended October 31, 2011

(b)

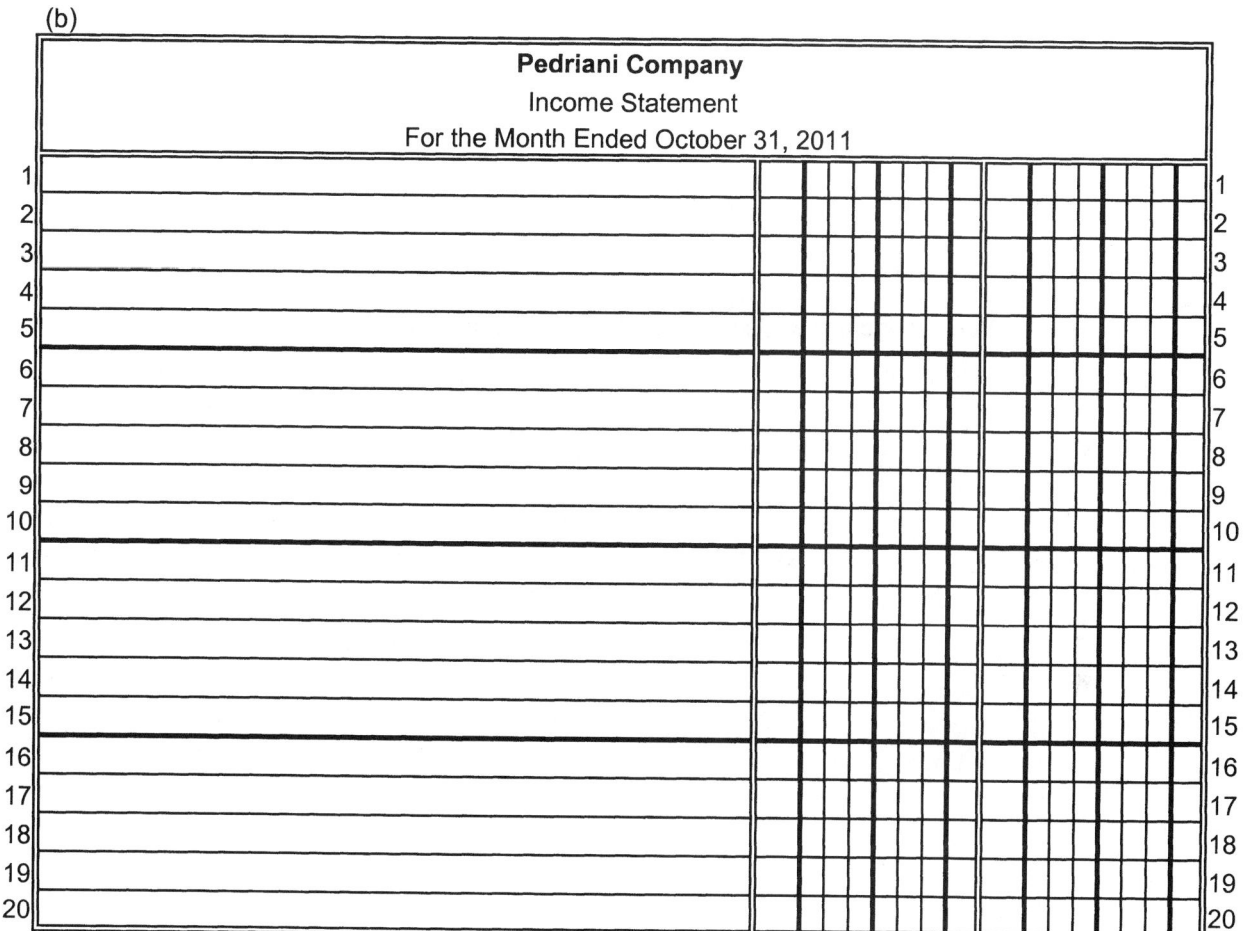

Pedriani Company

Income Statement

For the Month Ended October 31, 2011

You will find this working paper at the end of this booklet.

(b)

	Deglman Manufacturing Company																		
	Cost of Goods Manufactured Schedule																		
	For The Year Ended August 31, 2011																		
1																			1
2																			2
3																			3
4																			4
5																			5
6																			6
7																			7
8																			8
9																			9
10																			10
11																			11
12																			12
13																			13
14																			14
15																			15
16																			16
17																			17
18																			18
19																			19
20																			20
21																			21
22																			22
23																			23
24																			24
25																			25
26																			26
27																			27
28																			28
29																			29
30																			30
31																			31
32																			32
33																			33
34																			34
35																			35

(c)

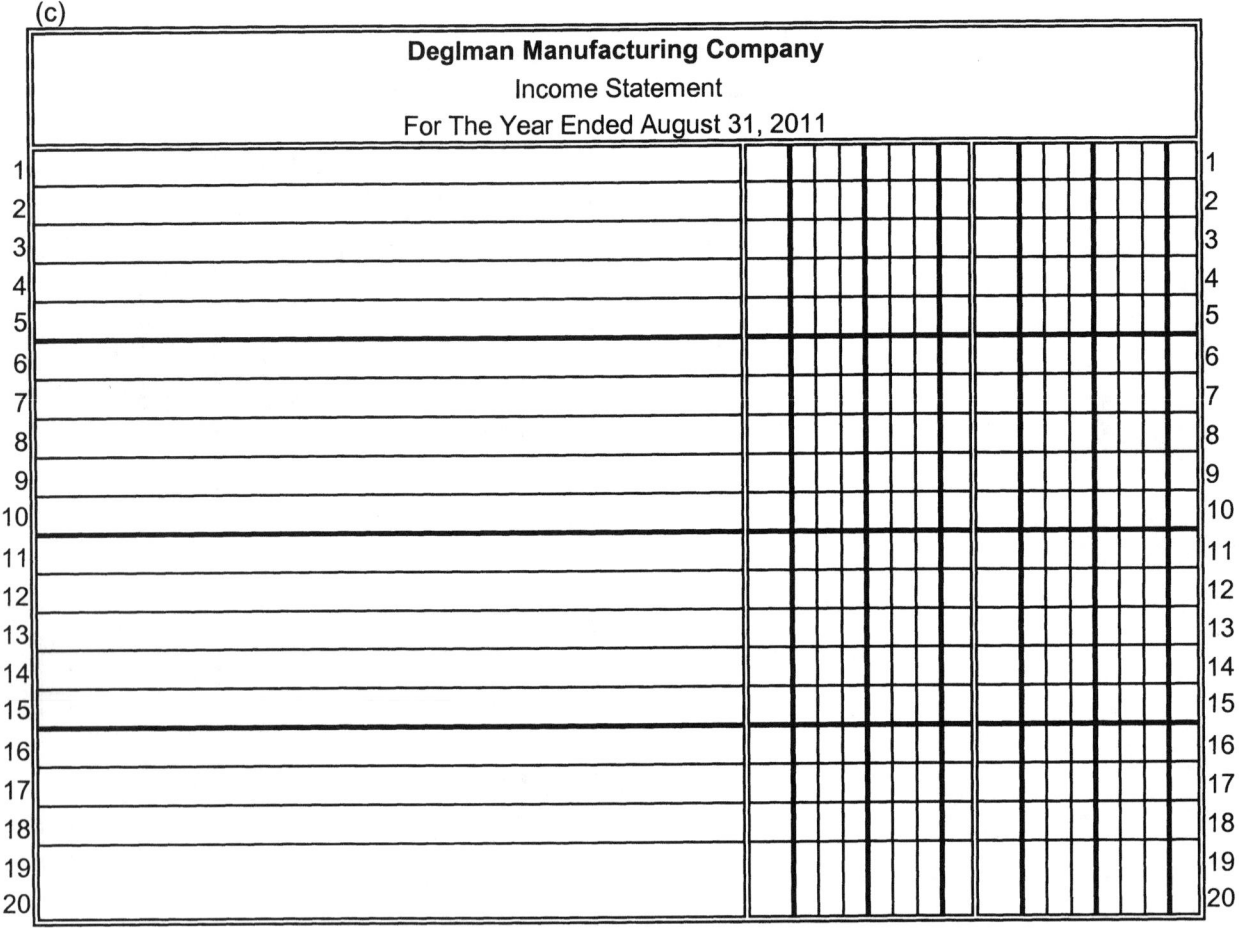

Deglman Manufacturing Company
Income Statement
For The Year Ended August 31, 2011

1		
2		
3		
4		
5		
6		
7		
8		
9		
10		
11		
12		
13		
14		
15		
16		
17		
18		
19		
20		

(e)

Manufacturing Summary

Income Summary

(c) Continued

	Deglman Manufacturing Company					
	Balance Sheet					
	August 31, 2011					
1	Assets						1
2							2
3							3
4							4
5							5
6							6
7							7
8							8
9							9
10							10
11							11
12							12
13							13
14							14
15							15
16	Liabilities and Stockholders' Equity						16
17							17
18							18
19							19
20							20
21							21
22							22
23							23
24							24
25							25
26							26
27							27
28							28
29							29
30							30
31							31
32							32
33							33

(d)

General Journal

	Date	Account Titles	Debit	Credit	
1	Aug. 31				1
2					2
3					3
4					4
5	31				5
6					6
7					7
8					8
9					9
10					10
11					11
12					12
13					13
14					14
15					15
16					16
17					17
18	31				18
19					19
20					20
21					21
22	31				22
23					23
24					24
25					25
26					26
27					27
28					28
29	31				29
30					30
31					31
32					32
33					33
34					34
35					35
36					36
37					37
38					38
39					39
40					40

Petra Company

(a)

Cost Item	Product Costs			Period Costs
	Direct Materials	Direct Labor	Manufacturing Overhead	
1 Maintenance costs on factory building				
2 Factory manager's salary				
3 Advertising for helmets				
4 Sales commissions				
5 Depreciation on factory building				
6 Rent on factory equipment				
7 Insurance on factory building				
8 Raw materials				
9 Utility costs for factory				
10 Supplies for general office				
11 Wages for assembly-workers				
12 Depreciation on office equipment				
13 Miscellaneous materials				
14 Totals				
15				
16				
17				

(b)

18 Total production costs:	
19	
20	
21	
22	
23	
24 Production cost per motorcycle helmet:	
25	

(a)

Cost Item	Product Costs			Period Costs
	Direct Materials	Direct Labor	Manufacturing Overhead	
1 Raw materials				
2 Wages for workers				
3 Rent on equipment				
4 Indirect materials				
5 Factory supervisor's salary				
6 Janitorial costs				
7 Advertising				
8 Depreciation on factory building				
9 Property taxes on factory building				
10 Totals				
11				
12				
13				
14				
15				
16				
17				

(b)

18 Total production costs:		
19		
20		
21		
22		
23		
24 Production cost per racket:		
25		

(a)

CASE 1

1		1
2		2
3		3
4		4
5		5
6		6
7		7
8		8
9		9
10		10
11		11
12		12
13		13
14		14
15		15
16		16
17		17
18		18
19		19
20		20

CASE 2

21		21
22		22
23		23
24		24
25		25
26		26
27		27
28		28
29		29
30		30
31		31
32		32
33		33
34		34
35		35
36		36
37		37
38		38
39		39
40		40

(b)

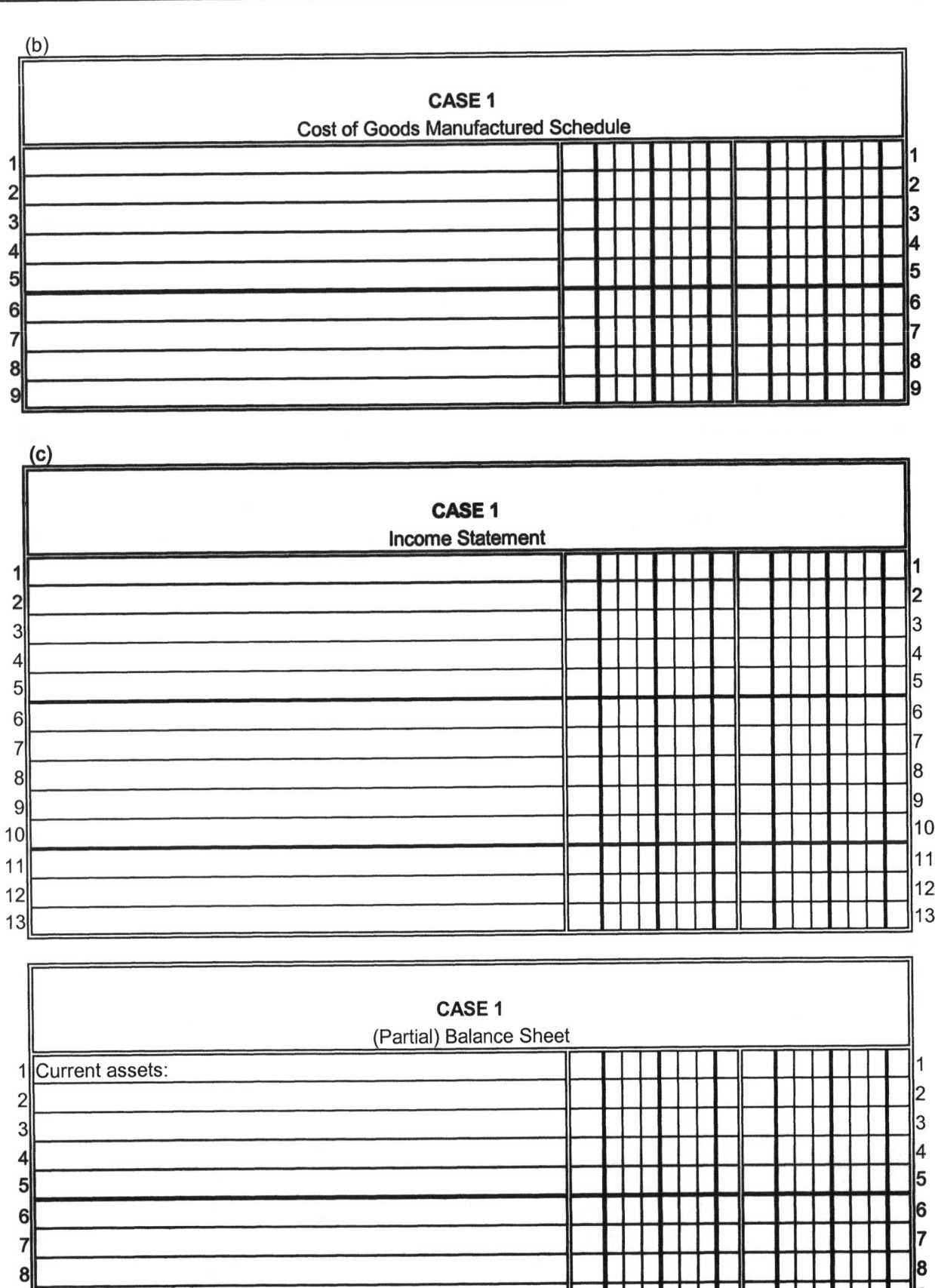

(c)

(a)

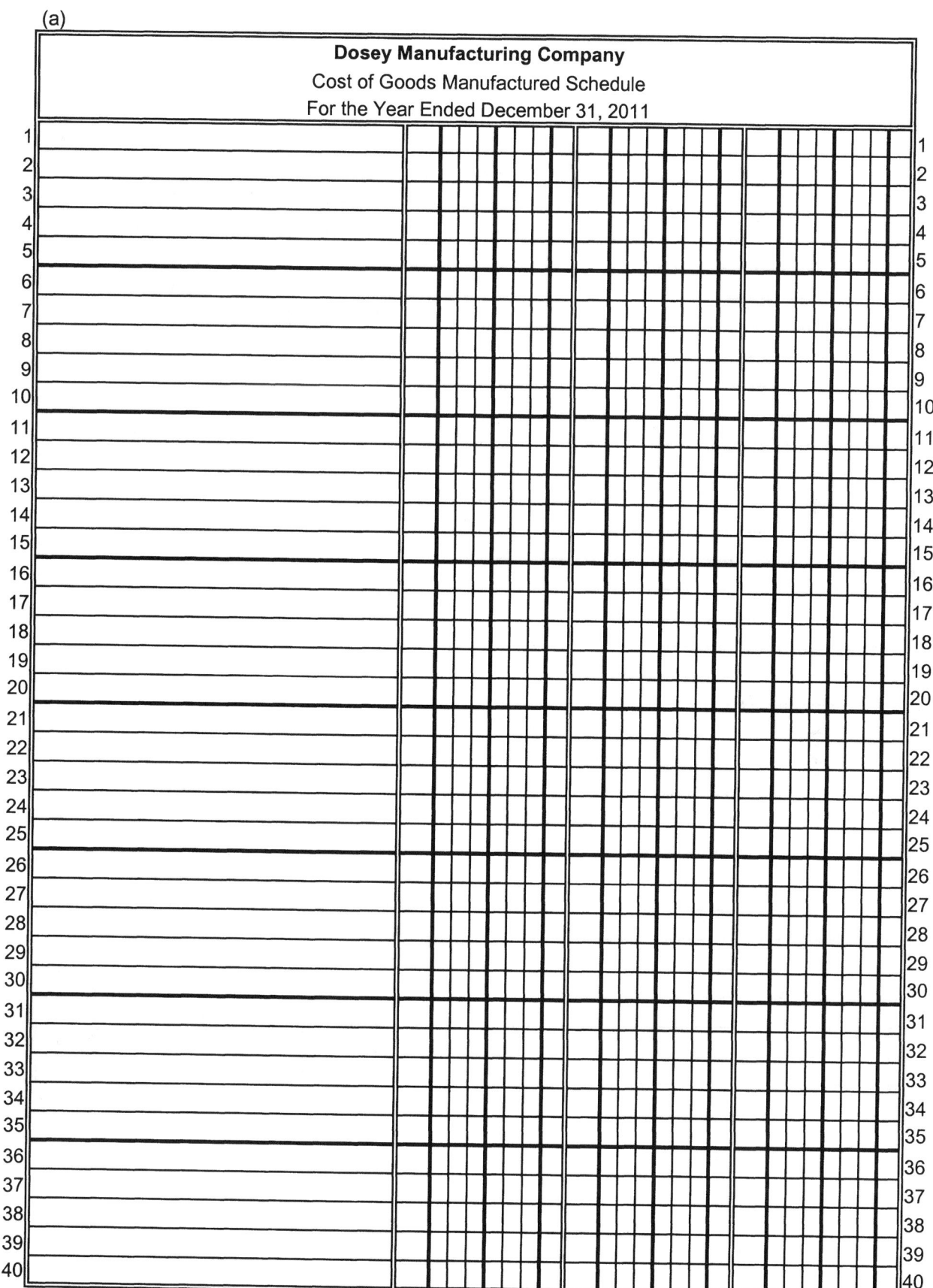

Dosey Manufacturing Company
Cost of Goods Manufactured Schedule
For the Year Ended December 31, 2011

(b)

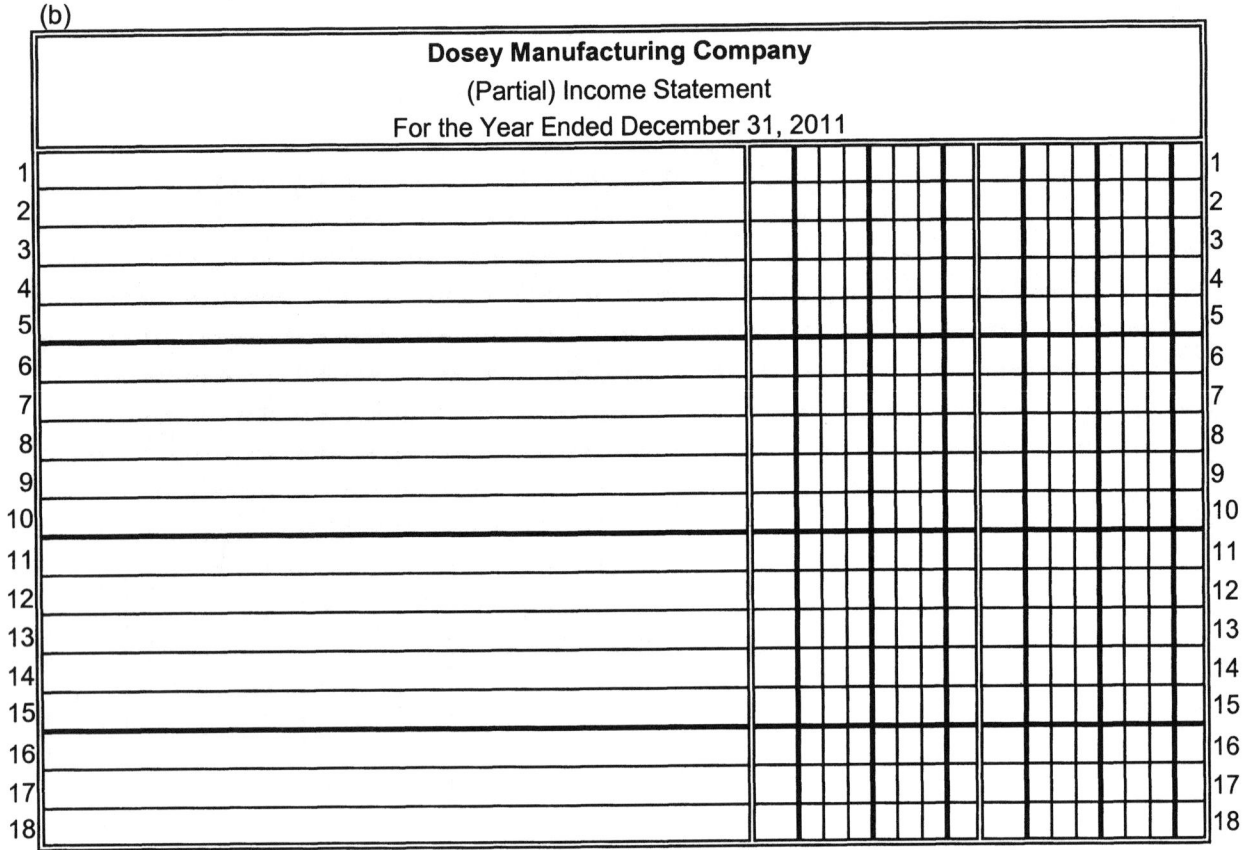

Dosey Manufacturing Company

(Partial) Income Statement

For the Year Ended December 31, 2011

(c)

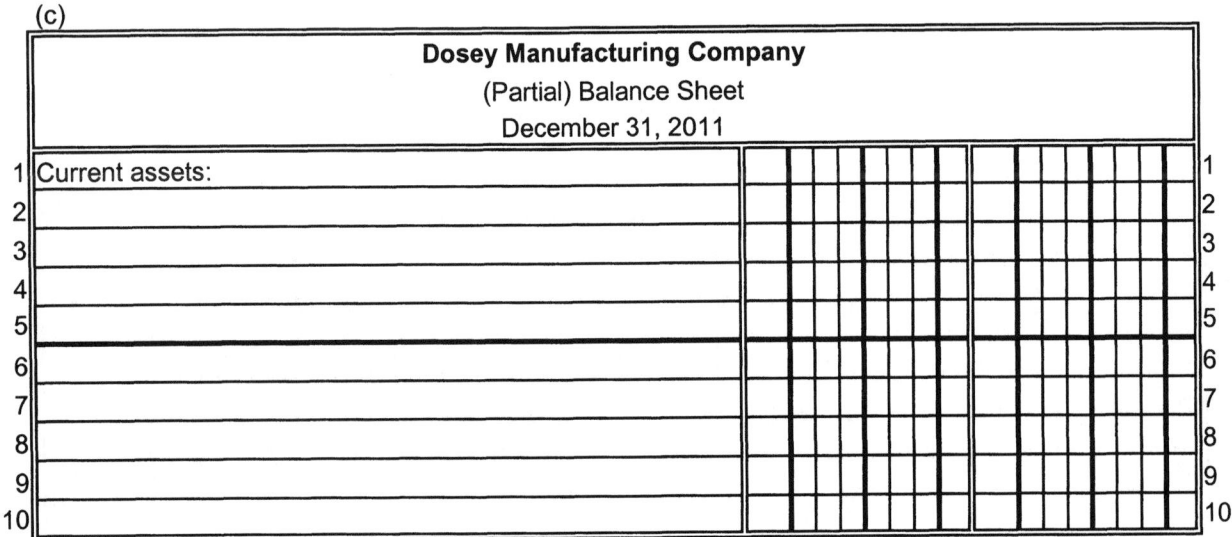

Dosey Manufacturing Company

(Partial) Balance Sheet

December 31, 2011

Current assets:

(a)

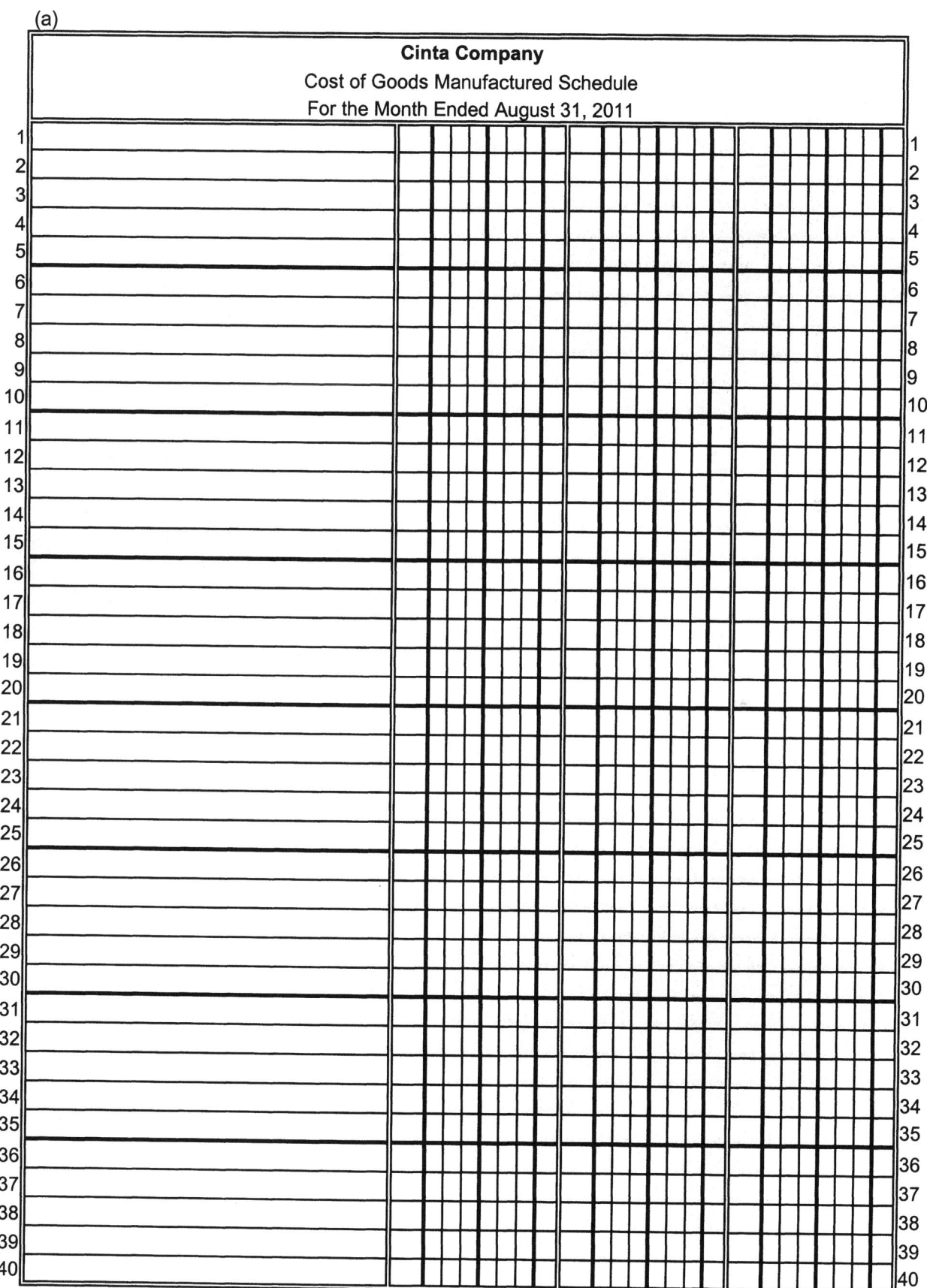

Cinta Company

Cost of Goods Manufactured Schedule

For the Month Ended August 31, 2011

(b)

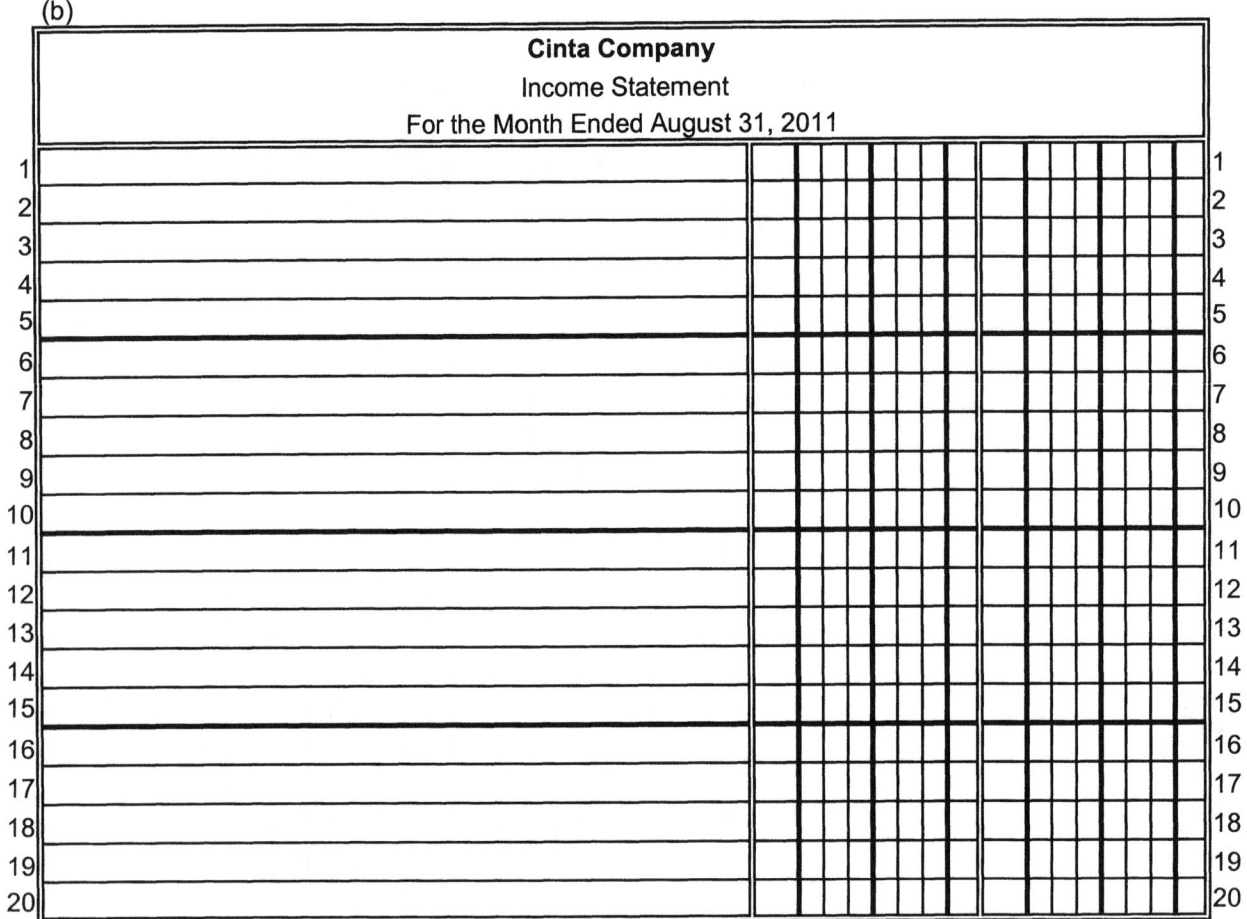

Cinta Company		
Income Statement		
For the Month Ended August 31, 2011		

BE2-2

	Date	Account Titles	Debit	Credit
1	Jan 31			
2				
3				
4	31			
5				
6				
7				
8	31			
9				
10				

BE2-3

	Date	Account Titles	Debit	Credit
11	Jan 31			
12				
13				
14				
15				
16				

BE2-4

	Date	Account Titles	Debit	Credit
17	Jan 31			
18				
19				
20				
21				
22				
23				
24				
25				

BE2-5

Job 1				Job 2		
Date	Direct Materials	Direct Labor		Date	Direct Materials	Direct Labor

Job 3		
Date	Direct Materials	Direct Labor

Name

Section

Date

BE2-7

	Date	Account Titles	Debit	Credit	
1	Jan 31				1
2					2
3					3
4					4
5	Feb 28				5
6					6
7					7
8					8
9					9
10	Mar 31				10
11					11
12					12
13					13
14					14
15	**BE2-8**				15
16	Mar 31				16
17					17
18					18
19					19
20	31				20
21					21
22					22
23					23
24					24
25	31				25
26					26
27					27
28					28
29					29
30					30
31					31
32					32
33					33
34					34
35					35
36					36
37					37
38					38
39					39
40					40

BE2-9

	Date	Account Titles	Debit	Credit	
1		Caroline Company			1
2	Dec 31				2
3					3
4					4
5		Criqui Company			5
6	Dec 31				6
7					7
8					8
9					9
10					10
11					11
12					12
13					13
14					14
15					15
16					16
17					17
18					18
19					19
20					20
21					21
22					22
23					23
24					24
25					25
26					26
27					27
28					28
29					29
30					30

DO IT! 2-1

		Account Titles	Debit	Credit	
1	(a)				1
2					2
3					3
4					4
5	(b)				5
6					6
7					7
8					8
9					9
10	(c)				10
11					11
12					12
13					13
14					14
15					15
16	**DO IT! 2-2**				16
17	The three summary entries are:				17
18					18
19					19
20					20
21					21
22					22
23					23
24					24
25					25
26					26
27					27
28					28
29					29
30					30
31					31
32					32
33					33
34					34
35					35
36					36
37					37
38					38
39					39
40					40

DO IT! 2-3

	Account Titles	Debit	Credit	
1				1
2				2
3				3
4				4
5				5
6				6
7				7
8				8
9				9
10				10
11				11
12				12
13				13
14				14
15				15
16				16
17				17
18				18
19				19
20				20
21				21
22				22
23				23
24				24
25				25
26				26
27				27
28				28
29				29
30				30

E2-1

	Date	Account Titles	Debit	Credit	
1	(a)				1
2					2
3					3
4					4
5					5
6					6
7					7
8	(b)				8
9					9
10					10
11					11
12					12
13					13
14					14
15					15

16	**E2-3**			16
17	(a) 1.			17
18				18
19				19
20				20
21	2.			21
22				22
23				23
24				24
25	(b)			25

	Date	Account Titles	Debit	Credit	
26	Date	Account Titles	Debit	Credit	26
27	Jan 31				27
28					28
29					29
30	31				30
31					31
32					32
33	31				33
34					34
35					35
36	31				36
37					37
38					38
39					39
40					40

(a)

	Date		Debit	Credit	
1	May 31				1
2					2
3					3
4					4
5					5
6	31				6
7					7
8					8
9					9
10					10
11	31				11
12					12
13					13
14					14
15					15
16	31				16
17					17
18					18
19					19
20					20

(b)

WORK IN PROCESS INVENTORY

Cost Sheets

Job No.	Beginning WIP	Direct Materials	Direct Labor	Manufacturing Overhead	Total	
						34
						35
						36
						37
						38
						39
						40

E2-5

1	(a)		1
2			2
3	(b)		3
4			4
5			5
6			6
7	(c)		7

	Date	Account Titles	Debit	Credit	
8					8
9					9
10					10
11					11
12					12
13					13
14					14
15					15

E2-6

16	E2-6		16
17	(a) (1) The source documents are:		17
18			18
19			19
20			20
21			21
22	(2)		22
23			23
24			24
25			25
26	(3) The total cost is:		26
27			27
28			28
29			29
30			30
31			31
32			32
33	(b)		33

	Date	Account Titles	Debit	Credit	
34	Date	Account Titles	Debit	Credit	34
35	July 31				35
36					36
37					37
38					38
39					39
40					40

	Trans-action	Account Titles	Debit	Credit	
1	1.				1
2					2
3					3
4	2.				4
5					5
6					6
7					7
8	3.				8
9					9
10					10
11					11
12	4.				12
13					13
14					14
15					15
16	5.				16
17					17
18					18
19					19
20					20
21	6.				21
22					22
23					23
24					24
25					25
26	7.				26
27					27
28					28
29					29
30					30
31	8.				31
32					32
33					33
34					34
35					35
36					36
37					37
38					38
39					39
40					40

Section

Date   Copa Printing Corp.

	Trans-action	Account Titles	Debit	Credit	
1	1.				1
2					2
3					3
4					4
5					5
6					6
7	2.				7
8					8
9					9
10					10
11					11
12					12
13					13
14					14
15	3.				15
16					16
17					17
18	4.				18
19					19
20					20
21					21
22	5.				22
23					23
24					24
25	6.				25
26					26
27					27
28					28
29					29
30					30
31					31
32					32
33	Computation of cost of jobs finished:				33

	Job Number	Direct Materials	Direct Labor	Manufacturing Overhead	Total	
34						34
35						35
36						36
37						37
38						38
39						39
40						40

(a)

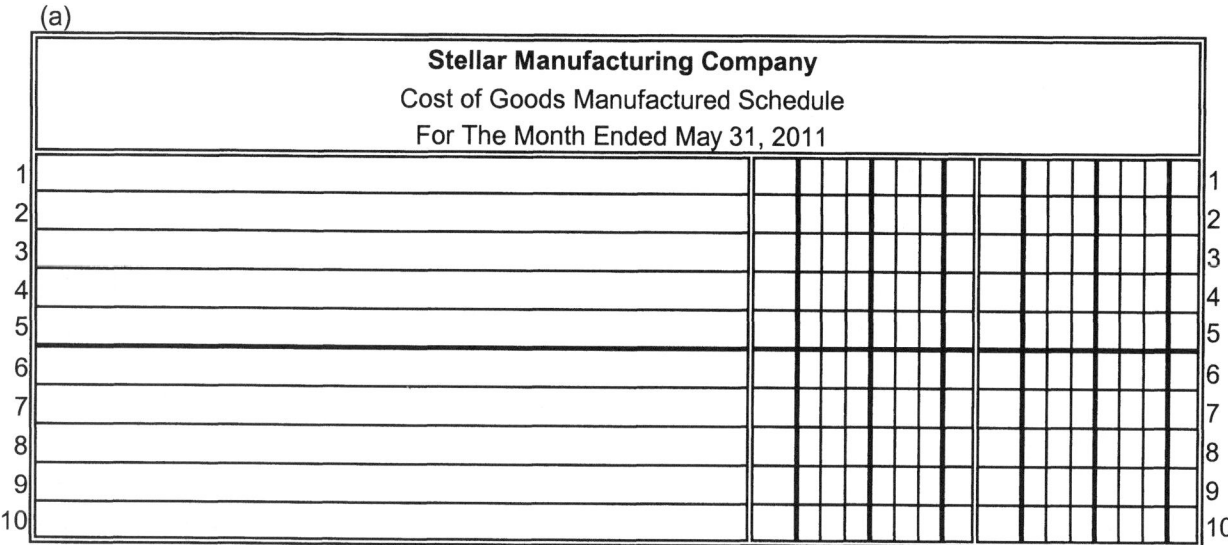

Stellar Manufacturing Company
Cost of Goods Manufactured Schedule
For The Month Ended May 31, 2011

(b)

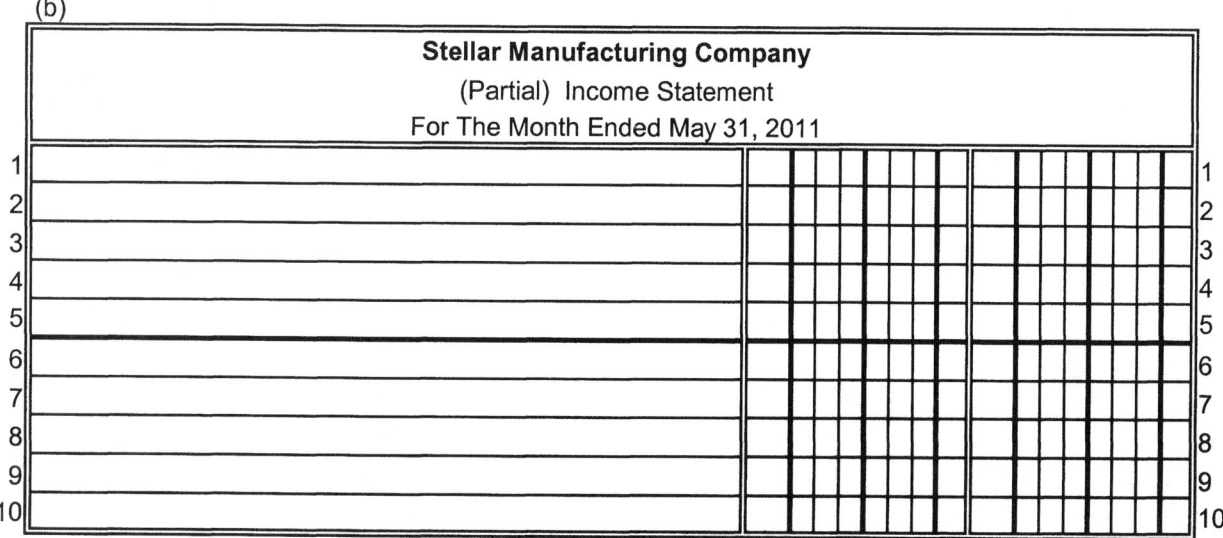

Stellar Manufacturing Company
(Partial) Income Statement
For The Month Ended May 31, 2011

(c)

(a)

1	Work in Process Inventory:	
2		
3		
4		
5		
6		
7		
8		
9		
10		
11	(b) Finished Goods Inventory:	
12		
13		
14		
15		
16		
17		
18		
19		
20		

(c) Gross Profit:

	Month	Job Number	Sales	Cost of Goods Sold	Gross Profit
26					
27					
28					
29					
30					
31					
32					
33					
34					
35					

(a)

Trans-action Number	Account Titles	Debit	Credit
1			
2			
3			
4			
5			
6			

(b)

WORK IN PROCESS INVENTORY

E2-12

(a)	Sara	Brian	Nick
1			
2			
3			
4			
5			
6			

(b)

(c)

E2-13

(a)   Predetermined overhead rate =

(b)   Applied overhead:

Account Titles	Debit	Credit

(c)   Under-or-overapplied overhead:

(a)

	1			1
1				1
2				2
3				3
4				4
5				5
6				6
7				7
8				8
9				9
10				10
11				11
12				12
13				13
14				14
15				15
16				16
17				17
18				18
19				19
20				20
21				21
22				22
23				23
24				24
25				25
26				26
27				27
28				28
29				29
30				30
31				31
32				32
33				33
34				34
35				35
36				36
37				37
38				38
39				39
40				40

(b) and (e)

Job Cost Sheets

JOB NO. 50

Date	Direct Materials	Direct Labor	Manu-facturing Overhead

Cost of completed job

JOB NO. 51

Date	Direct Materials	Direct Labor	Manu-facturing Overhead

Cost of completed job

JOB NO. 52

Date	Direct Materials	Direct Labor	Manu-facturing Overhead

	Account Titles	Debit	Credit	
1	(c)			1
2				2
3				3
4				4
5				5
6				6
7				7
8				8
9				9
10				10
11				11
12				12
13				13
14	(d)			14
15				15
16				16
17				17
18				18
19				19
20				20
21				21
22				22
23	(e)			23
24				24
25				25
26				26
27	(f)			27
28				28
29				29
30				30
31				31
32				32
33				33
34				34
35				35
36				36
37				37
38				38
39				39
40				40

(g)

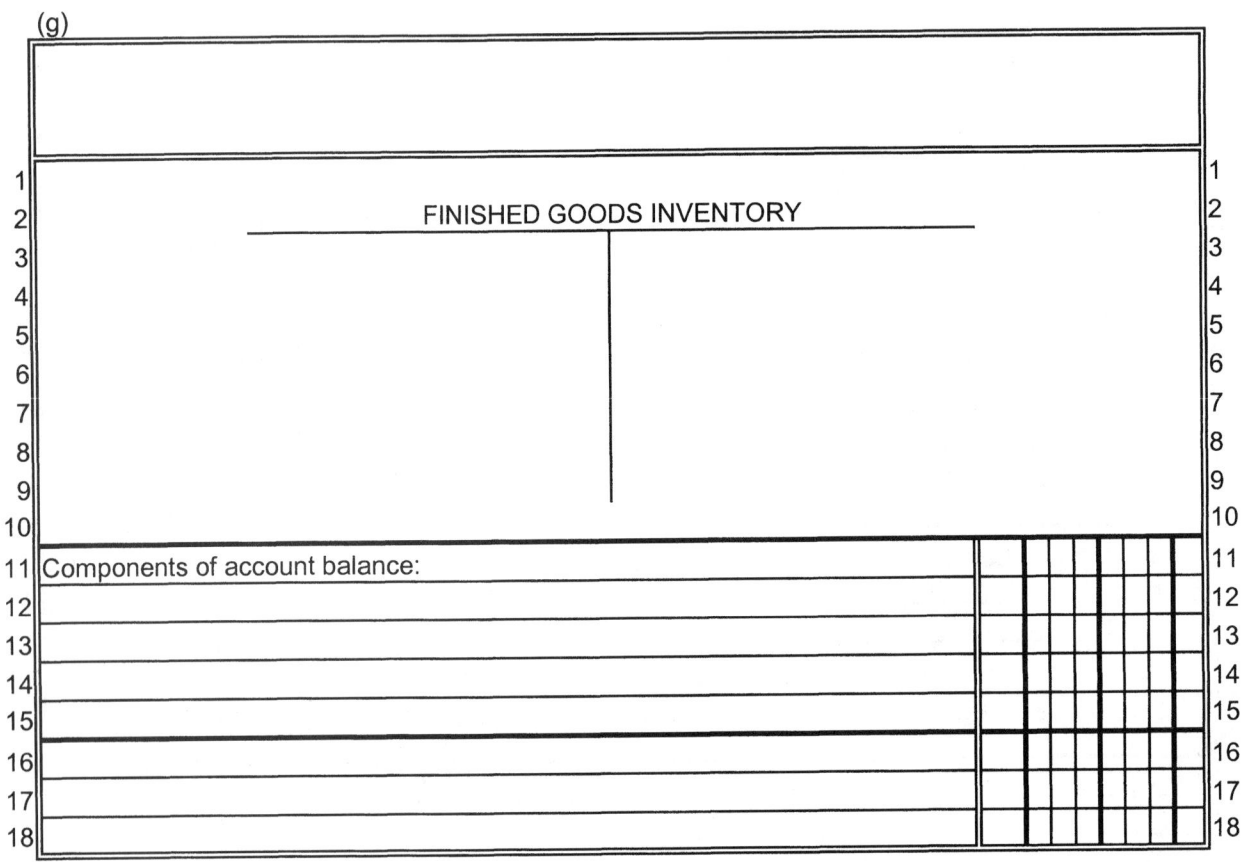

FINISHED GOODS INVENTORY

Components of account balance:

(h)

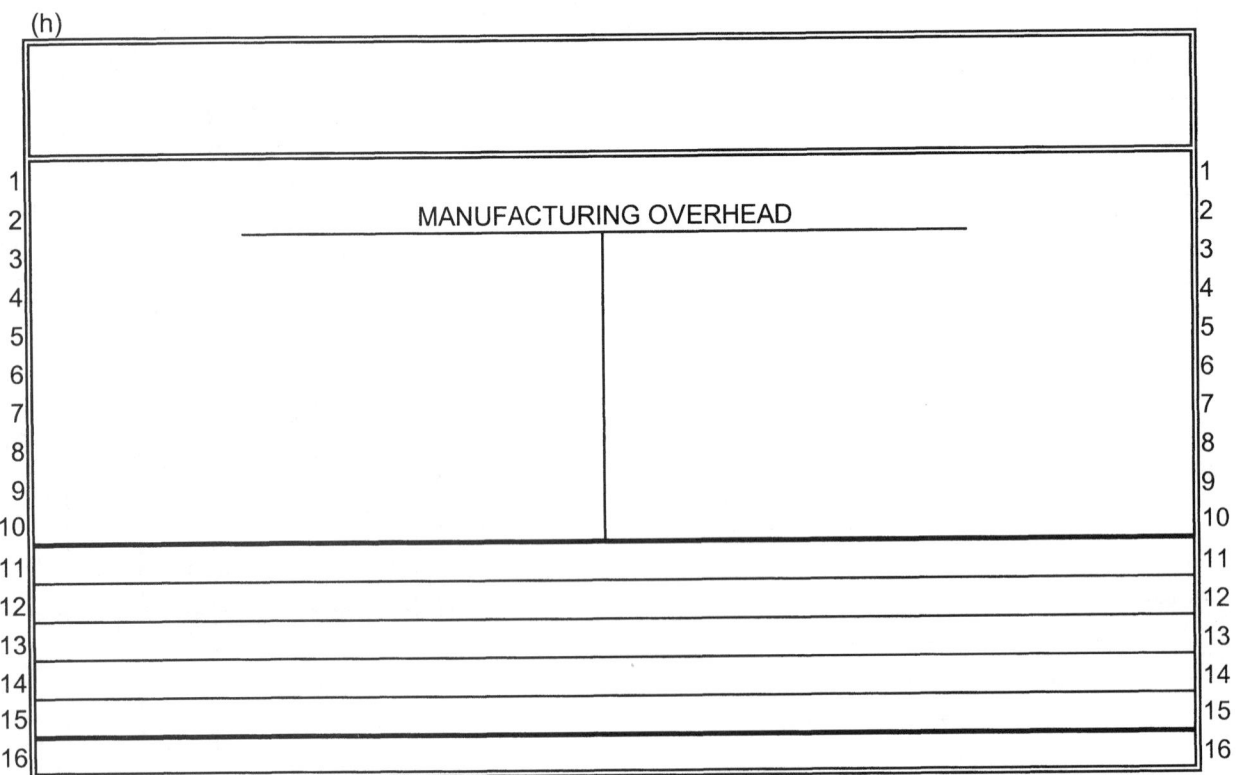

MANUFACTURING OVERHEAD

(a)

	WORK IN PROCESS INVENTORY		

Supporting calculations for five postings to Work In Process Inventory:

(1)		(3)	

(2)		(4)	

(5) (a) Job 7640

(b) Job 7641

(c) Total cost of completed work

(a) (Continued)

Proof of ending Work In Process Inventory balance:

1			1
2			2
3			3
4			4
5			5
6			6
7			7
8			8
9			9
10			10

(b)   Actual overhead costs

11			11
12			12
13			13
14			14
15			15
16			16
17			17

Applied overhead costs

18			18
19			19
20			20
21			21
22			22
23			23
24			24
25			25
26			26
27			27
28			28

	Date	Account Titles	Debit	Credit	
29					29
30					30
31					31
32					32

(c)

33			33
34			34
35			35
36			36
37			37
38			38
39			39
40			40

(a)

	Account Titles	Debit	Credit
1	(i)		
2			
3			
4			
5			
6			
7			
8			
9			
10	(ii)		
11			
12			
13			
14			
15			
16			
17			
18			
19			
20			
21	(iii)		
22			
23			
24			
25			
26			
27			
28			
29			
30			

	Job	Direct Materials	Direct Labor	Manufacturing Overhead	Total Cost
1					
2					
3					
4					
5					

(b)

WORK IN PROCESS INVENTORY

(c) Components of account balance:

(d)

Clarkson Inc.

Cost of Goods Manufactured Schedule

For The Month Ended June 30, 2011

(a)

	Computation of predetermined overhead rate:
1	Department D:
2	
3	
4	Department E:
5	
6	
7	Department K:
8	
9	
10	
11	
12	
13	
14	
15	
16	

(b)

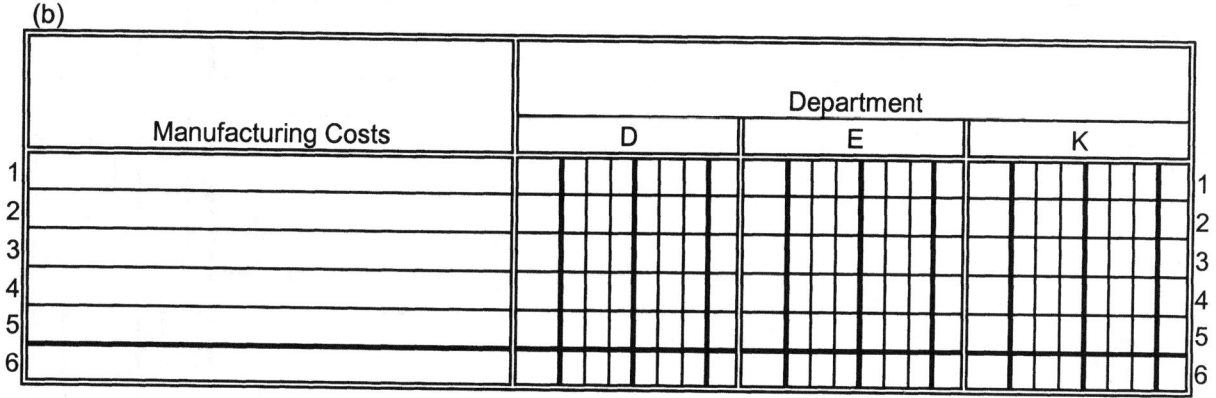

	Manufacturing Costs	Department		
		D	E	K
1				
2				
3				
4				
5				
6				

(c)

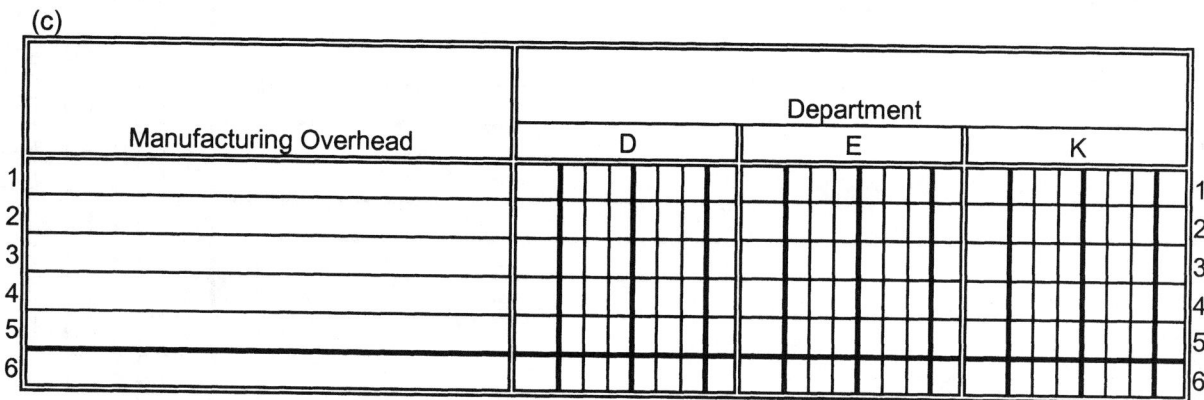

	Manufacturing Overhead	Department		
		D	E	K
1				
2				
3				
4				
5				
6				

(a) - (f)

1	(a)		1
2			2
3			3
4			4
5			5
6	(b)		6
7			7
8			8
9			9
10			10
11	(c)		11
12			12
13			13
14			14
15	(d)		15
16			16
17			17
18	(e)		18
19			19
20			20
21			21
22			22
23	(f)		23
24			24
25			25
26			26
27			27
28			28
29			29
30			30
31			31
32			32
33			33
34			34
35			35
36			36
37			37
38			38
39			39
40			40

(g) - (m)

1	(g)	1
2		2
3	(h)	3
4		4
5	(i)	5
6		6
7		7
8		8
9		9
10	(j)	10
11		11
12	(k)	12
13		13
14	(l)	14
15		15
16		16
17		17
18		18
19	(m)	19
20		20
21		21
22		22
23		23
24		24
25		25
26		26
27		27
28		28
29		29
30		30
31		31
32		32
33		33
34		34
35		35
36		36
37		37
38		38
39		39
40		40

Name

Section

Date

(a)

Name

Section

Date   Weinrich Manufacturing

(b) and (e)

Job Cost Sheets

JOB NO. 25

Date	Direct Materials			Direct Labor			Manu-facturing Overhead		

Cost of completed job

JOB NO. 26

Date	Direct Materials			Direct Labor			Manu-facturing Overhead		

Cost of completed job

JOB NO. 27

Date	Direct Materials		Direct Labor		Manu-facturing Overhead	

	Account Titles	Debit	Credit	
1	(c)			1
2				2
3				3
4				4
5				5
6				6
7				7
8				8
9				9
10				10
11				11
12				12
13				13
14	(d)			14
15				15
16				16
17				17
18				18
19				19
20				20
21				21
22				22
23	(e)			23
24				24
25				25
26				26
27	(f)			27
28				28
29				29
30				30
31				31
32				32
33				33
34				34
35				35
36				36
37				37
38				38
39				39
40				40

(g)

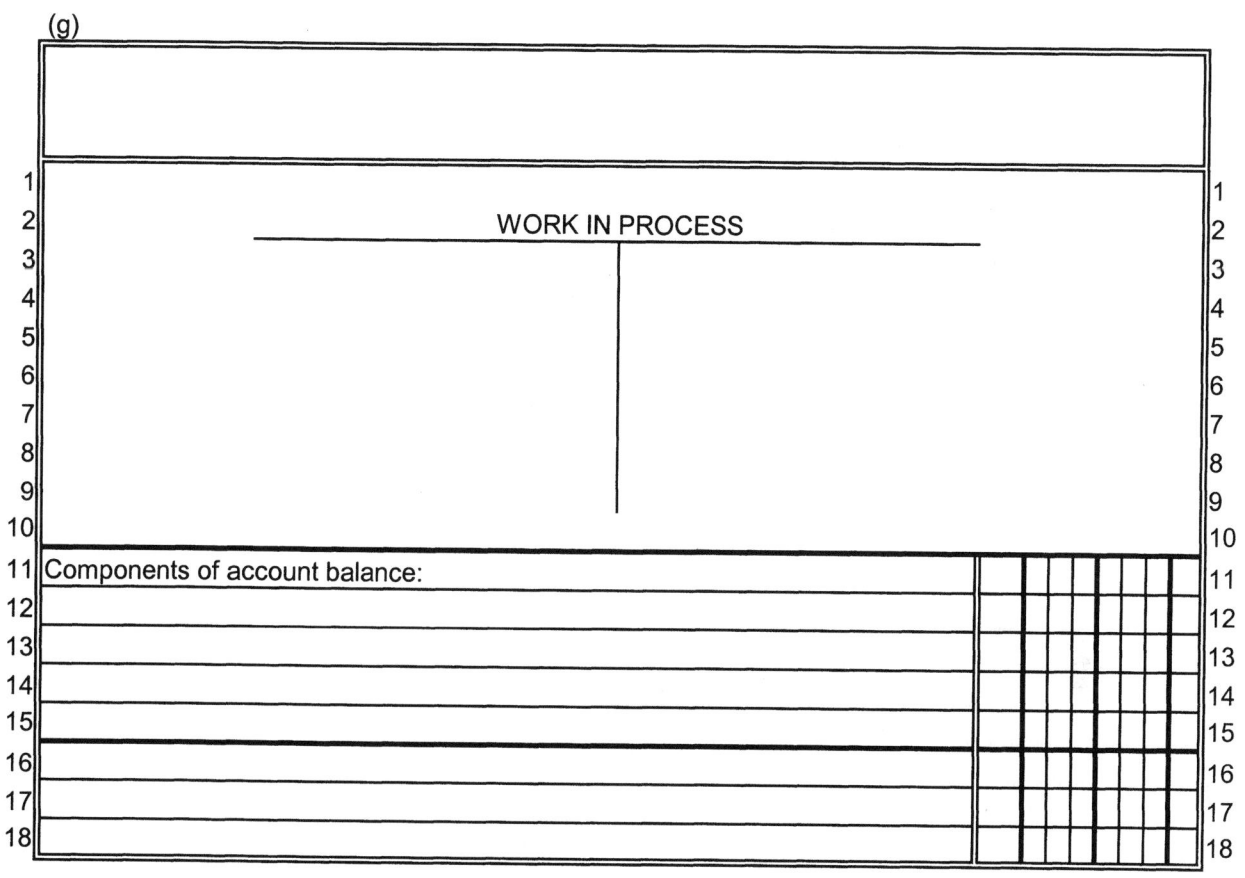

WORK IN PROCESS

Components of account balance:

(h)

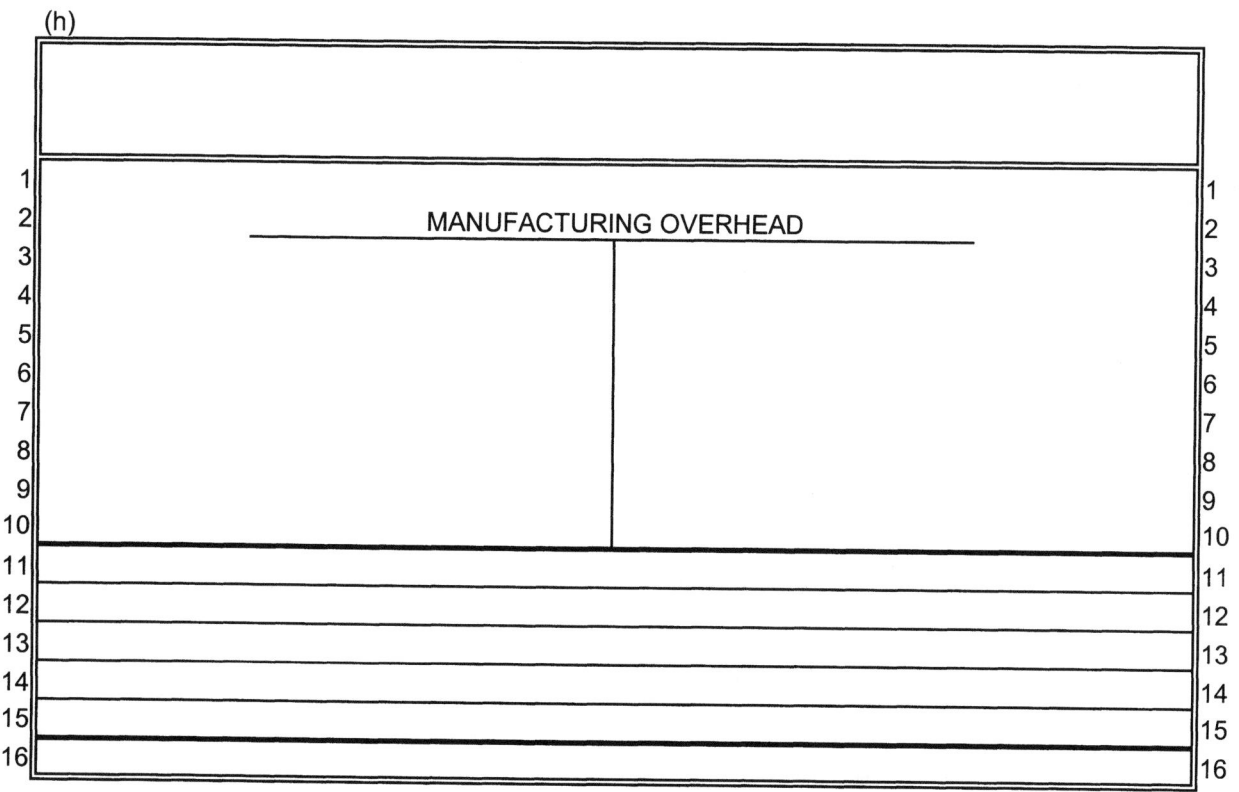

MANUFACTURING OVERHEAD

(a)

WORK IN PROCESS INVENTORY

Supporting calculations for five postings to Work In Process Inventory:

(1)   (3)

(2)   (4)

(5)   (a)   Job 7650

        (b)   Job 7651

        (c)   Total cost of completed work

(a) (Continued)

Proof of ending Work In Process Inventory balance:

	Date	Account Titles	Debit	Credit	
1					1
2					2
3					3
4					4
5					5
6					6
7					7
8					8
9					9
10					10

(b) Actual overhead costs

Applied overhead costs

(c)

(a)

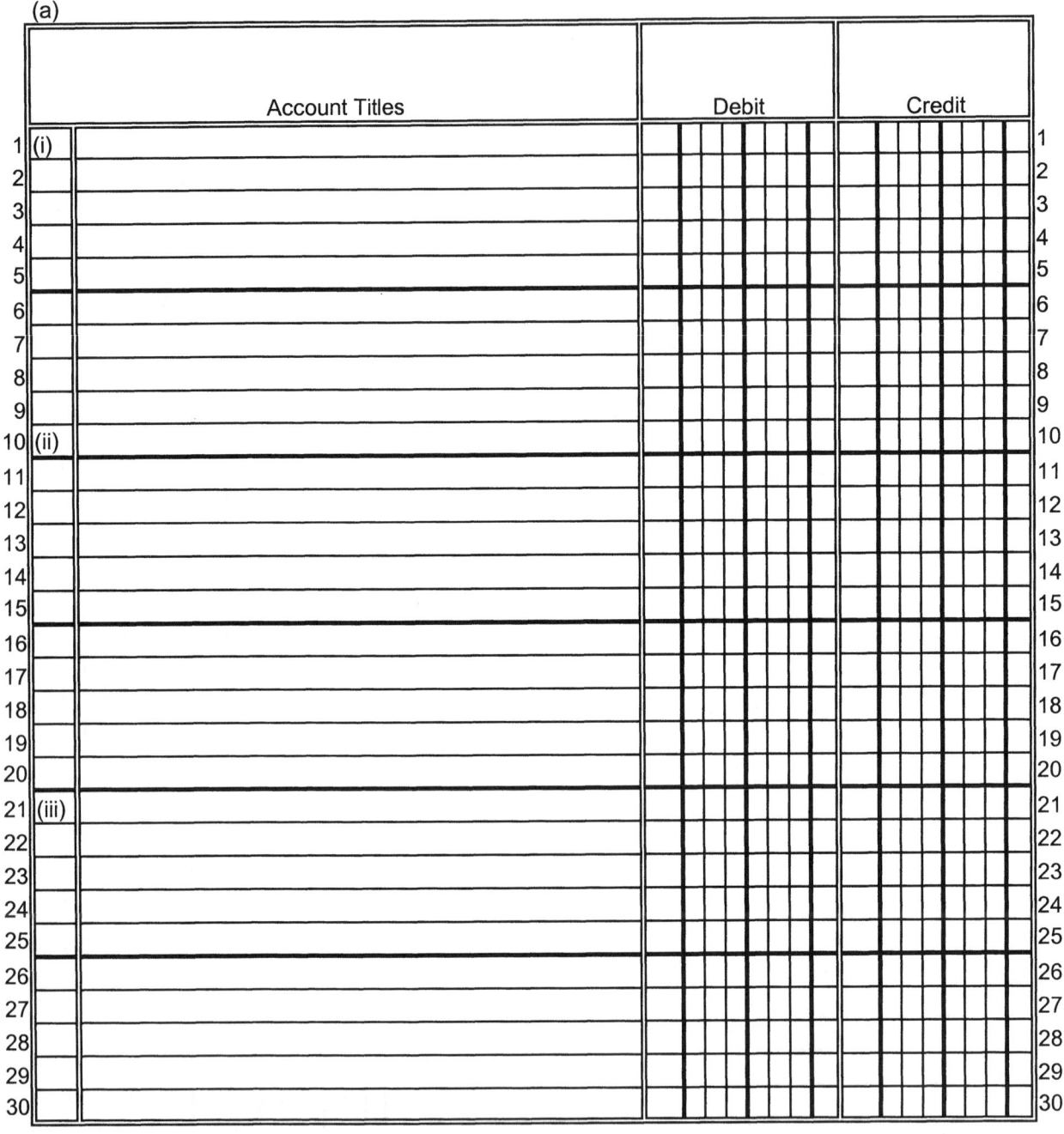

	Account Titles	Debit	Credit	
1	(i)			1
2				2
3				3
4				4
5				5
6				6
7				7
8				8
9				9
10	(ii)			10
11				11
12				12
13				13
14				14
15				15
16				16
17				17
18				18
19				19
20				20
21	(iii)			21
22				22
23				23
24				24
25				25
26				26
27				27
28				28
29				29
30				30

	Job	Direct Materials	Direct Labor	Manufacturing Overhead	Total Cost	
1						1
2						2
3						3
4						4
5						5

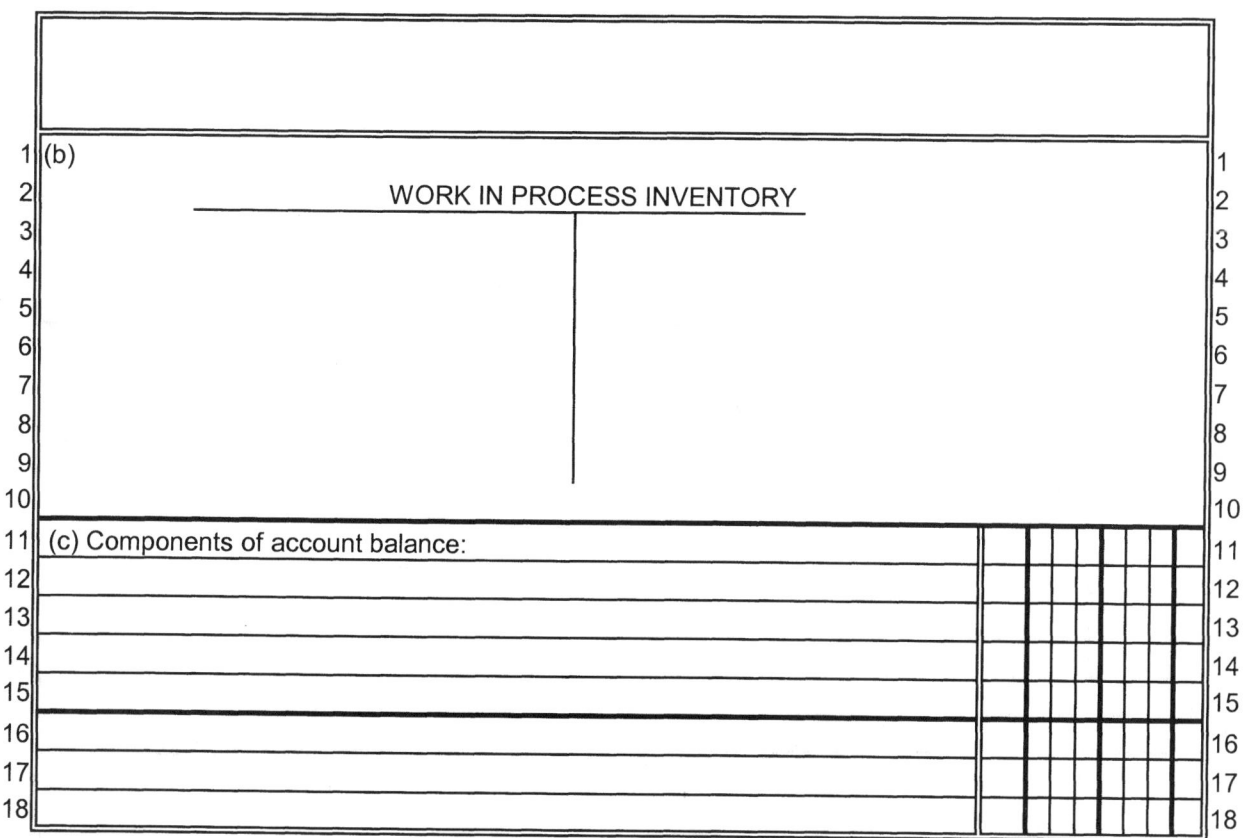

(b)

WORK IN PROCESS INVENTORY

(c) Components of account balance:

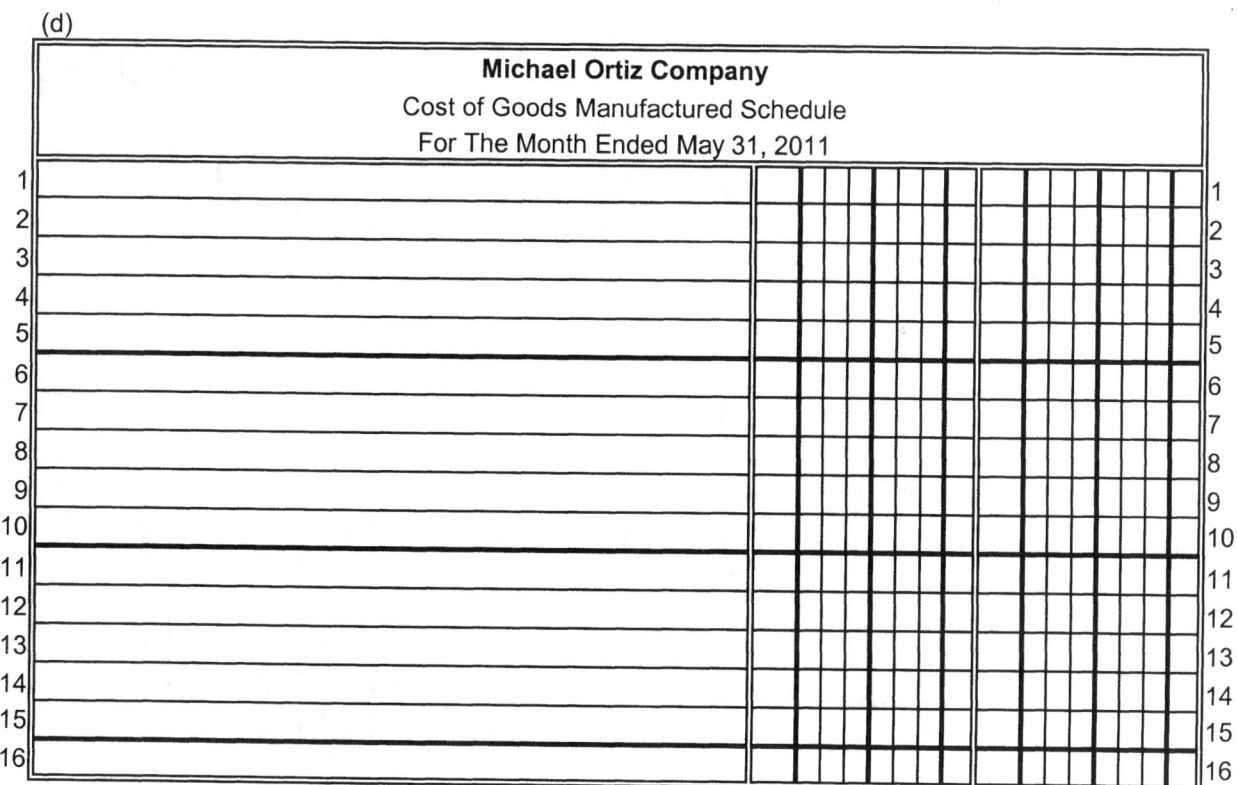

(d)

Michael Ortiz Company

Cost of Goods Manufactured Schedule

For The Month Ended May 31, 2011

(a)

Computation of predetermined overhead rates:

1	Department A:	
2		
3		
4	Department B:	
5		
6		
7	Department C:	
8		
9		
10		
11		
12		
13		
14		
15		
16		

(b)

	Manufacturing Costs	Department		
		A	B	C
1				
2				
3				
4				
5				
6				

(c)

	Manufacturing Overhead	Department		
		A	B	C
1				
2				
3				
4				
5				
6				

(a) - (g)

1	(a)							1
2								2
3								3
4								4
5	(b)							5
6								6
7								7
8								8
9								9
10	(c)							10
11								11
12								12
13	(e)							13
14								14
15	(f)							15
16								16
17								17
18								18
19								19
20								20
21	(g)							21
22								22
23								23
24								24
25								25
26								26
27								27
28								28
29								29
30								30
31								31
32								32
33								33
34								34
35								35
36								36
37								37
38								38
39								39
40								40

Name

Section

Date

(h) - (n)

1	(h)									1
2										2
3	(i)									3
4										4
5	(j)									5
6										6
7										7
8										8
9										9
10	(k)									10
11										11
12	(l)									12
13										13
14										14
15	(m)									15
16										16
17	(n)									17
18										18
19										19
20										20
21										21
22										22
23										23
24										24
25										25
26										26
27										27
28										28
29										29
30										30
31										31
32										32
33										33
34										34
35										35
36										36
37										37
38										38
39										39
40										40

(a)

(b)

(c)

	Costs	Quarter			
		1	2	3	4

	Account Titles	Debit	Credit	
1	FIRST ENTRY			1
2	(a)			2
3				3
4				4
5				5
6	(b)			6
7				7
8				8
9				9
10				10
11	SECOND ENTRY			11
12	(a)			12
13				13
14				14
15				15
16	(b)			16
17				17
18				18
19				19
20				20
21	THIRD ENTRY			21
22	(a)			22
23				23
24				24
25				25
26	(b)			26
27				27
28				28
29				29
30				30
31	FOURTH ENTRY			31
32	(a)			32
33				33
34				34
35				35
36	(b)			36
37				37
38				38
39				39
40				40

BE3-1

	Date	Account Titles	Debit	Credit	
1	Mar 31				1
2					2
3					3
4					4
5					5
6	31				6
7					7
8					8

BE3-2

	Date	Account Titles	Debit	Credit	
9					9
10	Mar 31				10
11					11
12					12
13					13
14	31				14
15					15
16					16
17					17

BE3-3

	Date	Account Titles	Debit	Credit	
18					18
19	Mar 31				19
20					20
21					21
22					22
23					23
24					24
25					25

BE3-4

		January	March	July	
26					26
27					27
28					28
29					29
30					30
31					31
32					32
33					33
34					34
35					35
36					36
37					37
38					38
39					39
40					40

BE3-5

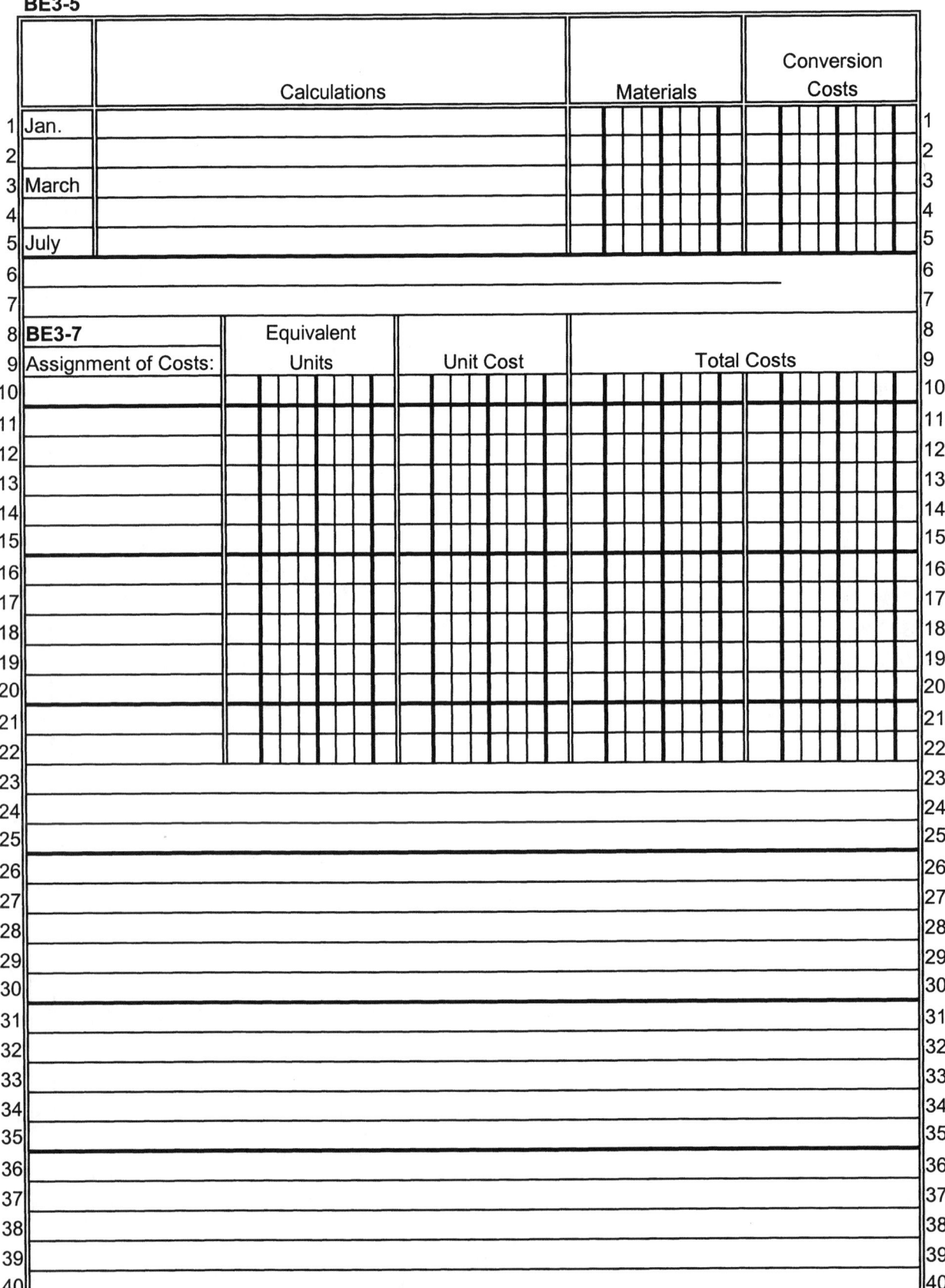

	Calculations	Materials	Conversion Costs	
1 Jan.				1
2				2
3 March				3
4				4
5 July				5

BE3-7	Equivalent Units	Unit Cost	Total Costs	
Assignment of Costs:				

BE3-9

Costs accounted for:		

BE3-10

	Materials	Conversion Costs

*BE3-11

	Costs to Be Assigned	Assignment of Costs	Equivalent Units	Unit Cost	Total Costs Assigned	
1						1
2						2
3						3
4						4
5						5
6						6
7						7
8						8
9						9
10						10

*BE3-12

		Equivalent Units	
		Materials	Conversion Costs
11				11
12				12
13				13
14				14
15				15
16	Units accounted for:			16
17				17
18				18
19				19
20				20
21				21
22				22
23				23
24				24
25				25
26				26
27				27
28				28
29				29
30				30
31				31
32				32
33				33
34				34
35				35
36				36
37				37
38				38
39				39
40				40

*BE3-12 (Continued)

	FONTILLAS COMPANY			
	(Partial) Production Cost Report			
	For the Month Ended March 31			
COSTS	Materials	Conversion Costs	Total	

Name

Section

Date

Boaz Company

	Account Titles	Debit	Credit
1			
2			
3			
4			
5			
6			
7			
8			
9			
10			
11			
12			
13			
14			
15			
16			
17			
18			
19			
20			
21			
22			
23			
24			
25			
26			
27			
28			
29			
30			
31			
32			
33			
34			
35			
36			
37			
38			
39			
40			

DO IT! 3-3

	Equivalent Units	
	(a) Materials	(b) Conversion Costs
1		
2		
3		
4		
5		
6		
7		
8		
9		

DO IT! 3-4

(a) Total units to be accounted for:	
11	
12	
13	
14	
15	
16	

(b)	Equivalent Units	
	Materials	Conversion Costs
17		
18		
19		
20		
21		
22		
23		
24		

(c) Cost reconciliation schedule		
25		
26		
27		
28		
29		
30		
31		
32		
33		
34		
35		
36		
37		
38		
39		
40		

	Date	Account Titles	Debit	Credit	
1	Apr 30				1
2					2
3					3
4					4
5	30				5
6					6
7					7
8					8
9	30				9
10					10
11					11
12					12
13	30				13
14					14
15					15
16					16
17					17
18					18
19					19
20					20
21					21
22					22
23					23
24					24
25					25
26					26
27					27
28					28
29					29
30					30
31					31
32					32
33					33
34					34
35					35
36					36
37					37
38					38
39					39
40					40

(a)

		1
		2
		3
		4
		5
		6

(b)

	Equivalent Units	
	Materials	Conversion Costs

| | Direct Materials | Conversion Costs |
| | | |

(c)

(d)

(e)

	Trans- action Number	Account Titles	Debit	Credit	
1	1.				1
2					2
3					3
4	2.				4
5					5
6					6
7	3.				7
8					8
9					9
10					10
11	4.				11
12					12
13					13
14					14
15	5.				15
16					16
17					17
18					18
19	6.				19
20					20
21					21
22					22
23	7.				23
24					24
25					25
26					26
27	8.				27
28					28
29					29
30					30
31	9.				31
32					32
33					33
34					34
35					35
36					36
37					37
38					38
39					39
40					40

E3-5

(a)

	January	May
1		
2		
3		
4		
5		
6		
7		
8		
9		

(b)

	Calculations	(1) Materials	(2) Conversion Costs
January			
March			
May			
July			

E3-6

(a)

	Materials	Conversion Costs

(b)

Materials:

Conversion costs:

Costs accounted for:

		Castillo Furniture Company			
		Production Cost Report - Sanding Department			
		For The Month Ended March 31, 2011			
			Equivalent Units		
Quantities:	Physical Units	Materials	Conversion Costs		
1					
2					
3					
4					
5					
6					
7					
8					
9					
10					
11 Costs:		Materials	Conversion Costs	Total	
12					
13					
14					
15					
16					
17					
18					
19					
20					
21					
22					
23 Cost Reconciliation Schedule:					
24					
25					
26					
27					
28					
29					
30					
31					
32					
33					
34					
35					
36					
37					

E3-8

	Materials	Conversion Costs
(a)		
1		
2		
3		
4		
5		

(b)	Materials	Conversion Costs	Total
6			
7			
8			
9			
10			
11			
12			

(c)		Materials	Conversion Costs	Total
13				
14				
15				
16				
17				
18				
19				
20				

E3-9

(a)   Materials:

Conversion costs:

(b)   Materials:

Conversion costs:

(c)   Units transferred out:

Units in ending work in process:

1	(a)	Materials:
2		
3		Conversion costs:
4		
5		
6	(b)	Materials:
7		
8		Conversion costs:
9		
10		
11	(c)	Units transferred out:
12		
13		Units in ending work in process:

(a)	Physical Units	Equivalent Units		
		Materials	Conversion Costs	
1				
2				
3				
4				
5				
6				
7				
8				
9				
10				
11				
12				
13				
14				
15				

(b)		Materials	Conversion Costs	Total
16				
17				
18				
19				
20				
21				
22				
23				
24				
25				
26				
27				
28				
29				
30				

(c)				
31				
32				
33				
34				
35				
36				
37				
38				
39				
40				

Kraiss Manufacturing Company

Welding Department

Production Cost Report

For The Month Ended February 28, 2011

Quantities:	Physical Units	Equivalent Units		
		Materials	Conversion Costs	
Costs:		Materials	Conversion Costs	Total
Cost Reconciliation Schedule:				

E3-14

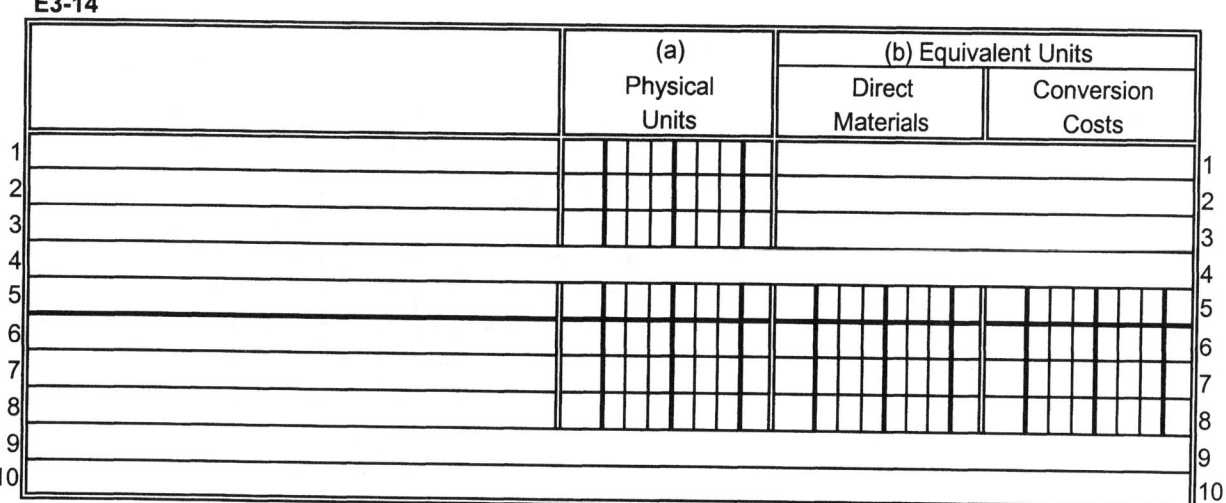

	(a) Physical Units	(b) Equivalent Units	
		Direct Materials	Conversion Costs
1			
2			
3			
4			
5			
6			
7			
8			
9			
10			

E3-15

	Equivalent Units	
(a)	Materials	Conversion Costs
1		
2		
3		
4		
(b) 5		
Materials 6		
7		
Conversion costs 8		
9		
Costs accounted for: 10		
11		
12		
13		
14		
15		
16		
17		
18		
19		
20		
21		
22		
23		
24		
25		

(a)	Physical Units	Equivalent Units	
		Materials	Conversion Costs
1 Applications completed:			
2			
3			
4			
5			
6			
7			
8 (b)			
9 Materials:			
10			
11 Conversion costs:			
12			
13			
14 Costs accounted for:			
15 Applications completed:			

(a) (1) Materials: Production Data	Physical Units	Materials Added This Period	Equivalent Units	
1				1
2				2
3				3
4				4
5				5
6 (2) Conversion Costs:				6
7 Production Data	Physical Units	Work Added This Period	Equivalent Units	7
8				8
9				9
10				10
11				11
12				12
13				13
14 (b) Unit costs are:				14
15 Materials:				15
16 Conversion Costs:				16
17 Total				17
18				18
19				19

20 Costs to Be Assigned	Assignment of Costs	Equivalent Units	Unit Cost	Total Costs Assigned	20
21					21
22					22
23 Tot. mfg. costs	Transferred out:				23
24					24
25					25
26					26
27	Work in process,				27
28	August 31				28
29					29
30					30
31					31
32					32
33					33
34					34
35					35
36					36
37					37
38					38
39					39
40					40

(a) (1) Materials	Physical Units	Materials Added This Period	Equivalent Units
1			
2			
3			
4			
5			

(2) Conversion Costs	Physical Units	Work Added This Period	Equivalent Units

(b) Unit costs are:

Materials:

Conversion Costs:

Total

(c)

Costs to Be Assigned	Assignment of Costs	Equivalent Units	Unit Cost	Total Costs Assigned
Tot. mfg. costs	Transferred out:			
	Work in process, 9/30			

(a)

	1
	2
	3
	4
	5
	6

(b)   Materials:

Production Data:	Physical Units	Materials Added This Period	Equivalent Units
Unit cost			

(c)   Conversion costs:

Production Data:	Physical Units	Work Added This Period	Equivalent Units
Unit cost			

(d)

(e)

(f)

Mortellaro Manufacturing Company
Welding Department
Production Cost Report
For The Month Ended February 28, 2011

Quantities	Physical Units	Equivalent Units		Total
		Materials	Conversion Costs	
1 Units to be accounted for				
2				
3				
4				
5				
6 Units accounted for				
7				
8				
9				
10				
11				
12				
13				
14 Costs				
15 Unit costs				
16				
17				
18				
19				
20 Costs to be accounted for				
21				
22				
23				
24 Cost Reconciliation Schedule:				
25 Costs accounted for				
26				
27				
28				
29				
30				
31				
32				
33				
34				
35				
36				

		Account Titles	Debit	Credit	
1	1.				1
2					2
3					3
4	2.				4
5					5
6					6
7					7
8	3.				8
9					9
10					10
11	4.				11
12					12
13					13
14					14
15	5.				15
16					16
17					17
18	6.				18
19					19
20					20
21					21
22	7.				22
23					23
24					24
25	8.				25
26					26
27					27
28	9.				28
29					29
30					30
31					31
32					32
33					33
34					34
35					35
36					36
37					37
38					38
39					39
40					40

(a)

1 Physical units:

2

3

4

5

6

7

8

9

10

(b) Equivalent units:

11

12

13 | | Materials | Conversion Costs |

14

15

16

17

18

19

20

(c) Unit costs:

21

22

23 | | Materials | Conversion Costs | Total |

24

25

26

27

28

29

(d) Costs accounted for:

	Equivalent Units	Unit Cost	Total Costs Assigned
Transferred out			
Work in process, June 30:			

(e)

Harrington Company				
Production Cost Report - Molding Department				
For The Month Ended June 30, 2011				
	Physical Units	Equivalent Units		
		Materials	Conversion Costs	
1 Quantities:				
2 Units to be accounted for				
3				
4				
5				
6				
7 Units accounted for				
8				
9				
10				
11				
12 Costs:			Conversion	
13 Unit costs:		Materials	Costs	Total
14				
15				
16				
17				
18 Costs to be accounted for				
19				
20				
21				
22				
23				
24 Cost reconciliation schedule:				
25 Costs accounted for				
26				
27				
28				
29				
30				
31				
32				
33				
34				
35				
36				
37				

(a)

	T12 Tables	C10 Chairs
1 (1) Physical units:		
2		
3		
4		
5		
6		
7		
8		
9		
10		
11		

(2) Equivalent units:	T12 Tables	
	Materials	Conversion Costs

	C10 Chairs	
	Materials	Conversion Costs

(3) Unit costs:	T12 Tables	C10 Chairs

(a) Continued

(4)	T12 Tables	
Costs accounted for:		
	C10 Chairs	
Costs accounted for:		

(b)

		Mallett Industries Inc. - Plant 1			
		Production Cost Report - Cutting Department			
		For The Month Ended July 31, 2011			

		Physical Units	Equivalent Units		
			Materials	Conversion Costs	
1	Quantities:				
2	Units to be accounted for				
3					
4					
5					
6					
7	Units accounted for				
8					
9					
10					
11					
12	Costs:			Conversion	
13	Unit costs:		Materials	Costs	Total
14					
15					
16					
17					
18	Costs to be accounted for				
19					
20					
21					
22					
23	Cost Reconciliation Schedule:				
24	Costs accounted for				
25					
26					
27					
28					
29					
30					
31					
32					
33					
34					
35					
36					
37					

(a)	Physical Units	Equivalent Units	
		Materials	Conversion Costs
1 Units to be accounted for:			
2			
3			
4			
5			
6			
7 Units accounted for:			
8			
9			
10			
11			
12 Costs:			
13			
14			
15			
16			
17			
18 Cost per unit			
19			
20 (b)			
21 Costs accounted for:			
22			
23			
24			
25			
26			
27			
28			
29			
30			
31			
32			
33			
34			
35			
36			
37			
38			
39			
40			

(b)

	Cortez Company				
	Assembly Department				
	Production Cost Report				
	For The Month Ended November 30, 2011				

		Physical Units	Equivalent Units		
			Materials	Conversion Costs	
1	Quantities:				
2	Units to be accounted for				
3					
4					
5					
6					
7	Units accounted for				
8					
9					
10					
11					
12	Costs:			Conversion	
13	Unit costs:		Materials	Costs	Total
14					
15					
16					
17					
18	Costs to be accounted for				
19					
20					
21					
22					
23	Cost Reconciliation Schedule:				
24	Costs accounted for				
25					
26					
27					
28					
29					
30					
31					
32					
33					
34					
35					
36					

(a) (1)	Physical Units	Equivalent Units	
		Materials	Conversion Costs
1 Units to be accounted for:			
2			
3			
4			
5			
6			
7 Units accounted for:			
8			
9			
10			
11 (2)			
12 Costs:			
13			
14			
15			
16			
17			
18 Cost per unit			
19			
20 (3)			
21 Costs accounted for:			
22			
23			
24			
25			
26			
27			
28			
29			
30			
31			
32			
33			
34			
35			
36			
37			
38			
39			
40			

(b)

			Ghost Company		
			Basketball Department		
			Production Cost Report		
			For The Month Ended July 31, 2011		

		Physical Units	Equivalent Units		
			Materials	Conversion Costs	
1	Quantities:				
2	Units to be accounted for				
3					
4					
5					
6					
7	Units accounted for				
8					
9					
10					
11					
12	Costs:			Conversion	
13	Unit costs:		Materials	Costs	Total
14					
15					
16					
17					
18	Costs to be accounted for				
19					
20					
21					
22					
23	Cost Reconciliation Schedule:				
24	Costs accounted for				
25					
26					
27					
28					
29					
30					
31					
32					
33					
34					
35					
36					

		Physical Units	Equivalent Units	
			Materials	Conversion Costs
1	(a) Computation of equivalent units:			
2				
3				
4				
5				
6				
7				
8				
9				
10				
11				
12	Computation of October unit costs:			
13				
14				
15				
16				
17				
18				
19				
20				
21	(b) Cost Reconciliation Schedule:			
22				
23				
24				
25				
26				
27				
28				
29				
30				
31				
32				
33				
34				
35				
36				
37				
38				
39				
40				

(a) Bicycles

(1) Equivalent units - Materials

	Physical Units	% Added This Period	Equivalent Units
1			
2			
3			
4			
5			

Equivalent units - Conversion

	Physical Units	% Added This Period	Equivalent Units
6			
7			
8			
9			
10			
11			

(2) Unit Costs:

	Materials	Conversion
12		
13		
14		
15		
16		
17		
18		

(3) Assignment of Costs:

Costs to Be Assigned	Assignment of Costs	Equivalent Units	Unit Cost	Total Costs Assigned

(a) Continued

Tricycles (1) Equivalent units - Materials	Physical Units	% Added This Period	Equivalent Units
1			
2			
3			
4			
5			

6 Equivalent units - Conversion			
7			
8			
9			
10			
11			

12 (2) Unit Costs:		Materials	Conversion
13			
14			
15			
16			
17			
18			

(3) Assignment of Costs:

Costs to Be Assigned	Assignment of Costs	Equivalent Units	Unit Cost	Total Costs Assigned
23				
24				
25				
26				
27				
28				
29				
30				
31				
32				
33				
34				
35				

(b)

		Pacocha Company
		Bicycles Department
		Production Cost Report
		For The Month Ended March 31

	Physical Units	Equivalent Units		
		Materials	Conversion Costs	
1 Quantities:				
2 Units to be accounted for				
3				
4				
5				
6				
7 Units accounted for				
8				
9				
10				
11				
12 Costs:			Conversion	
13 Unit costs:		Materials	Costs	Total
14				
15				
16				
17				
18 Costs to be accounted for				
19				
20				
21				
22				
23 Cost Reconciliation Schedule:				
24 Costs accounted for				
25				
26				
27				
28				
29				
30				
31				
32				
33				
34				
35				
36				

	Trans-action	Account Titles	Debit	Credit	
1	1.				1
2					2
3					3
4	2.				4
5					5
6					6
7					7
8	3.				8
9					9
10					10
11	4.				11
12					12
13					13
14					14
15	5.				15
16					16
17					17
18	6.				18
19					19
20					20
21					21
22	7.				22
23					23
24					24
25	8.				25
26					26
27					27
28	9.				28
29					29
30					30
31					31
32					32
33					33
34					34
35					35
36					36
37					37
38					38
39					39
40					40

(a)

1	Physical units:	
2		
3		
4		
5		
6		
7		
8		
9		
10		

(b) Equivalent units:

		Materials	Conversion Costs
11			
12			
13			
14			
15			
16			
17			
18			
19			
20			

(c) Unit costs:

		Materials	Conversion Costs	Total
21				
22				
23				
24				
25				
26				
27				
28				
29				

(d) Costs accounted for:

		Equivalent Units	Unit Cost	Total Costs Assigned
30				
31				
32				
33				
34	Transferred out			
35	Work in process, June 30:			
36				
37				
38				
39				
40				

(e)

		Walters Company					
		Production Cost Report - Molding Department					
		For The Month Ended January 31, 2011					

	Physical Units	Equivalent Units			
		Materials	Conversion Costs		
1	Quantities:				
2	Units to be accounted for				
3					
4					
5					
6					
7	Units accounted for				
8					
9					
10					
11					
12	Costs:			Conversion	
13	Unit costs:		Materials	Costs	Total
14					
15					
16					
17					
18	Costs to be accounted for				
19					
20					
21					
22					
23					
24	Cost reconciliation schedule:				
25	Costs accounted for				
26					
27					
28					
29					
30					
31					
32					
33					
34					
35					
36					
37					

(a)

	R12 Refrigerators	F24 Freezers
(1) Physical units:		

(2) Equivalent units:	R12 Refrigerators	
	Materials	Conversion Costs

	F24 Freezers	
	Materials	Conversion Costs

(3) Unit costs:	R12 Refrigerators	F24 Freezers

(a) Continued

(4)		R12 Refrigerators	
Costs accounted for:			
		F24 Freezers	
Costs accounted for:			

(b)

Slocum Corporation - Plant A					
Production Cost Report - Stamping Department					
For The Month Ended June 30, 2011					
	Physical Units	Equivalent Units			
		Materials	Conversion Costs		
Quantities:					
Units to be accounted for					
Units accounted for					
Costs:		Materials	Conversion Costs	Total	
Unit costs:					
Costs to be accounted for					
Cost Reconciliation Schedule:					
Costs accounted for					

(a)	Physical Units	Equivalent Units	
		Materials	Conversion Costs
1 Units to be accounted for:			
2			
3			
4			
5			
6			
7 Units accounted for:			
8			
9			
10			
11			
12 Costs:			
13			
14			
15			
16			
17			
18 Cost per unit			
19			
20 (b)			
21 Costs accounted for:			
22			
23			
24			
25			
26			
27			
28			
29			
30			
31			
32			
33			
34			
35			
36			
37			
38			
39			
40			

(b)

McNair Company

Assembly Department

Production Cost Report

For The Month Ended October 31, 2011

	Physical Units	Equivalent Units		
		Materials	Conversion Costs	
1 Quantities:				
2 Units to be accounted for				
3				
4				
5				
6				
7 Units accounted for				
8				
9				
10				
11				
12 Costs:			Conversion	
13 Unit costs:		Materials	Costs	Total
14				
15				
16				
17				
18 Costs to be accounted for				
19				
20				
21				
22				
23 Cost Reconciliation Schedule:				
24 Costs accounted for				
25				
26				
27				
28				
29				
30				
31				
32				
33				
34				
35				
36				

(a) (1)	Physical Units	Equivalent Units	
		Materials	Conversion Costs
1 Units to be accounted for:			
2			
3			
4			
5			
6			
7 Units accounted for:			
8			
9			
10			
11 (2)			
12 Costs:			
13			
14			
15			
16			
17			
18 Cost per unit			
19			
20 (3)			
21 Costs accounted for:			
22			
23			
24			
25			
26			
27			
28			
29			
30			
31			
32			
33			
34			
35			
36			
37			
38			
39			
40			

(b)

		Marte Company				
		Bicycle Department				
		Production Cost Report				
		For The Month Ended May 31, 2011				

	Physical Units	Equivalent Units			
		Materials	Conversion Costs		
1 Quantities:					1
2 Units to be accounted for					2
3					3
4					4
5					5
6					6
7 Units accounted for					7
8					8
9					9
10					10
11					11
12 Costs:			Conversion		12
13 Unit costs:		Materials	Costs	Total	13
14					14
15					15
16					16
17					17
18 Costs to be accounted for					18
19					19
20					20
21					21
22					22
23 Cost Reconciliation Schedule:					23
24 Costs accounted for					24
25					25
26					26
27					27
28					28
29					29
30					30
31					31
32					32
33					33
34					34
35					35
36					36

	Physical Units	Equivalent Units	
		Materials	Conversion Costs
(a) Computation of equivalent units:			
Computation of March unit costs:			
(b) Cost Reconciliation Schedule:			

(a) Basketballs	Physical Units	% Added This Period	Equivalent Units
(1) Equivalent units - Materials			

Equivalent units - Conversion			

(2) Unit Costs:

	Materials	Conversion

(3) Assignment of Costs:

Costs to Be Assigned	Assignment of Costs	Equivalent Units	Unit Cost	Total Costs Assigned

(a) Continued

Soccer balls (1) Equivalent units - Materials	Physical Units	% Added This Period	Equivalent Units
1			
2			
3			
4			
5			

Equivalent units - Conversion			
7			
8			
9			
10			
11			

(2) Unit Costs:

	Materials	Conversion
13		
14		
15		
16		
17		
18		

(3) Assignment of Costs:

Costs to Be Assigned	Assignment of Costs	Equivalent Units	Unit Cost	Total Costs Assigned

(b)

Stangel Company				
Basketballs Department				
Production Cost Report				
For The Month Ended August 31				
	Physical Units	Equivalent Units		
		Materials	Conversion Costs	
1 Quantities:				
2 Units to be accounted for				
3				
4				
5				
6				
7 Units accounted for				
8				
9				
10				
11				
12 Costs:			Conversion	
13 Unit costs:		Materials	Costs	Total
14				
15				
16				
17				
18 Costs to be accounted for				
19				
20				
21				
22				
23 Cost Reconciliation Schedule:				
24 Costs accounted for				
25				
26				
27				
28				
29				
30				
31				
32				
33				
34				
35				
36				

(a)

(b)

(b)

		Sunshine Beach Company		
		Mixing Department		
		Production Cost Report		
		For The Month Ended July 31, 2011		

	Physical Units	Equivalent Units Materials	Conversion Costs	
1 Quantities:				
2 Units to be accounted for				
3				
4				
5				
6				
7 Units accounted for				
8				
9				
10				
11				
12 Costs:		Materials	Conversion Costs	Total
13 Unit costs:				
14				
15				
16				
17				
18 Costs to be accounted for				
19				
20				
21				
22				
23 Cost Reconciliation Schedule:				
24 Costs accounted for				
25				
26				
27				
28				
29				
30				
31				
32				
33				
34				
35				
36				

BE4-6

Activity Cost Pool	Estimated Overhead	Expected Use of Cost Drivers per Activity	Activity-Based Overhead Rates
1. Designing	$ 4 5 0 0 0 0	12,000 Designer hours	
2. Sizing and cutting	4 0 0 0 0 0	160,000 Machine hours	
3. Stitching and trimming	1 4 4 0 0 0	80,000 Labor hours	
4. Wrapping and packing	3 3 6 0 0 0	32,000 Finished units	
5.			

BE4-7

Activity Cost Pool	Estimated Overhead	Expected Use of Cost Drivers per Activity	Activity-Based Overhead Rates
	$ 9 0 0 0 0		
Ordering and receiving	4 8 0 0 0	15,000 orders	
Etching	1 7 6 0 0 0	60,000 Machine hours	
Soldering		440,000 Labor hours	

	Cost Drivers	Overhead Rates	Total Overhead Applied
	11,000 Orders		
	50,000 Machine hours		
	500,000 Labor hours		

BE4-9

Value-added Activities	Hours

Non-value-added Activites	Hours

BE4-12

(a) Activity Cost Pool	Estimated Overhead	Expected Use of Cost Drivers per Activity	Activity-Based Overhead Rates	
1				1
2 Product design	$ 50000	10 changes		2
3 Machining	300000	150,000 Machine hours		3
4 Material handling	100000	100 set-ups		4
5				5
6				6

(b)		
Activity	Level of Activity	7 8
Product design		9
Machining		10
Material handling		11

(a)   Computations of activity-based overhead rates per cost driver:

Activity Cost Pool	Estimated Overhead	Expected Use of Cost Drivers per Activity	Activity-Based Overhead Rates
1 Machine setup	$ 20000	40 setups	
2 Machining	110000	5,000 Machine hours	
3 Packing	30000	500 orders	
4	$160000		

(b)   Assignment of each activity's overhead cost to products using ABC:

See next page

(c)   Computation of overhead cost per unit:

	BC113	AD908
Total costs assigned		
Total units produced		
Overhead cost per unit		

(d)

Name _____

Section _____

Date _____

Weber Industries

(b)

Activity Cost Pools	BC113		AD908	
	Expected Use of Cost Drivers per Product	Activity-Based Overhead Rates	Cost Assigned	Expected Use of Cost Drivers per Product	Activity-Based Overhead Rates	Cost Assigned
1 Machine setup						
2 Machining						
3 Packing and shipping						
4 Total assigned costs						
5						
6						
7						
8						
9						
10						

	Estimated Overhead	Direct Labor Costs	Overhead Rate	
(a)				

(b) Activity Cost Pool	Estimated Overhead	Expected Use of Cost Drivers per Activity	Activity-Based Overhead Rates
Machining			
Machine setup			

(c) Traditional Costing		Standard		Custom
Activity-based costing		Standard		Custom
Machining:				
Machine setup:				

(a) Traditional costing system:

	Product 540X	Product 137Y	Product 249S
Sales			
Costs			
Operating income			

(b) Activity-based costing system:

	Product 540X	Product 137Y	Product 249S
Sales			
Costs			
Operating income			

(c)

Product 540X:

Product 137Y:

Product 249S:

(d)

(a)

Activity Cost Pool	Estimated Overhead	Expected Use of Cost Drivers per Activity	Activity-Based Overhead Rates
1			
2			
3			
4			
5			

Activity-based costing		Wool		Cotton	
6					
7 Cutting					
8					
9					
10					
11 Design					
12					
13					
14					
15					
16					

(b)

	Estimated Overhead	Direct Labor Hours	Overhead Rate	
17				
18				
19				
20				
21				
22				
23				

Traditional costing		Wool		Cotton	
24					
25					
26					
27					
28					
29					
30					
31					
32					
33					
34					
35					
36					
37					
38					
39					
40					

(a)

1	Direct labor hours for car wheels		
2	Direct labor hours for truck wheels		
3	Total direct labor hours		
4			

	Estimated Overhead	Direct Labor Hours	Overhead Rate
5			
6			
7			
8			
9			
10			

11	Overhead assigned:	
12	Car wheels	
13	Truck wheels	
14	Total overhead	
15		

(b)

	Activity Cost Pools	Estimated Overhead	Expected Use of Cost Drivers	ABC Overhead Rate
17				
18				
19	Machine setup			
20	Assembling			
21	Inspection			
22				

(c)   Car Wheels

	Activiy Cost Pools	Expected Use of Cost Driver	Overhead Rate	Cost Assigned
24				
25				
26	Setting up machines			
27	Assembling			
28	Inspection			
29	Total costs assigned			
30				

Truck Wheels

		Expected Use of Cost Driver	Overhead Rate	Cost Assigned
32	Setting up machines			
33	Assembling			
34	Inspection			
35	Total costs assigned			
36				

(d)

38	
39	
40	

(a) Activity Cost Pool	Estimated Overhead	Expected Use of Cost Drivers per Activity	Activity-Based Overhead Rates	
1 Scheduling and travel				
2 Setup time				
3 Supervision				
4				
5 Commercial				
6 Cost Pools		Cost Drivers per	ABC OH Rate	OH Costs
7 Scheduling and travel				
8 Setup time				
9 Supervision				
10 Total commercial overhead				
11				
12 Residential				
13 Cost Pools		Cost Drivers	ABC OH Rate	OH Costs
14 Scheduling and travel				
15 Setup time				
16 Supervision				
17 Total residential overhead				
18				
19				

(b)	Commercial	Residential
20		
21 Revenues		
22 Direct material cost		
23 Direct labor costs		
24 Overhead cost		
25 Operating income (loss)		

26

27 (c)

28

29

30

31

32

33

34

35

36

37

38

39

40

1	(a) Traditional costing:	1
2	Overhead rate =	2
3		3
4	(1) One mobile safe:	4
5		5
6		6
7		7
8	(2) One walk-in safe:	8
9		9
10		10
11		11
12	(b) Activity-based costing:	12
13	(1) Material handing costs rate =	13
14		14
15	(a) One mobile safe:	15
16		16
17		17
18		18
19	(b) One walk-in safe:	19
20		20
21		21
22		22
23	(2) Purchasing activity costs rate =	23
24		24
25	(a) One mobile safe:	25
26		26
27		27
28		28
29	(b) One walk-in safe:	29
30		30
31		31
32		32

		Traditional Costing	Activity-based Costing	
33	(c)			33
34				34
35				35
36	Mobile safe			36
37	Walk-in safe			37
38				38
39				39
40				40

(a)

Activity	Expected Use of Cost Drivers		Overhead Rate
	Overhead		
1 Material handling			
2 Machine setups			
3 Quality inspections			
4			
5			

(b)

Cost Driver	Instruments		Gauges		Total
	Number	Cost	Number	Cost	Overhead
6					
7 Requisitions					
8 Setups					
9 Inspections					
10 Total costs					
11					
12 Total units					
13					
14 Cost per unit					
15					
16					
17					
18					
19					
20					

(c)

1		1
2		2
3		3
4		4
5		5
6		6
7		7
8		8
9		9
10		10
11		11
12		12
13		13
14		14
15		15
16		16
17		17
18		18
19		19
20		20
21		21
22		22
23		23
24		24
25		25
26		26
27		27
28		28
29		29
30		30
31		31
32		32
33		33
34		34
35		35
36		36
37		37
38		38
39		39
40		40

(a)

(1)

	(2) Activity Cost Pool	Cost Drivers Used	Overhead Rate	Overhead Cost Assigned	
6	Sales commissions				
7	Advertising - TV/Radio				
8	Advertising - Newspaper				
9	Catalogs				
10	Cost of catalog sales				
11	Credit and collection				
12	Total assigned cost				
13	for March				

(b)

(c)

(a)

	Activity Cost Pool	Cost Drivers Used	Overhead Rate	Overhead Cost Assigned	
1	(1)				
2					
3					
4					
5					
6	(2)				
7	Activity Cost Pool				
8	Inspections of material received				
9	In-process inspections				
10	FDA certification				
11	Total assigned cost				
12	for June				

(b)

(c)

(a) and (b)

(a)

Manufacturing Costs	Products		
	Home Model	Commercial Model	

(b)

Activity Cost Pool	Estimated Overhead	Expected Use of Cost Driver		Activity- Based Overhead Rate	
		Number	Driver	Rate	Per
Receiving					
Forming					
Assembling					
Testing					
Painting					
Packing and shipping					
Total					

(c)

Activity Cost Pool	Home Model			Commercial Model		
	Expected Use of Drivers	Overhead Rate	Cost Assigned	Expected Use of Drivers	Overhead Rate	Cost Assigned
1 Receiving						
2 Forming						
3 Assembling						
4 Testing						
5 Painting						
6 Packing and shipping						
7 Total assigned cost						
8						
9						
10 Units produced						
11						
12 Overhead cost per unit						
13						
14						
15						
16						
17						
18						
19						
20						

(d)

	Products	
	Home Model	Commercial Model
1		
2		
3		
4		
5		
6		
7		

(e)

Activity	Value- vs Non-value-Added

(f) (1)

(2)

(a) Allocation of total manufacturing overhead using ABC-

	Overhead Rate	Royale		Majestic		Total Overhead
		Drivers Used	Cost Assigned	Drivers Used	Cost Assigned	
Purchase orders						
Machine setups						
Machine hours						
Inspections						
Total assigned costs						
Units produced						
Cost per unit						

(b) Per unit cost and gross profit under ABC costing were:

	Royale	Majestic

(c)

(a), (b), and (d)

1	(a) Predetermined overhead rate using machine hours:
2	
3	
4	
5	
6	(b) Manufacturing cost per stair under traditional costing:
7	
8	
9	
10	
11	
12	
13	
14	
15	
16	
17	
18	
19	
20	
21	(d)
22	
23	
24	
25	
26	
27	
28	
29	
30	
31	
32	
33	
34	
35	
36	
37	
38	
39	
40	

(c)

Manufacturing cost per stair under activity-based costing:					
Computation of Activity-based Overhead Rates					
Activity Cost Pool	Total Estimated Overhead	Expected Use of Cost Drivers per Activity		Activity-Based Overhead	
		Number	Driver	Rate	Per
Purchasing					
Handling materials					
Production					
Setting up machines					
Inspecting					
Inventory control					
Utilities					
Total					

Assignment of Overhead to Order of 280 Stairs				
Activity Cost Pool	Expected Used of Driver		Activity Based Overhead Rate	Cost Assigned
	Number	Driver		
Purchasing				
Handling materials				
Production				
Setting up machines				
Inspecting				
Inventory control				
Utilities				
Total overhead assigned				

Total manufacturing cost per stair under ABC:	

(a) and (b)

(a)   Computation of unit costs - traditional costing

Overhead cost per labor hour:

	Products		
Manufacturing Costs	CoolDay	LiteMist	

(b)

ty Cost Pool	Estimated Overhead	Expected Use of Cost Driver Number	Activity- Based Overhead	
			Rate	Per
Grape processing				
Aging				
Bottling and corking				
Labeling and boxing				
Maintain and inspect equipment				
Total				

(c)

Activity Cost Pool	CoolDay			LiteMist		
	Expected Use of Drivers	Overhead Rate	Cost Assigned	Expected Use of Drivers	Overhead Rate	Cost Assigned
1 Grape processing						
2 Aging						
3 Bottling and corking						
4 Labeling and boxing						
5 Maintain and inspect equipment						
6 Totals						
7						
8 Liters produced						
9						
10 Overhead cost per liter						
11						
12						
13						
14						
15						
16						
17						
18						
19						
20						

(d)

Manufacturing Costs	Products	
	CoolDay	LiteMist
1		
2		
3		
4		
5		

(e)

(a), (c), and (d)

(a)	
Overhead rate assigned to audit:	
Overhead rate assigned to tax:	

(c)		Value-Added vs.
	Activity	Nonvalue-Added

(d) Overhead assigned to the two service lines:	Audit	Tax

Name

Section

Date

(b) (1) Computation of activity-based overhead rates:

Activity Cost Pool	Estimated Overhead	Total Expected Use of Cost Drivers		Activity-Based Overhead	
		Amount	Driver	Rate	Per
1 Employee training					1
2 Typing and secretarial					2
3 Computing					3
4 Facility rental					4
5 Travel					5
6 Total					6
7					7
8					8

(2) Assignment of overhead to audit and tax services:

Activity Cost Pool	Audit			Tax		
	Expected Use of Driver	Overhead Rate	Cost Assigned	Expected Use of Driver	Overhead Rate	Cost Assigned
1 Employee training						1
2 Typing and secretarial						2
3 Computing						3
4 Facility rental						4
5 Travel						5
6 Overhead asigned						6
7						7
8						8

(a) and (b)

(a)	Products		
	Deluxe Model	Standard Model	
1 Manufacturing Costs			
2			
3			
4			
5			
6			
7			
8			
9			
10			
11			
12			
13			
14			
15			

(b)		Expected Use of Cost Driver		Activity- Based Overhead Rate	
Activity Cost Pool	Estimated Overhead	Number	Driver	Rate	Per
20 Purchasing					
21 Receiving					
22 Assembling					
23 Testing					
24 Finishing					
25 Packing and shipping					
26 Total					
27					
28					
29					
30					

Name

Section

Date

VideoPlus, Inc.

(c)

Activity Cost Pool	Deluxe Model			Standard Model		
	Expected Use of Drivers	Overhead Rate	Cost Assigned	Expected Use of Drivers	Overhead Rate	Cost Assigned
1 Purchasing						
2 Receiving						
3 Assembling						
4 Testing						
5 Finishing						
6 Packing and shipping						
7 Total assigned cost						
8						
9						
10 Units produced						
11						
12 Overhead cost per unit						
13						
14						
15						
16						
17						
18						
19						
20						

(d)

	Products	
	Deluxe Model	Standard Model
1		
2		
3		
4		
5		
6		
7		
8		

(e)

Activity	Value- vs Non-value-Added

(f) (1)

(2)

(a) Allocation of total manufacturing overhead using ABC-

	Elite		Preferred		Total Overhead
Overhead Rate	Drivers Used	Cost Assigned	Drivers Used	Cost Assigned	
Purchase orders					
Machine setups					
Machine hours					
Inspections					
Total assigned costs					
Units produced					
Cost per unit					

(b) and (c)

(b) Per unit cost and gross profit under ABC costing were:

	Elite	Preferred

(c)

(a), (b), and (d)

1	(a) Predetermined overhead rate using machine hours:
2	
3	
4	
5	
6	(b) Manufacturing cost per armoire under traditional costing:
7	
8	
9	
10	
11	
12	
13	
14	
15	
16	
17	
18	
19	
20	
21	(d)
22	
23	
24	
25	
26	
27	
28	
29	
30	
31	
32	
33	
34	
35	
36	
37	
38	
39	
40	

(c)

Manufacturing cost per armoire under activity-based costing:

Computation of Activity-based Overhead Rate

Activity Cost Pool	Total Estimated Overhead	Total Estimated Drivers		Activity-Based Overhead	
		Number	Driver	Rate	Per
Purchasing					
Handling materials					
Production					
Setting up machines					
Inspecting					
Inventory control					
Utilities					
Total					

Assignment of Overhead to Order of 10 armoires

Activity Cost Pool	Expected Used of Driver		Activity Based Overhead Rate	Cost Assigned
	Number	Driver		
Purchasing				
Handling materials				
Production				
Setting up machines				
Inspecting				
Inventory control				
Utilities				
Total overhead assigned				

Total manufacturing cost per armoire under ABC:

(a) and (b)

(a)   Computation of unit costs - traditional costing

Overhead cost per labor hour:

Manufacturing Costs	Products		
	Valley Fresh	Venuchi Valley	

(b)

Activity Cost Pool	Estimated Overhead	Expected Use of Cost Driver Number	Activity- Based Overhead	
			Rate	Per
Grape processing				
Aging				
Bottling and corking				
Labeling and boxing				
Maintain and inspect equipment				
Total				

(c)

Activity Cost Pool	Valley Fresh			Venuchi Valley		
	Expected Use of Drivers	Overhead Rate	Cost Assigned	Expected Use of Drivers	Overhead Rate	Cost Assigned
1 Grape processing						
2 Aging						
3 Bottling and corking						
4 Labeling and boxing						
5 Maintain and inspect equipment						
6 Totals						
7						
8 Gallons produced						
9						
10 Overhead cost per gallon						
11						
12						
13						
14						
15						
16						
17						
18						
19						
20						

(d)

Manufacturing Costs	Products	
	Valley Fresh	Valley Venuchi
1		
2		
3		
4		
5		

(e)

(a), (c), and (d)

1	**(a)**
2	Computation of total overhead cost using direct labor hours:
3	
4	
5	
6	Overhead assigned to corporate:
7	Overhead assigned to individual:
8	
9	
10	

(c)		
	Activity	Value-Added vs. Nonvalue-Added
13		
14		
15		
16		
17		
18		
19		
20		
21		
22		
23		
24		
25		

(d) Overhead is assigned to the two service lines as follows:	Corporate	Individual
Traditional costing		
ABC		
Difference		

Name _____

Section _____

Date _____

(b) (1) Computation of activity-based overhead rates:

Activity Cost Pool	Estimated Overhead	Total Expected Use of Cost Drivers		Activity-Based Overhead Rates	
		Amount	Driver	Rate	Per
1 Employee training					
2 Typing and secretarial					
3 Computing					
4 Facility rental					
5 Travel					
6 Total					
7					
8					

(2) Assignment of overhead to corporate and individual services:

Activity Cost Pool	Corporate			Individual		
	Expected Use of Driver	Overhead Rate	Cost Assigned	Expected Use of Driver	Overhead Rate	Cost Assigned
1 Employee training						
2 Typing and secretarial						
3 Computing						
4 Facility rental						
5 Travel						
6 Total overhead assigned						
7						
8						

(a) Computation of activity-based overhead rate:

Activity Cost Pool	Total Estimated Overhead	Expected Used of Cost Driver		Activity-Based Overhead	
		Number	Driver	Rate	Per
Market analysis					
Product design					
Product development					
Prototype testing					

(b) Computation of charges to in-house manufacturing department-

Activity Cost Pool	Cost Drivers Used		Overhead Rate	Cost Assigned
	Amount	Driver		
Market analysis				
Product design				
Product development				
Prototype testing				
Total overhead assigned				

(c) Computation of charges to outside R&D contractor -

Activity Cost Pool	Cost Drivers Used		Overhead Rate	Cost Assigned
	Amount	Driver		
Market analysis				
Product design				
Product development				
Prototype testing				
Total overhead assigned				

(d)

BE5-4	High	Low	Difference	Variable Cost per Mile

	High	Low

BE5-5	High	Low	Difference	Variable Cost per Unit

	High	Low

BE5-6

Russel Manufacturing Inc.

CVP Income Statement

For the Quarter Ended March 31, 2011

(a)

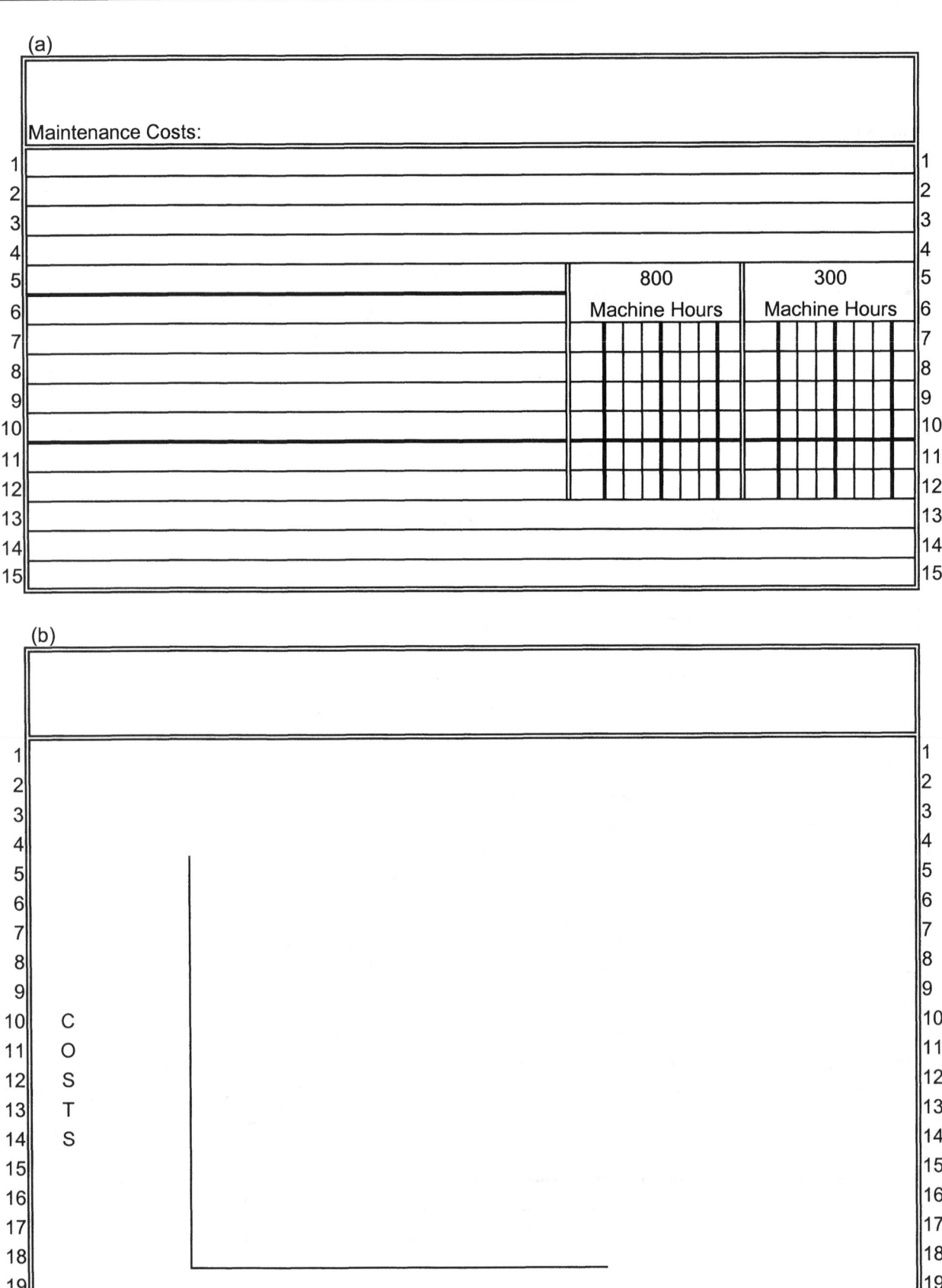

Maintenance Costs:	800 Machine Hours	300 Machine Hours

(b)

COSTS

Machine Hours

(a)

Maintenance Costs:

			Activity Level		
			High	Low	
1					1
2					2
3					3
4					4
5					5
6					6
7					7
8					8
9					9
10					10
11					11
12					12
13					13
14					14
15					15

(b)

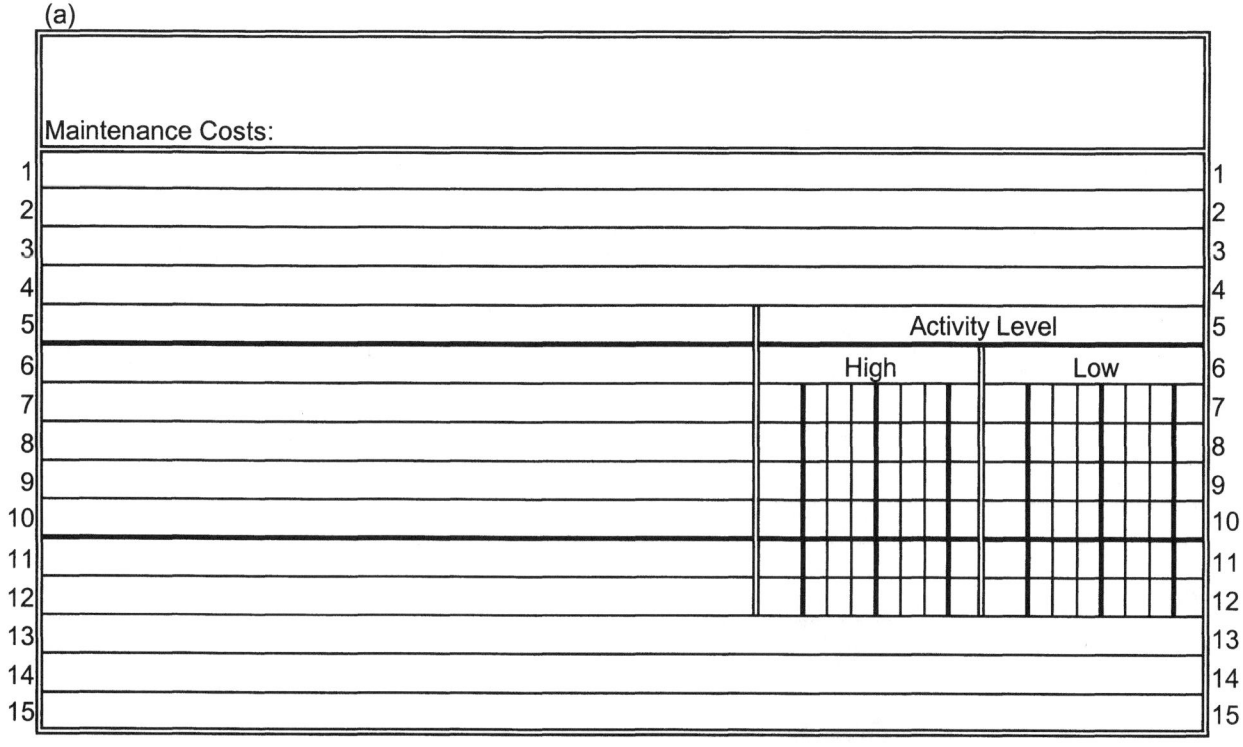

C
O
S
T
S

Machine Hours

(a)

Sannes Company

CVP Income Statement

For the Month Ended September 30, 2011

	Total	Per Unit
1			1
2			2
3			3
4			4
5			5
6			6
7			7
8			8
9			9
10			10

(b)

1	1
2	2
3	3
4	4
5	5

(c)

Sannes Company

CVP Income Statement

For the Month Ended September 30, 2011

	Total	Per Unit
1			1
2			2
3			3
4			4
5			5
6			6
7			7
8			8
9			9
10			10
11			11
12			12
13			13
14			14
15			15

1	(a) Variable cost (per haircut)	Fixed cost (per month)	1
2			2
3			3
4			4
5			5
6			6
7			7
8			8
9			9
10	(b) Break-even sales in units Break-even sales in dollars		10
11			11
12			12
13			13
14			14
15			15
16	(c) CVP graph		16
17			17
18			18
19			19
20			20
21			21
22	D		22
23	O		23
24	L		24
25	L		25
26	A		26
27	R		27
28	S		28
29	(000)		29
30			30
31			31
32			32
33			33
34			34
35		Number of Haircuts	35
36	(d) Net income		36
37			37
38			38
39			39
40			40

(a)

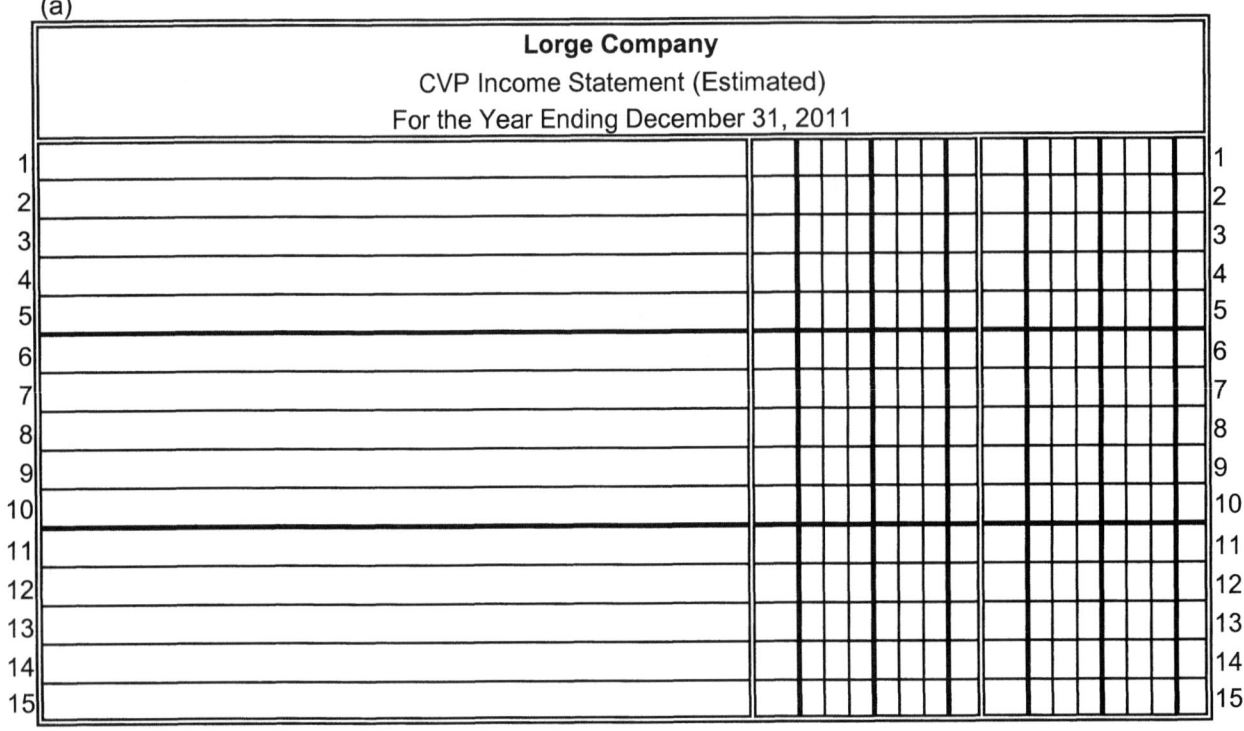

Lorge Company		
CVP Income Statement (Estimated)		
For the Year Ending December 31, 2011		

(b), (c), and (d)

(b)

(1) Break-even sales in units   (2) Break-even sales in dollars

(c) Contribution margin ratio

Margin of safety ratio

(d) Required sales

(a) and (b)

1	(a) Current break-even point:
2	
3	
4	
5	
6	
7	
8	New break-even point:
9	
10	
11	
12	
13	(b) Current margin-of-safety ratio:
14	
15	
16	
17	
18	New margin-of-safety ratio:
19	
20	
21	
22	

(c)

Value Shoe Store
Comparative CVP Income Statement

	Current	New
1		
2		
3		
4		
5		
6		
7		
8		
9		
10		
11		
12		
13		

(a)

	Current Year
(1)	
1	
2	
3	
4	
5	
6	
7	
8	
9	
10	
11	
12	

	Current Year		Projected Year
13			
14			
15			
16			
17			
18			
19			
20			
21			
22			
23			
24			
25			
26			
27			

(2)	Current Year	Projected Year
Fixed costs:		
30		
31		
32		
33		
34		
35		
36		
37		
38		
39		
40		

(b)

1	1
2	2
3	3
4	4
5	5
6	6
7	7
8	8
9	9
10	10
11	11
12 (c)	12
13	13
14	14
15	15
16	16
17	17
18	18
19	19
20 (d)	20
21	21
22	22
23	23
24	24
25	25
26	26
27	27
28	28
29	29
30	30
31	31
32	32
33	33
34	34
35	35
36	36
37	37
38	38
39	39
40	40

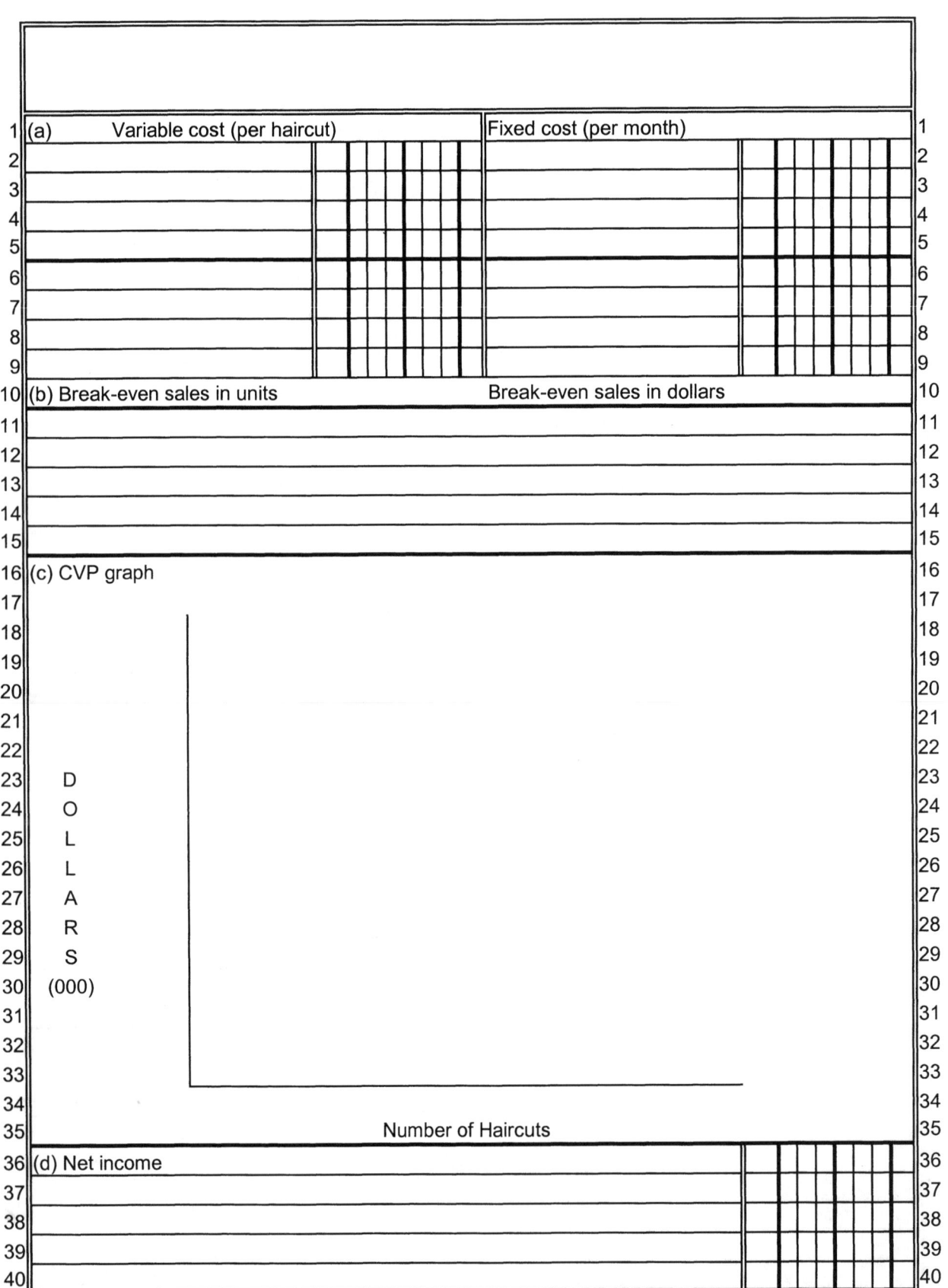

(a)   Variable cost (per haircut)   Fixed cost (per month)

(b) Break-even sales in units   Break-even sales in dollars

(c) CVP graph

D
O
L
L
A
R
S
(000)

Number of Haircuts

(d) Net income

(a)

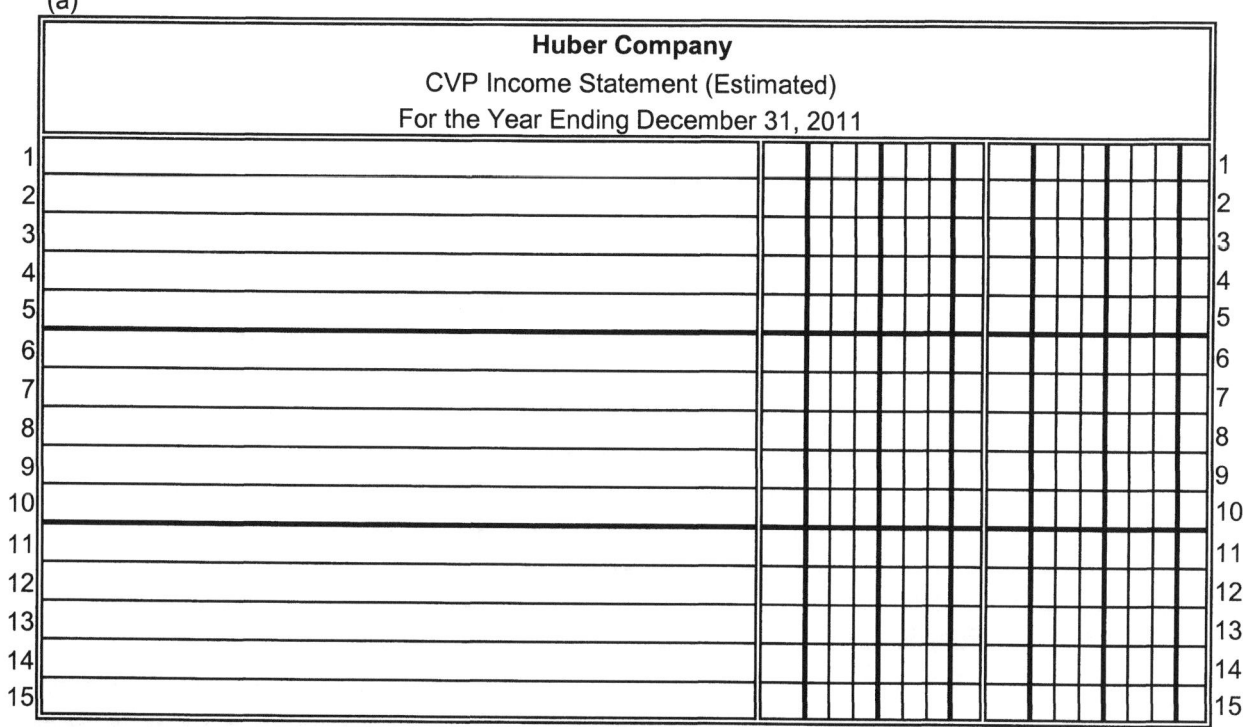

Huber Company

CVP Income Statement (Estimated)

For the Year Ending December 31, 2011

(b), (c), and (d)

(b)

(1) Break-even sales in units   (2) Break-even sales in dollars

(c) Contribution margin ratio

Margin of safety ratio

(d) Required sales

(a) and (b)

1	(a) Current break-even point:
2	
3	
4	
5	
6	
7	
8	New break-even point:
9	
10	
11	
12	
13	(b) Current margin-of-safety ratio:
14	
15	
16	
17	
18	New margin-of-safety ratio:
19	
20	
21	
22	

(c)

Payless Shoe Store
Comparative CVP Income Statement

	Current	New
1		
2		
3		
4		
5		
6		
7		
8		
9		
10		
11		
12		
13		
14		

(a)

	(1)	Current Year
1		
2		
3		
4		
5		
6		
7		
8		
9		
10		
11		
12		

		Current Year		Projected Year
13				
14				
15				
16				
17				
18				
19				
20				
21				
22				
23				
24				
25				
26				
27				

	(2) Fixed costs:	Current Year	Projected Year
28			
29			
30			
31			
32			
33			
34			
35			
36			
37			
38			
39			
40			

(b)

1	1
2	2
3	3
4	4
5	5
6	6
7	7
8	8
9	9
10	10
11	11

12 (c)   Sales dollars required for

13   target net income =

20 (d)   Margin of safety ratio =

25 (e) (1)   Projected Year

(e) (Continued)

1	(2) Contribution margin ratio =
2	
3	
4	
5	(3) Break-even point in dollars =
6	
7	
8	
9	
10	
11	
12	
13	
14	
15	
16	
17	
18	
19	
20	
21	
22	
23	
24	
25	
26	
27	
28	
29	
30	
31	
32	
33	
34	
35	
36	
37	
38	
39	
40	

Name

Chapter 5 Decision Making Across the Organization

Gagliano Company

(a) (1)

	CAPITAL INTENSIVE			(2)		LABOR INTENSIVE	

1 Fixed costs:

2

3

4

5

6 Unit contribution margin:

7

8

9

10

11

12

13

14

15 Break-even Point in units:

16

17

18 (b)

19

20

21

22

(c)

1	1
2	2
3	3
4	4
5	5
6	6
7	7
8	8
9	9
10	10
11	11
12	12
13	13
14	14
15	15
16	16
17	17
18	18
19	19
20	20
21	21
22	22
23	23
24	24
25	25
26	26
27	27
28	28
29	29
30	30
31	31
32	32
33	33
34	34
35	35
36	36
37	37
38	38
39	39
40	40

Name

Section

Date

(a) and (b)

1	(a) Variable costs per unit:	1
2		2
3		3
4		4
5		5
6		6
7	Fixed costs are:	7
8		8
9		9
10		10
11		11
12		12
13	The break-even points are:	13
14		14
15		15
16		16
17		17
18		18
19		19
20		20
21		21
22		22
23	(b)	23
24		24
25		25
26		26
27		27
28	Net income computation:	28
29		29
30		30
31		31
32		32
33		33
34		34
35		35
36		36
37		37
38		38
39		39
40		40
41		41

(b) (Continued), (c), and (d)

1	(b) (Continued) - New break-even point in dollars:
2	
3	
4	
5	
6	
7	
8	(c) Computations:
9	
10	
11	
12	
13	
14	Net income calculation:
15	
16	
17	
18	
19	
20	
21	
22	
23	
24	
25	
26	
27	
28	
29	
30	
31	New break-even point in dollars:
32	
33	
34	
35	
36	
37	
38	(d)
39	
40	

BE6-2

	Pesavento Manufacturing Inc.
	Income Statement
	For the Quarter Ended March 31, 2011

1			
2			
3			
4			
5			
6			
7			
8			
9			
10			
11			
12			
13			
14			

BE6-7

	Model	Sales Mix Percentage	Unit Contribution Margin	Weighted-Average Unit Contribution Margin
	A12			
	B22			
	C124			

BE6-8

Total break-even sales in units:

Units of A12 =	
Units of B22 =	
Units of C124 =	

BE6-9

1	Weighted average contribution	1
2	margin ratio =	2
3		3
4		4
5	Total break-even point in dollars =	5
6		6
7		7
8	Birthday	8
9	Standard tapered	9
10	Large scented	10
11		11
12		12

BE6-11

		Product A	Product B	
13				13
14				14
15				15
16				16
17				17
18				18

BE6-13

		Break-even Point in Dollars		
19		Turgro Co.	Meriden Co.	19
20				20
21				21
22				22
23				23
24				24
25				25
26				26
27				27
28				28
29				29

BE6-15

		Product 1	Product 2	
30				30
31				31
32				32
33				33
34				34
35				35
36				36
37				37
38				38
39				39
40				40

*BE6-16

Variable Costing

*BE6-17

Absorption Costing

*BE6-18

(a) Absorption Costing:

(b) Variable Costing:

	Naylor Manufacturing Inc. Income Statement For the Month Ended January 31, 2011		
1			
2			
3			
4			
5			
6			
7			
8			
9			
10			
11			
12			
13			
14			
15	Contribution margin per unit:		
16			
17	Contribution margin ratio:		
18			
19			
20			
21			
22			
23			
24			
25			
26			
27			
28			
29			
30			
31			
32			
33			
34			
35			
36			
37			
38			
39			
40			

DO IT! 6-3

			Basic	Basic Plus	Premium
1	(a)	The sales mix percenatges as a function of units sold is:			
7	(b)	The weighted-average unit contribution margin is:			
11	(c)	The break-even point in units is:			
14	(d)	The break-even units to produce for each product are:			
15		Basic:			
16		Basic Plus:			
17		Premium:			

DO IT! 6-4

			Good	Better	Best
21	(a)				
25	(b)	The contribution margin per unit of limited resource is:			
32	(c)				

E6-2

1	(a)	Contrubution margin in dollars:
2		
3		
4		
5		
6		Contribution margin per unit:
7		
8		Contribution margin ratio:
9		
10	(b)	Break-even point in dollars:
11		
12		
13		Break-even point in units:
14		
15		
16	(c)	Margin of safety in dollars:
17		
18		
19		Margin of safety ratio:
20		
21		

E6-3

	August Results (Base Amounts)	Alternative 1 — Increase Selling Price by 10%	Alternative 2 — Decrease Variable Costs to 58% of Sales	Alternative 3 — Reduce Fixed Costs by $20,000
Sales	$ 300000			
Less: Variable Costs	210000			
Fixed Costs	70000			
Net Income	$ 20000			

1	(a) (1)		1
2			2
3			3
4			4
5			5
6			6
7	(2)		7
8			8
9			9
10			10
11			11
12			12
13			13
14	(b)		14
15			15
16			16
17			17
18	(c)		18
19			19
20			20
21			21
22			22
23			23
24			24
25			25
26			26
27			27
28			28
29			29
30			30
31			31
32			32
33			33
34			34
35			35
36			36
37			37
38			38
39			39
40			40

E6-5 (a)

Mozena Company		
CVP Income Statement (Current)		
For the Year Ended December 31, 2011		
	Total	Per Unit
1		
2		
3		
4		
5		
6		

(b)

Mozena Company		
CVP Income Statement (With Changes)		
For the Year Ended December 31, 2011		
	Total	Per Unit
1		
2		
3		
4		
5		
6		
7		
8		

E6-6

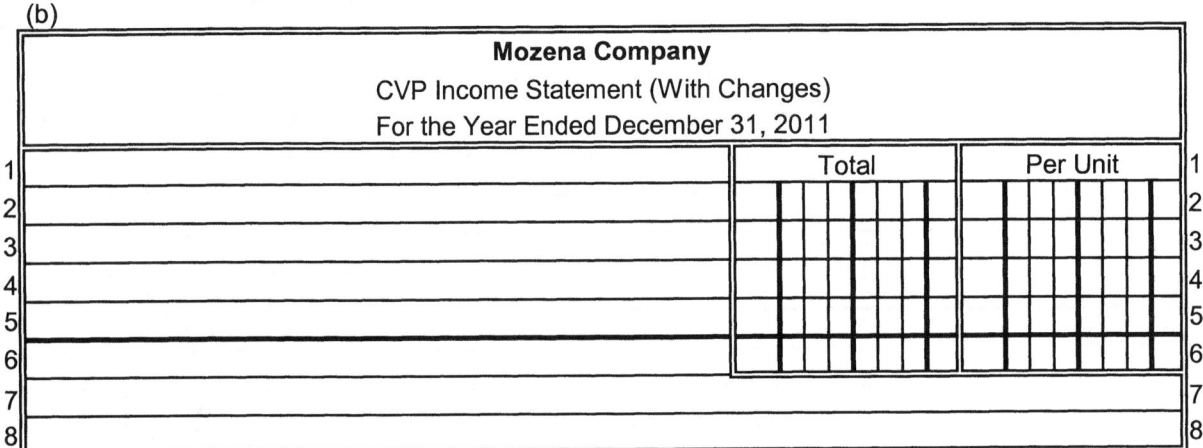

	Sales Mix %	Contribution Margin Per Unit	Wtd.- Ave. Contribution Margin
1 Lawnmowers			
2 Weed-Trimmers			
3 Chainsaws			
4			
5			
6 Total break-even sales in units =			
7			
8			

	Sales Mix %	Total Break-even Sales in Units	Sales Units Needed Per Product
9			
10			
11			
12 Lawnmowers			
13 Weed-trimmers			
14 Chainsaws			
15 Total units			
16			

(a)	Sales Mix %	Contribution Margin Ratio	Wtd. -Ave Contribution Margin Ratio	
1 Oil changes				1
2 Brake repair				2
3				3
4				4
5 Total break-even sales in dollars =				5
6				6
7				7

	Sales Mix %	Total Break-even Sales Dollars	Sales Dollars Needed Per Product	
8				8
9				9
10				10
11 Oil changes				11
12 Brake repair				12
13 Total sales				13
14				14

(b)				
15				15
16 Sales to achieve target net income =				16
17				17
18				18

	Sales Mix %	Total Sales Needed	Sales Dollars Needed Per Product Per Store	
19				19
20				20
21				21
22				22
23 Oil changes				23
24 Brake repair				24
25				25
26				26
27				27
28				28
29				29
30				30
31				31
32				32
33				33
34				34
35				35
36				36
37				37
38				38
39				39
40				40

(a)

	Sales Mix %	Contribution Margin Ratio	Wtd.- Ave. Contribution Margin Ratio	
1 Mail pouches and				1
2 small boxes				2
3 Non-standard boxes				3
4				4
5				5
6 Total break-even sales in dollars =				6
7				7
8				8

	Sales Mix %	Total Break-even Sales Dollars	Sales Dollars Needed Per Product	
9				9
10				10
11				11
12 Mail pouches and				12
13 small boxes				13
14 Non-standard boxes				14
15 Total sales				15
16				16
17				17

(b)

	Sales Mix %	Contribution Margin Ratio	Wtd. Ave. Contribution Margin Ratio	
18				18
19				19
20				20
21 Mail pouches and				21
22 small boxes				22
23 Non-standard boxes				23
24				24
25				25
26 Total break-even sales in dollars =				26
27				27
28				28

	Sales Mix %	Sales in Dollars	Sales Dollars Per Product	
29				29
30				30
31 Mail pouches and				31
32 small boxes				32
33 Non-standard boxes				33
34 Total sales				34
35				35
36				36
37				37
38				38
39				39
40				40

	(a)		
1	Weighted average unit		1
2	contribution margin =		2
3			3
4	Break-even point in units =		4
5			5
6	(b)		6
7	Shoes		7
8	Gloves		8
9	Range finders		9
10			10
11			11
12	(c)		12
13	Shoes		13
14	Gloves		14
15	Range finders		15
16	Total contribution margin		16
17	Fixed costs		17
18	Net income		18
19			19
20			20
21			21
22			22
23			23
24			24
25			25
26			26
27			27
28			28
29			29
30			30
31			31
32			32
33			33
34			34
35			35
36			36
37			37
38			38
39			39
40			40

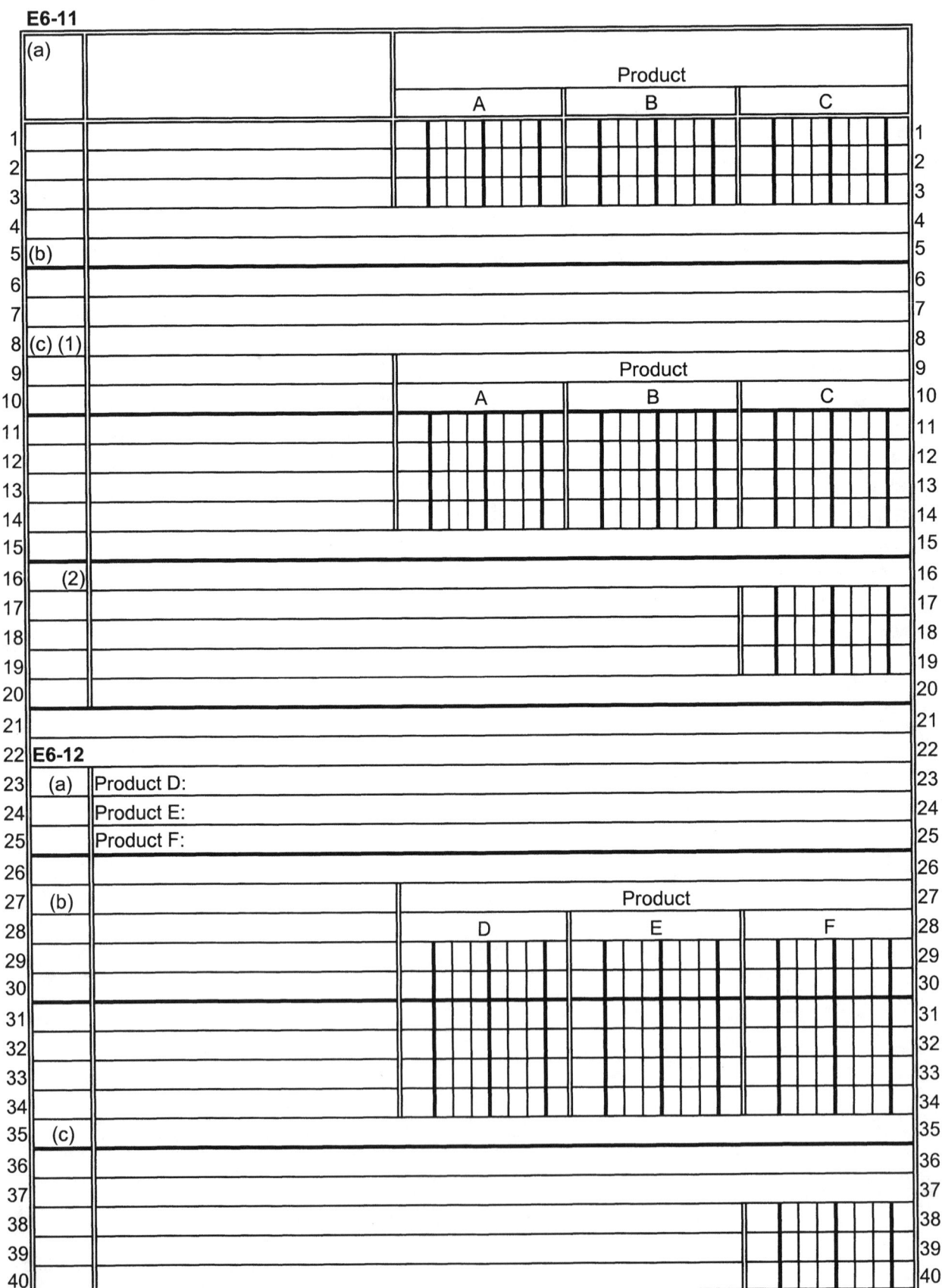

		Product	
(a)		Basic	Deluxe
1			
2			
3			
4			
5			
6			
7			
(b) 8			
9			
10			
(c) 11			

(1)	Basic	Deluxe	Total
12			
13			
14			
15			
16			
17			

(2)	Basic	Deluxe	Total
18			
19			
20			
21			
22			
23			

E6-14

(a)	Contribution Margin	Net Income	Degree of Operating Leverage	
1 Grissom				
2 Moran				
3				
4 Interpretation:				
5				
6				
7				

(b)	Grissom Company	Moran Company	
8			
9			
10 Sales revenue			
11 Variable costs			
12 Contribution margin			
13 Fixed costs			
14 Net income			
15			

(c)	
16	
17	
18	
19	
20	

E6-15

(a)	Contribution Margin	Net Income	Degree of Operating Leverage	
1 Manual system				
2 Computerized system				
3				

(b)	
4	
5	
6	
7	
8	

	Manual System	Computerized System	
9			
10			
11 Sales			
12 Variable costs			
13 Contribution margin			
14 Fixed costs			
15 Net income			

E6-15 (Continued)

(c)	(Actual Sales -	Break-even Sales) ÷	Actual Sales =	Margin of Safety Ratio	
1 Manual system					1
2 Computerized system					2
3					3
4					4
5					5

E6-16

(a)	Contribution Margin ÷	Net Income =	Degree of Operating Leverage		
1 Old Fashion					1
2 Mech-Apple					2
3					3
4					4
5					5
6					6
7					7
8					8
9					9
10					10
11					11
12					12

(b)	% Change in Sales x	Degree of Operating Leverage =	% Change in Net Income		
13					13
14					14
15					15
16 10% decrease:					16
17 Old Fashion					17
18 Mech-Apple					18
19					19
20 5% incease:					20
21 Old Fashion					21
22 Mech-Apple					22
23					23
24 (c)					24
25					25
26					26
27					27
28					28
29					29
30					30

(a)   Unit Cost

(b)

Matt's Company

Income Statement - Variable Costing

For the Year Ended December 31, 2011

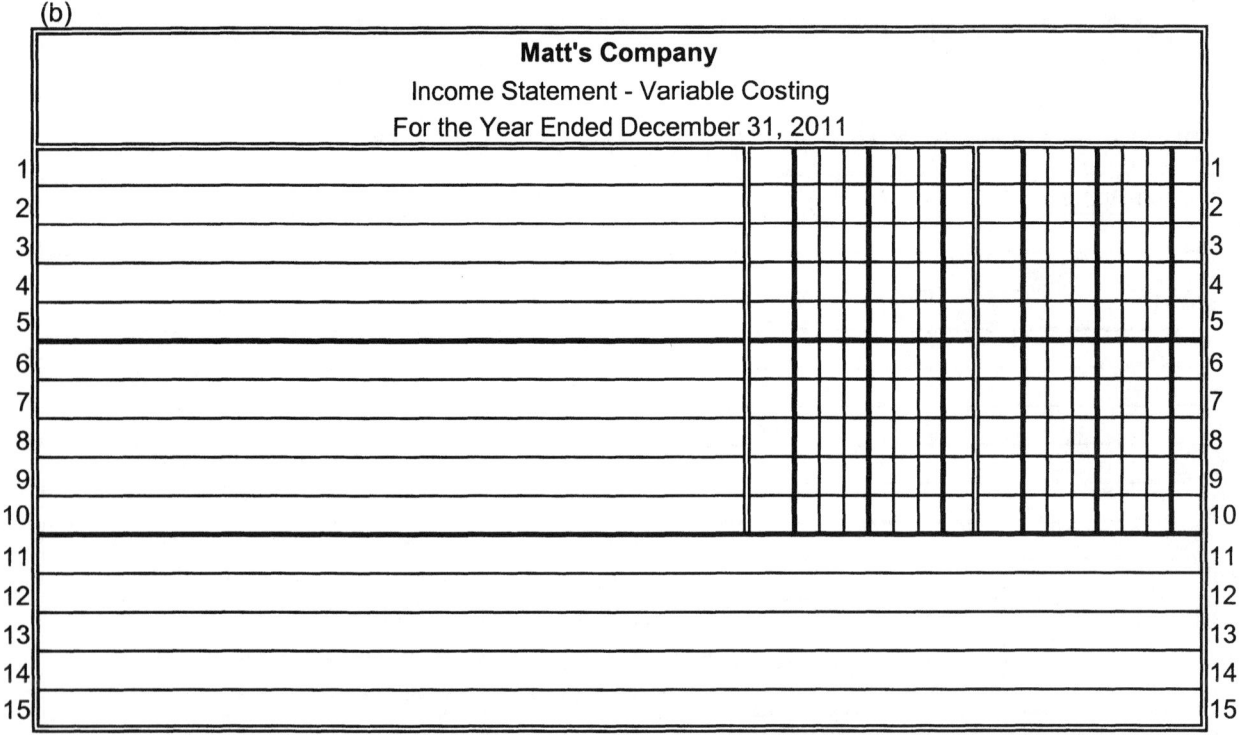

(c)   Unit Cost

(d)

Matt's Company			
Income Statement - Absorption Costing			
For the Year Ended December 31, 2011			
1			
2			
3			
4			
5			
6			
7			
8			

*E6-18

(a)

1 Finished goods inventory cost (variable costing):		
2		
3		
4		
5		
6		
7 Variable manufacturing cost per unit =		
8		
9 Finished goods inventory cost =		
10		
11 (b)		
12		
13		
14		
15		
16		
17		
18		
19		
20		
21		
22		
23		
24		
25		
26		
27		

(a)

	Utility Expense		
1	Variable utilities:		1
2			2
3			3
4			4
5	Fixed utilities:		5
6			6
7			7
8			8
9	Variable Costing		9
10			10
11			11
12			12
13			13
14			14
15			15
16			16
17			17
18			18
19	(b)		19
20	Absorption Costing		20
21			21
22			22
23			23
24			24
25			25
26			26
27			27
28			28
29			29
30			30
31			31
32			32
33			33
34	(c)		34
35			35
36			36
37			37
38			38
39			39
40			40

(a)

	(1)		Current Year
1			
2			
3			
4			
5			
6			
7			
8			
9			
10			
11			
12			

			Current Year		Projected Year
13					
14					
15					
16					
17					
18					
19					
20					
21					
22					
23					
24					
25					
26					
27					

	(2)		Current Year	Projected Year
28				
29		Fixed costs:		
30				
31				
32				
33				
34				
35				
36				
37				
38				
39				
40				

(b)

1			1
2			2
3			3
4			4
5			5
6			6
7			7
8			8
9			9
10			10
11			11
12	(c)	Sales dollars required for	12
13		target net income =	13
14			14
15			15
16	(d)	Margin of safety ratio =	16
17			17
18			18
19			19
20	(e) (1)		Current	20
21			Year	21
22				22
23				23
24				24
25				25
26				26
27				27
28				28
29				29
30				30
31				31
32				32
33				33
34				34
35				35
36				36
37				37
38	(2)	Contribution margin ratio =	38
39			39
40			40

(e) (3)

1		Break-even point in dollars =
2		
3		
4		
5		Comments:
6		
7		
8		
9		
10		
11		
12		
13		
14		
15		
16		
17		
18		
19		
20		
21		
22		
23		
24		
25		
26		
27		
28		
29		
30		
31		
32		
33		
34		
35		
36		
37		
38		
39		
40		

(a)

		Product		
		Economy	Standard	Deluxe
1				
2				
3				
4				
5				
6				
7				
8				

(b)

		Product		
		Economy	Standard	Deluxe

(c)

(a)

	Sales Mix %	Contribution Margin Ratio	Wtd.- Ave. Contribution Margin Ratio	
1 Appetizers				1
2 Main entrees				2
3 Desserts				3
4 Beverages				4
5				5
6				6
7 Total sales required to				7
8 achieve target net income =				8
9				9
10				10

	Sales Mix %	Total Sales	Sales From Each Product	
11				11
12				12
13 Appetizers				13
14 Main entrees				14
15 Desserts				15
16 Beverages				16
17				17
18				18

(b)

	Sales Mix %	Contribution Margin Ratio	Wtd.- Ave. Contribution Margin Ratio	
1 Appetizers				1
2 Main entrees				2
3 Desserts				3
4 Beverages				4
5				5
6				6
7				7
8 Total sales required to				8
9 achieve target net income =				9
10				10

	Sales Mix %	Contribution Margin Ratio	Sales Dollars Per Product	
11				11
12				12
13 Appetizers				13
14 Main entrees				14
15 Desserts				15
16 Beverages				16
17				17

(c)

	Sales Mix %	Contribution Margin Ratio	Wtd.- Ave. Contribution Margin Ratio	
1 Appetizers				1
2 Main entrees				2
3 Desserts				3
4 Beverages				4
5				5
6				6
7 Total sales required to				7
8 achieve target net income =				8
9				9
10				10

	Sales Mix %	Total Sales	Sales From Each Product	
11				11
12				12
13 Appetizers				13
14 Main entrees				14
15 Desserts				15
16 Beverages				16
17				17
18				18
19				19
20				20
21				21
22				22
23				23
24				24
25				25
26				26
27				27
28				28
29				29
30				30
31				31
32				32
33				33
34				34
35				35
36				36
37				37
38				38
39				39
40				40

(a)

	Contribution Margin	Sales	Contribution Margin Ratio	
1 Old Company				1
2 New Company				2
3				3
4				4

	Fixed Costs	Contribution Margin Ratio	Break-even Point in Dollars	
5				5
6				6
7				7
8 Old Company				8
9 New Company				9
10				10
11				11

	Actual Sales	Break-even Sales	Actual Sales	Margin of Safety Ratio	
12					12
13					13
14 Old Company					14
15 New Company					15
16					16
17					17
18					18
19					19
20					20

(b)

	Contribution Margin	Net Income	Degree of Operating Leverage	
1 Old Company				1
2 New Company				2
3				3
4				4
5				5
6				6
7				7
8				8
9				9
10				10
11				11
12				12
13				13
14				14
15				15

(c)

	Old Company	New Company
1 Sales		
2 Variable costs		
3 Contribution margin		
4 Fixed costs		
5 Net income		
6		
7		
8		
9		
10		

(d)

	Old Company	New Company
1 Sales		
2 Variable costs		
3 Contribution margin		
4 Fixed costs		
5 Net income		
6		
7		
8		

(e)

1	
2	
3	
4	
5	
6	
7	
8	
9	
10	
11	
12	

(a)

	(All amounts are in $000s)			
1				
2				
3				
4				
5				
6				
7	Contribution margin ratio =			
8				
9	Break-even point =			
10				
11				

(b)

12				
13				
14				
15				
16				
17				
18	Contribution margin ratio =			
19				
20	Break-even point =			
21				
22				

(c)

23			
24	(1)	Current situation: from part (a)	
25			
26			
27	(2)	Proposed situation: from part (b)	
28			
29			
30			
31			
32			
33			
34			
35			
36			
37			
38			
39			
40			

(c) (Continued)

1		1
2		2
3		3
4		4
5		5
6		6
7		7
8		8
9		9
10		10
11		11
12		12
13		13
14	(d)	14
15		15
16		16
17		17
18		18
19		19
20		20
21		21
22		22
23		23
24		24
25		25
26		26
27		27
28		28
29		29
30		30
31		31
32		32
33		33
34		34
35		35
36		36
37		37
38		38
39		39
40		40

(a)

Marotta Company Income Statement - Variable Costing For the Year Ended December 31,		2010		2011	
1					1
2					2
3					3
4					4
5					5
6					6
7					7
8					8
9					9
10					10
11					11
12					12
13					13
14					14
15					15
16					16
17					17
18					18
19					19
20					20
21					21
22					22
23					23
24					24
25					25
26					26
27					27
28					28
29					29
30					30

(b)

Marotta Company
Income Statement - Absorption Costing
For the Year Ended December 31,

	2010	2011
1		
2		
3		
4		
5		
6		
7		
8		
9		
10		
11		
12		
13		
14		
15		

(c)

	2010	2011
1 Variable costing net inc.		
2 Fixed manufacturing OH		
3 expensed with variable		
4 costing		
5 Less: Fixed manufacturing		
6 overhead expensed with		
7 absorption costing		
8 Difference		
9 Absorption costing net inc.		

(d)

1	
2	
3	
4	
5	

(a)

Basic Electric Motors Division		
Income Statement - Absorption Costing		
For the Year Ended December 31, 2011		
	50,000 Produced	80,000 Produced

(b)

Basic Electric Motors Division		
Income Statement - Variable Costing		
For the Year Ended December 31, 2011		
	50,000 Produced	80,000 Produced

(c)

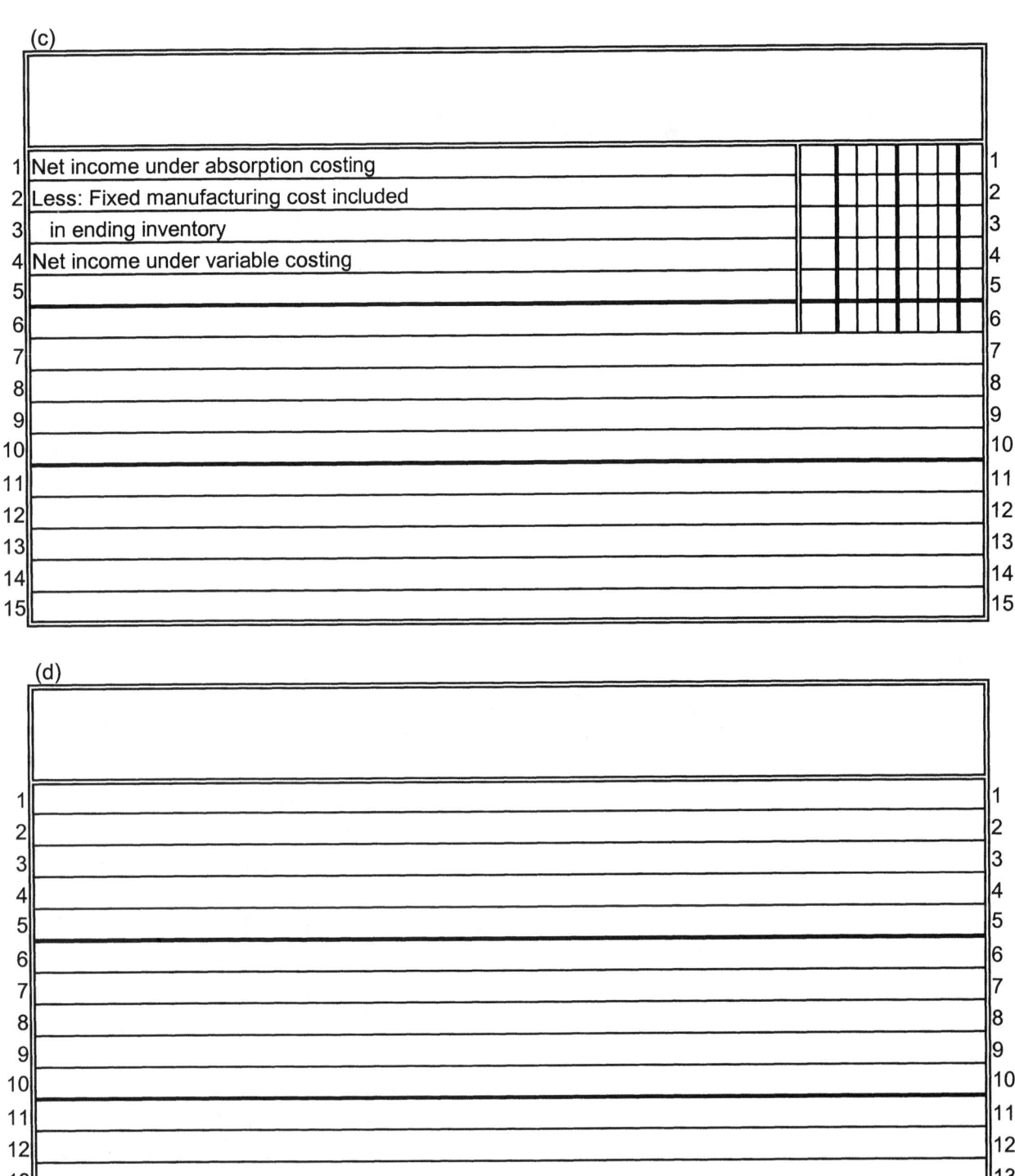

1	Net income under absorption costing	1
2	Less: Fixed manufacturing cost included	2
3	in ending inventory	3
4	Net income under variable costing	4
5		5
6		6
7		7
8		8
9		9
10		10
11		11
12		12
13		13
14		14
15		15

(d)

(a)

	(1)		Current Year
1			
2			
3			
4			
5			
6			
7			
8			
9			
10			
11			
12			

		Current Year		Projected Year
13				
14				
15				
16				
17				
18				
19				
20				
21				
22				
23				
24				
25				
26				
27				

	(2)		Current Year	Projected Year
28				
29		Fixed costs:		
30				
31				
32				
33				
34				
35				
36				
37				
38				
39				
40				

(b)

(c)   Sales dollars required for

       target net income =

(d)   Margin of safety ratio =

(e) (1)

	Current Year

   (2) Contribution margin ratio =

(e) (3)

1	Break-even point in dollars =
2	
3	
4	
5	Comments:
6	
7	
8	
9	
10	
11	
12	
13	
14	
15	
16	
17	
18	
19	
20	
21	
22	
23	
24	
25	
26	
27	
28	
29	
30	
31	
32	
33	
34	
35	
36	
37	
38	
39	
40	

(a)

		Product		
		Economy	Standard	Deluxe
1				
2				
3				
4				
5				
6				
7				
8				
9				

(b)

		Product		
		Economy	Standard	Deluxe
11				
12				
13				
14				
15				
16				
17				
18				
19				

(c)

21	
22	
23	
24	
25	
26	
27	
28	
29	
30	
31	
32	
33	
34	
35	
36	
37	
38	
39	
40	

(a)

	Sales Mix %	Contribution Margin Ratio	Wtd.- Ave. Contribution Margin Ratio	
1 Appetizers				1
2 Main entrees				2
3 Desserts				3
4 Beverages				4
5				5
6				6
7 Total sales required to				7
8 achieve target net income =				8
9				9
10				10

	Sales Mix %	Total Sales	Sales From Each Product	
11				11
12				12
13 Appetizers				13
14 Main entrees				14
15 Desserts				15
16 Beverages				16
17				17
18				18

(b)

	Sales Mix %	Contribution Margin Ratio	Wtd.- Ave. Contribution Margin Ratio	
1 Appetizers				1
2 Main entrees				2
3 Desserts				3
4 Beverages				4
5				5
6				6
7				7
8 Total sales required to				8
9 achieve target net income =				9
10				10

	Sales Mix %	Contribution Margin Ratio	Sales Dollars Per Product	
11				11
12				12
13 Appetizers				13
14 Main entrees				14
15 Desserts				15
16 Beverages				16
17				17

(c)

	Sales Mix %	Contribution Margin Ratio	Wtd.- Ave. Contribution Margin Ratio	
1 Appetizers				1
2 Main entrees				2
3 Desserts				3
4 Beverages				4
5				5
6				6
7 Total sales required to				7
8 achieve target net income =				8
9				9
10				10

	Sales Mix %	Total Sales	Sales From Each Product	
11				11
12				12
13 Appetizers				13
14 Main entrees				14
15 Desserts				15
16 Beverages				16
17				17
18				18
19				19
20				20
21				21
22				22
23				23
24				24
25				25
26				26
27				27
28				28
29				29
30				30
31				31
32				32
33				33
34				34
35				35
36				36
37				37
38				38
39				39
40				40

(a)

	Contribution Margin	Sales	Contribution Margin Ratio	
1 Yesterday Company				1
2 Tomorrow Company				2
3				3
4				4

	Fixed Costs	Contribution Margin Ratio	Break-even Point in Dollars	
5				5
6				6
7				7
8 Yesterday Company				8
9 Tomorrow Company				9
10				10
11				11

	Actual Sales	Break-even Sales	Actual Sales	Margin of Safety Ratio	
12					12
13					13
14 Yesterday Company					14
15 Tomorrow Company					15
16					16
17					17
18					18
19					19
20					20

(b)

	Contribution Margin	Net Income	Degree of Operating Leverage	
1 Yesterday Company				1
2 Tomorrow Company				2
3				3
4				4
5				5
6				6
7				7
8				8
9				9
10				10
11				11
12				12
13				13
14				14
15				15

(c)

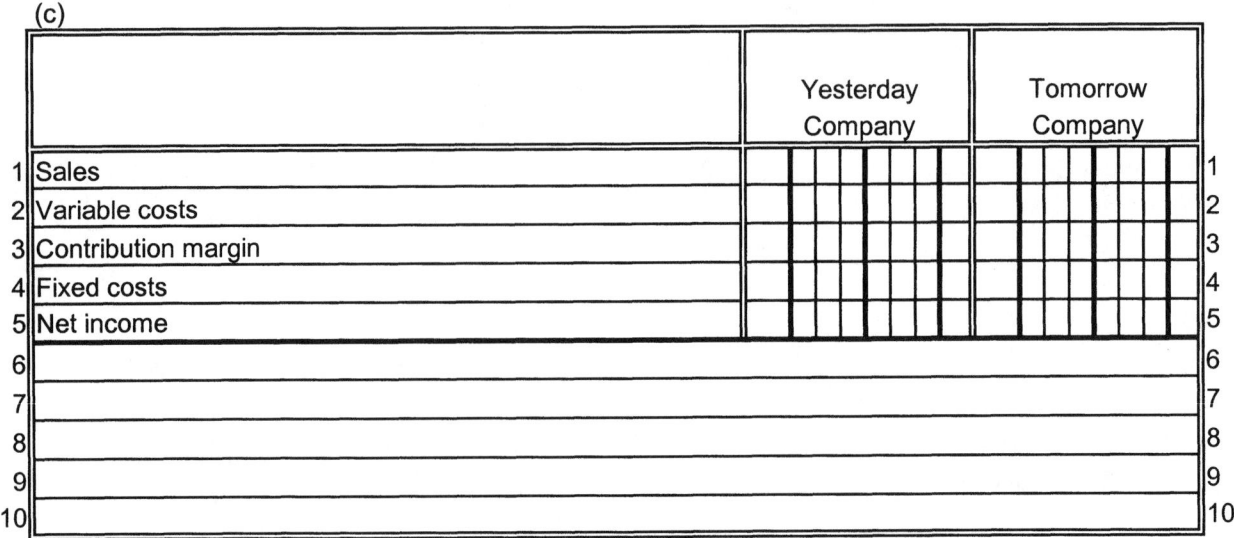

	Yesterday Company	Tomorrow Company	
1 Sales			1
2 Variable costs			2
3 Contribution margin			3
4 Fixed costs			4
5 Net income			5
6			6
7			7
8			8
9			9
10			10

(d)

	Yesterday Company	Tomorrow Company	
1 Sales			1
2 Variable costs			2
3 Contribution margin			3
4 Fixed costs			4
5 Net income			5
6			6
7			7
8			8

(e)

1		1
2		2
3		3
4		4
5		5
6		6
7		7
8		8
9		9
10		10
11		11
12		12

(a)

(All amounts are in $000s)

Contribution margin ratio =

Break-even point =

(b)

Contribution margin ratio =

Break-even point =

(c)

(1) Current situation: from part (a)

(2) Proposed situation: from part (b)

(c) (Continued)

1			1
2			2
3			3
4			4
5			5
6			6
7			7
8			8
9			9
10			10
11			11
12			12
13			13
14	(d)		14
15			15
16			16
17			17
18			18
19			19
20			20
21			21
22			22
23			23
24			24
25			25
26			26
27			27
28			28
29			29
30			30
31			31
32			32
33			33
34			34
35			35
36			36
37			37
38			38
39			39
40			40

(a)

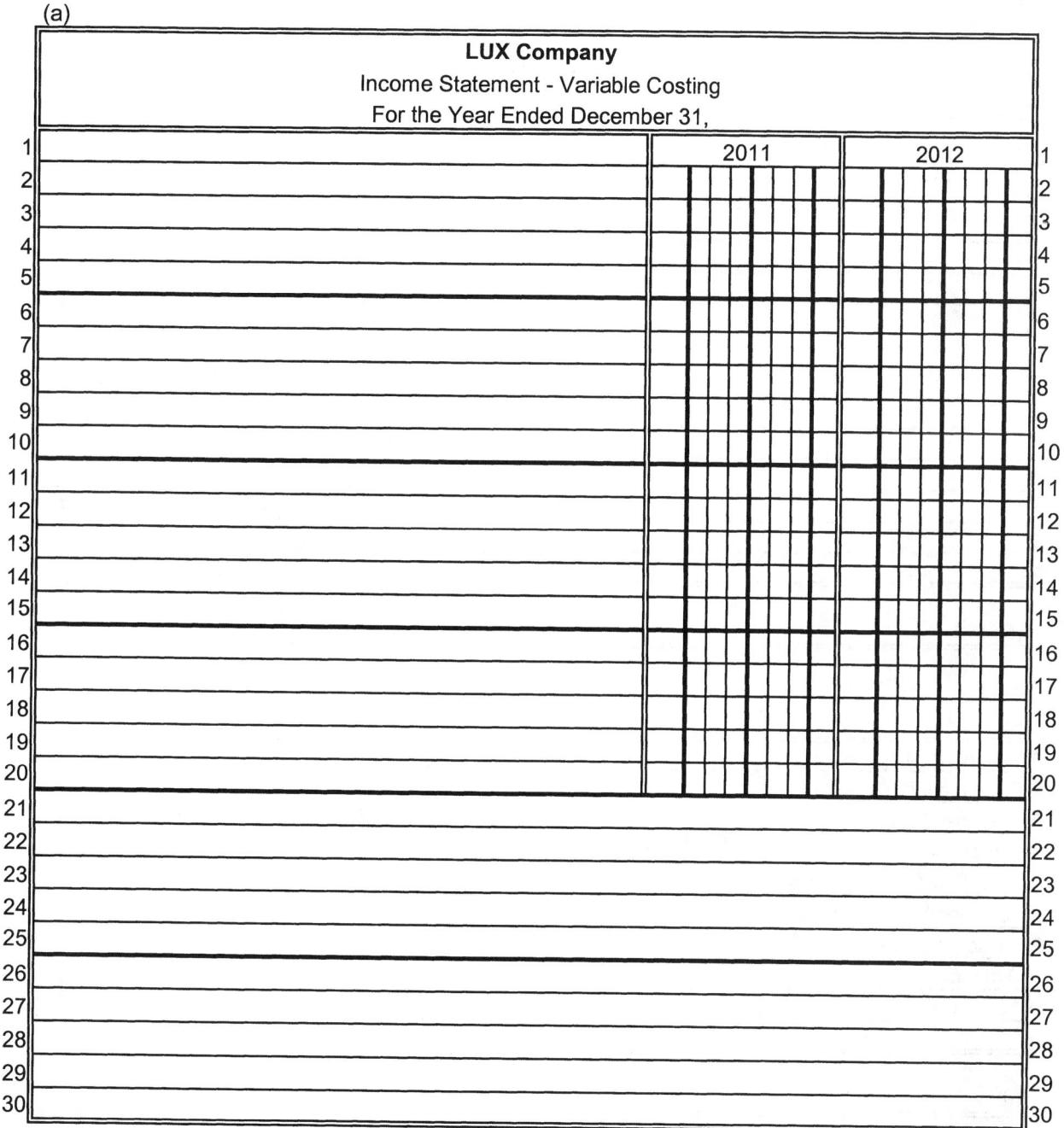

LUX Company

Income Statement - Variable Costing

For the Year Ended December 31,

	2011	2012

(b)

LUX Company Income Statement - Absorption Costing For the Year Ended December 31,	2011	2012
1		
2		
3		
4		
5		
6		
7		
8		
9		
10		
11		
12		
13		
14		
15		

(c)

	2011	2012
1 Variable costing net inc.		
2 Fixed manufacturing OH		
3 expensed with variable		
4 costing		
5 Less: Fixed manufacturing		
6 overhead expensed with		
7 absorption costing		
8 Difference		
9 Abs. costing net inc.		
10		

(d)

1	
2	
3	
4	
5	

(a)

	Electricswitch Division	
Income Statement - Absorption Costing		
For the Year Ended December 31, 2011		
	200,000 Produced	250,000 Produced
1		
2		
3		
4		
5		
6		
7		
8		
9		
10		
11		
12		
13		
14		
15		

(b)

	Electricswitch Division	
Income Statement - Variable Costing		
For the Year Ended December 31, 2011		
	200,000 Produced	250,000 Produced
1		
2		
3		
4		
5		
6		
7		
8		
9		
10		
11		
12		
13		
14		
15		
16		
17		
18		
19		
20		

(c)

1	Net income under absorption costing	
2	Less: Fixed manufacturing cost included	
3	in ending inventory	
4	Net income under variable costing	
5		
6		
7		
8		
9		
10		
11		
12		
13		
14		
15		

(d)

1		
2		
3		
4		
5		
6		
7		
8		
9		
10		
11		
12		
13		
14		
15		

(a)

1	Sales		1
2	Less: Variable costs		2
3	Contribution margin		3
4	Less: Fixed costs		4
5	Net income		5

(b)

1	Contribution margin ratio =	1
2		2
3	Break-even point in dollars =	3
4		4
5	Margin of safety ratio =	5
6		6
7	Degree of operating leverage =	7
8		8

(c)

1	Sales		1
2	Less: Variable costs		2
3	Contribution margin		3
4	Less: Fixed costs		4
5	Net income		5

(d)

1	Contribution margin ratio =	1
2		2
3	Break-even point in dollars =	3
4		4
5	Margin of safety ratio =	5
6		6
7	Degree of operating leverage =	7

(e)

1	1
2	2
3	3
4	4
5	5
6	6
7	7
8	8
9	9
10	10
11	11
12	12
13	13
14	14
15	15
16	16
17	17
18	18
19	19
20	20
21	21
22	22
23	23
24	24
25	25
26	26
27	27
28	28
29	29
30	30
31	31
32	32
33	33
34	34
35	35
36	36
37	37
38	38
39	39
40	40

(a)

($ in millions)	Consumer Products	Pet Products	Soup and Infant Feeding Products	
1 Sales				1
2 Variable costs				2
3 Contribution margin				3
4				4
5 Contribution margin				5
6 ÷ Sales				6
7 Contribution margin ratio				7
8				8
9 Division sales				9
10 ÷ Total sales				10
11 Sales mix percentage				11
12				12

(b)

	Sales Mix %	Contribution Margin Ratio	Wtd.- Ave. Contribution Margin Ratio	
1 Consumer products				1
2 Pet products				2
3 Soup and infant feeding				3
4 products				4
5				5
6				6
7 Total sales required to				7
8 break-even (in millions)				8
9				9
10				10

	Sales Mix %	Total Sales	Sales From Each Product (in millions)	
11				11
12				12
13				13
14 Consumer products				14
15 Pet products				15
16 Soup and infant feeding				16
17 products				17
18				18
19				19
20				20
21				21
22				22
23				23

(a)

1		1
2		2
3		3
4		4
5		5
6		6
7		7
8		8
9		9
10		10

(b)   (in millions of $)

	FedEx Ground		
	Income Statement - Variable Costing		
	For the Year Ended May 31, 2008		
1	Revenues		1
2	Variable costs:		2
3	Salaries and employee benefits		3
4	Purchased transportation		4
5	Fuel		5
6	Maintenance and repairs		6
7	Intercompany charges		7
8	Contribution margin		8
9	Fixed costs:		9
10	Rentals		10
11	Depreciation and amortization		11
12	Other		12
13	Net income		13
14			14
15			15
16	Contribution margin ratio =		16
17			17
18			18
19	Break-even point in dollars =		19
20			20
21			21
22			22
23			23
24			24
25			25

(c)

(i)	2008	2006
FedEx Express		
FedEx Ground		
FedEx Freight		
FedEx Services		

(ii)	2008	2006
FedEx Express		
FedEx Ground		
FedEx Freight		
FedEx Services		

(iii)

BE7-2

	Alternative A	Alternative B	Net Income Increase (Decrease)
1			
2			
3			
4			
5			
6			
7			

BE7-3

	Reject Order	Accept Order	Net Income Increase (Decrease)
8			
9			
10			
11			
12			
13			
14			
15			
16			
17			

BE7-4

	Make	Buy	Net Income Increase (Decrease)
18			
19			
20			
21			
22			
23			
24			
25			
26			

BE7-5

	Sell	Process Further	Net Income Increase (Decrease)
27			
28			
29			
30			
31			
32			
33			
34			
35			
36			
37			
38			
39			
40			

BE7-7

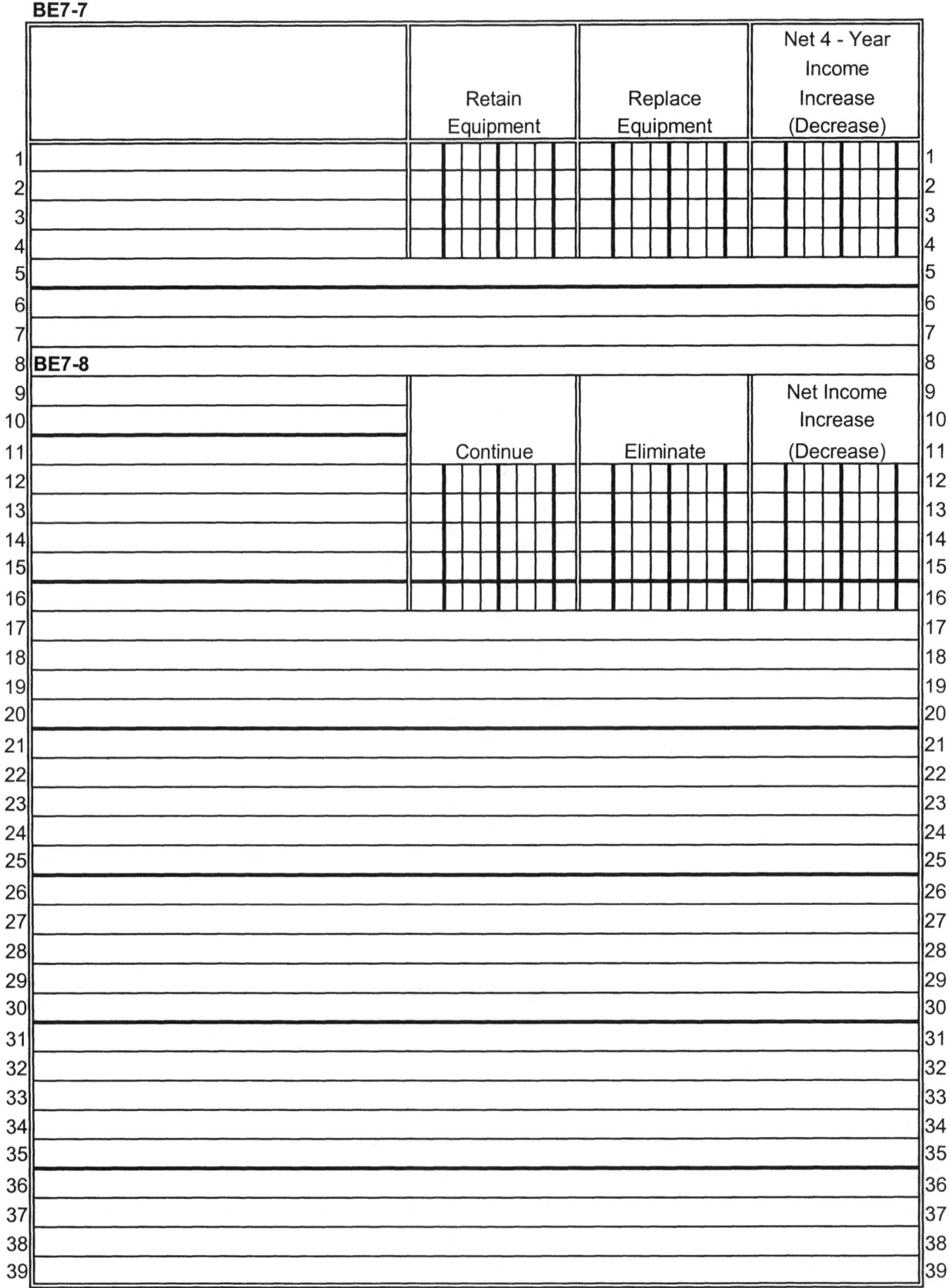

	Retain Equipment	Replace Equipment	Net 4 - Year Income Increase (Decrease)	
1				1
2				2
3				3
4				4
5				5
6				6
7				7

BE7-8

	Continue	Eliminate	Net Income Increase (Decrease)	
8				8
9				9
10				10
11				11
12				12
13				13
14				14
15				15
16				16
17				17
18				18
19				19
20				20
21				21
22				22
23				23
24				24
25				25
26				26
27				27
28				28
29				29
30				30
31				31
32				32
33				33
34				34
35				35
36				36
37				37
38				38
39				39

DO IT! 7-1

	Reject	Accept	Net Income Increase (Decrease)
1			
2			
3			
4			
5			
6			
7			

DO IT! 7-2

(a)	Make	Buy	Net Income Increase (Decrease)
12			
13			
14			
15			
16			
17			
18			
19			
20			
21			

(b)	Make	Buy	Net Income Increase (Decrease)
25			
26			
27			
28			
29			
30			
31			
32			
33			
34			
35			
36			
37			
38			
39			
40			

DO IT! 7-3

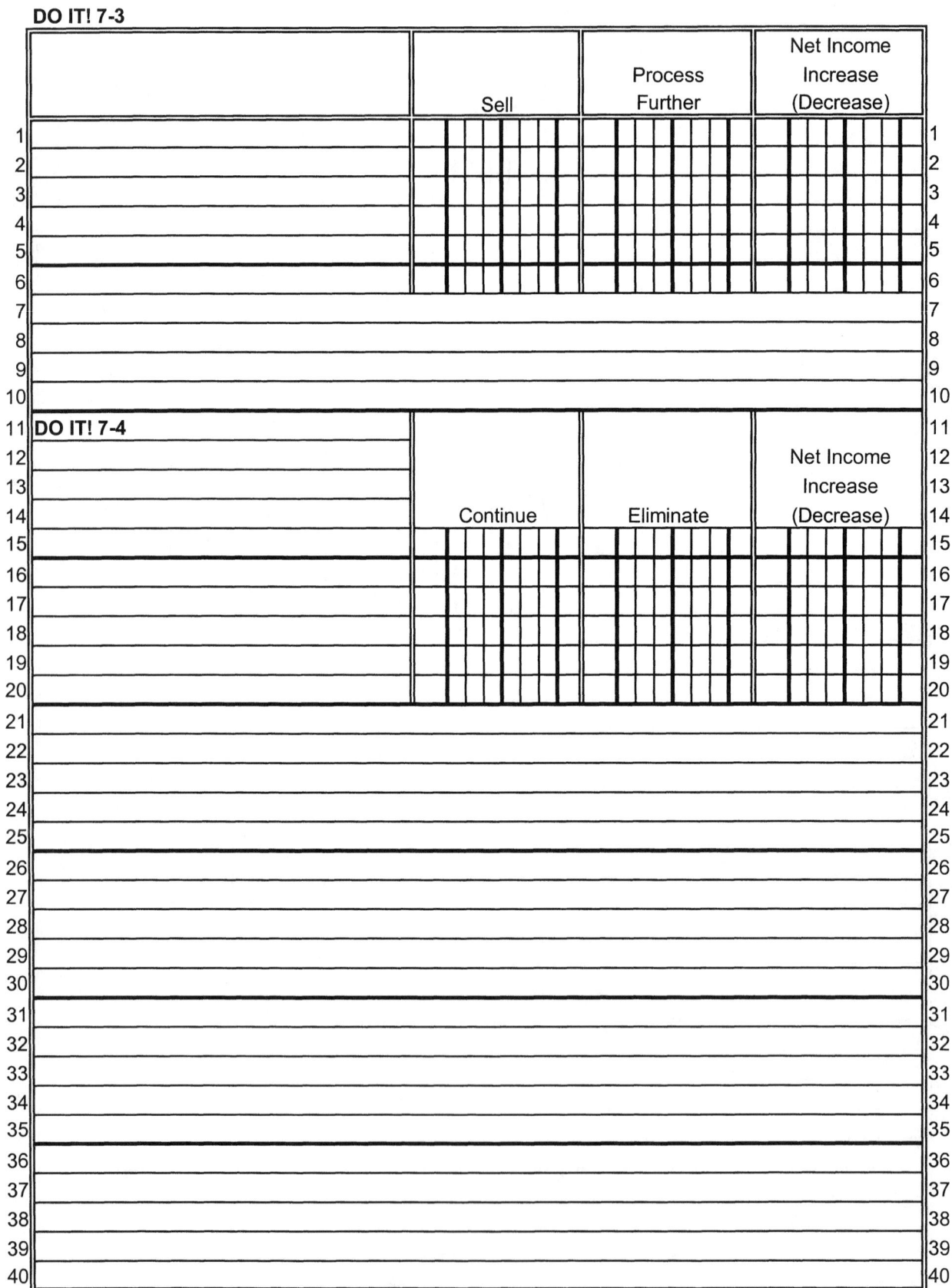

		Sell	Process Further	Net Income Increase (Decrease)	
1					1
2					2
3					3
4					4
5					5
6					6
7					7
8					8
9					9
10					10

DO IT! 7-4

11		Continue	Eliminate	Net Income Increase (Decrease)	11
12					12
13					13
14					14
15					15
16					16
17					17
18					18
19					19
20					20
21					21
22					22
23					23
24					24
25					25
26					26
27					27
28					28
29					29
30					30
31					31
32					32
33					33
34					34
35					35
36					36
37					37
38					38
39					39
40					40

(a)	Reject Order	Accept Order	Net Income Effect
1			
2			
3			
4			
5			
6			
7			
8			
9			
10			

(b)

(c)

E7-3

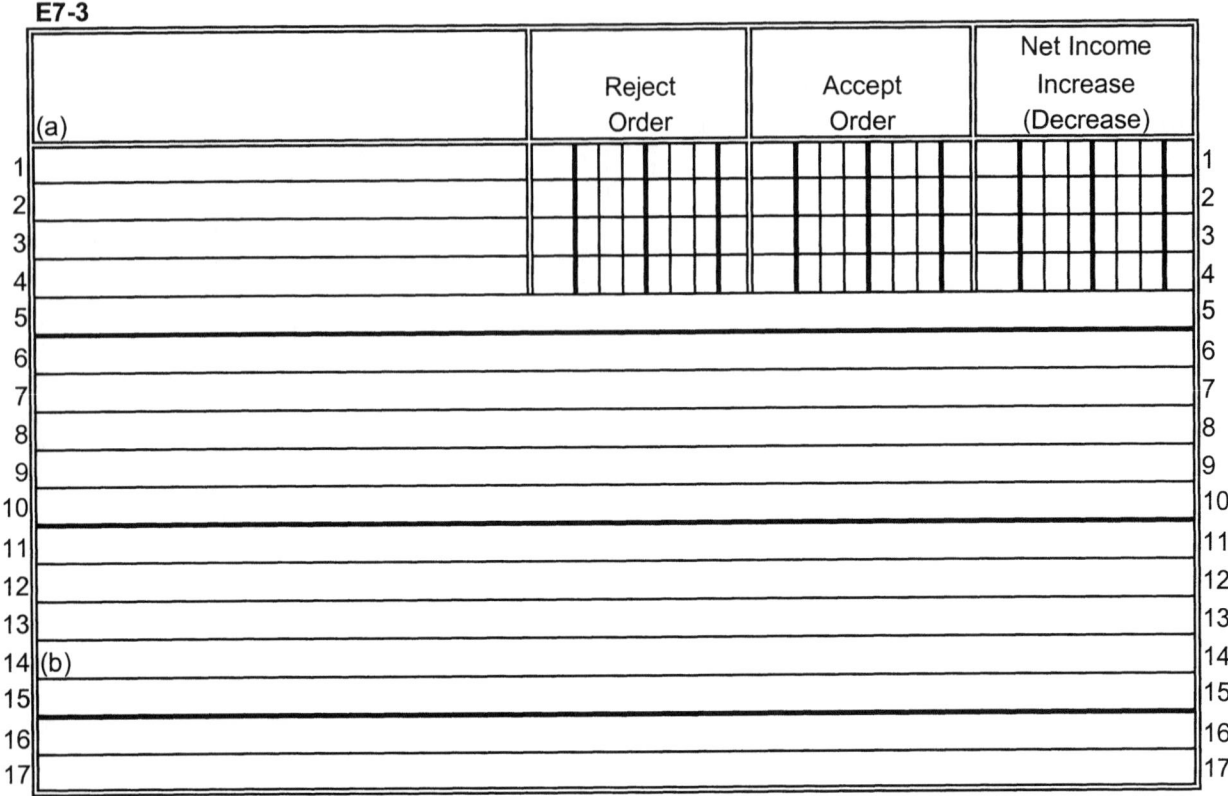

	Reject Order	Accept Order	Net Income Increase (Decrease)	
(a)				
1				1
2				2
3				3
4				4
5				5
6				6
7				7
8				8
9				9
10				10
11				11
12				12
13				13
14 (b)				14
15				15
16				16
17				17

E7-4

	Reject Order	Accept Order	Net Income Increase (Decrease)	
1				1
2				2
3				3
4				4
5				5
6				6
7				7
8				8
9				9
10				10
11				11
12				12
13				13
14				14
15				15
16				16
17				17
18				18

E7-5

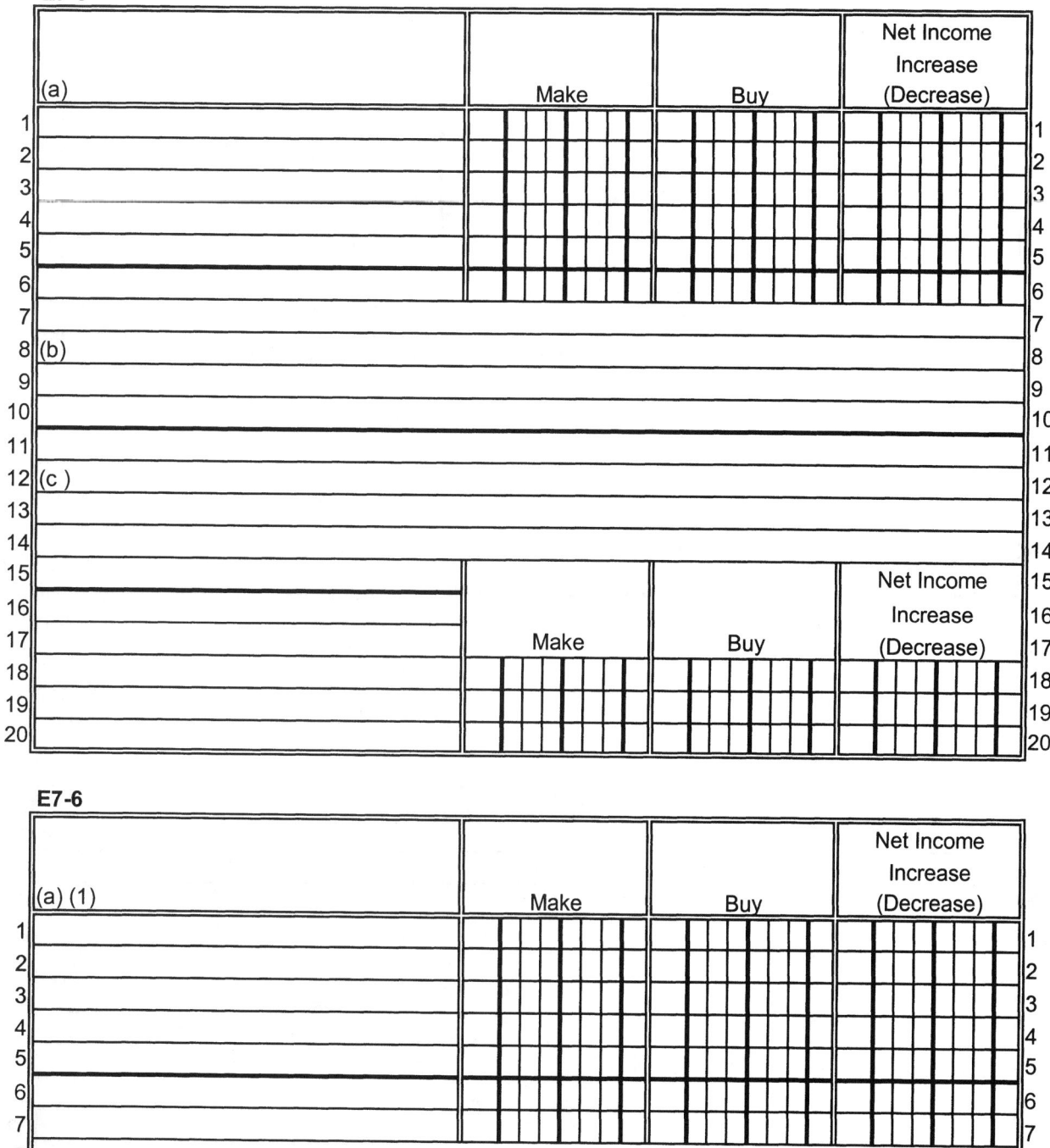

(a)		Make	Buy	Net Income Increase (Decrease)
1				
2				
3				
4				
5				
6				
7				
(b) 8				
9				
10				
11				
(c) 12				
13				
14				
15		Make	Buy	Net Income Increase (Decrease)
16				
17				
18				
19				
20				

E7-6

(a) (1)		Make	Buy	Net Income Increase (Decrease)
1				
2				
3				
4				
5				
6				
7				
8				
9				
10				
11				
12				
13				
14				
15				

(a) (Continued)

(a) (2)	Make	Buy	Net Income Increase (Decrease)
1			
2			
3			
4			
5			
6			
7			
8			
9			
10			

(b)

(a)		Make Sails	Buy Sails	Net Income Increase (Decrease)	
1					1
2					2
3					3
4					4
5					5
6					6
7					7
8					8
9					9
10					10
11					11
12					12
13					13
14					14

(b)	Per Unit	Make	Buy	Net Income Increase (Decrease)	
15 (Based on 1,200 units)					15
16					16
17					17
18					18
19					19
20					20
21					21
22					22
23					23

(c)		
24		24
25		25
26		26
27		27
28		28
29		29
30		30
31		31
32		32
33		33
34		34
35		35
36		36
37		37
38		38
39		39
40		40

(a)

	Make IMC2	Buy IMC2	Net Income Increase (Decrease)
1			
2			
3			
4			
5			
6			

7

8

9

10

11

(b)

12

13

14

15

16

17

18

19

20

(c)

21

22

23

24

25

26

27

28

29

30

31

32

33

34

35

36

37

38

39

40

	Sell Basic Kit	Process Further Stage 2 Kit	Net Income Increase (Decrease)
1			
2			
3			
4			
5			
6			
7			
8			
9			
10			
11			
12			
13			
14			
15			
16			
17			
18			
19			
20			
21			
22			
23			
24			
25			
26			
27			
28			
29			
30			
31			
32			
33			
34			
35			
36			
37			
38			
39			
40			

(a)

Sales	
Joint costs	
Net income	

(b)

Sales	
Joint costs	
Additional costs	
Net income	

(c)

	Product 12	Product 14	Product 16
Incremental revenue			
Incremental costs			
Incremental profit (loss)			

(d)

Sales	
Joint costs	
Additional costs	
Net income	

E7-11

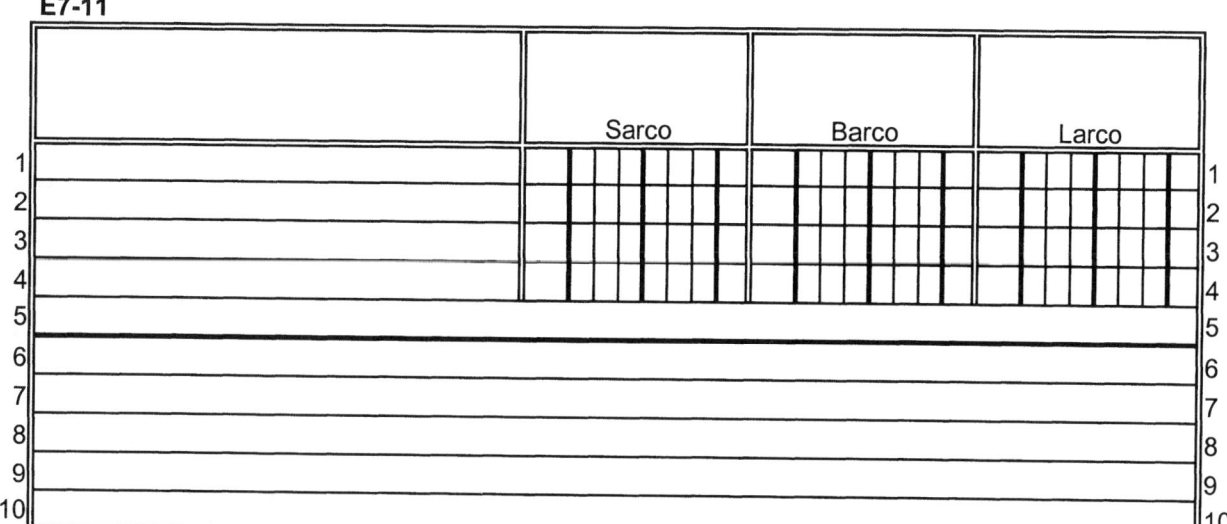

	Sarco	Barco	Larco
1			
2			
3			
4			
5			
6			
7			
8			
9			
10			

E7-12

(a)		
(b)	Revenue after further processing:	
	Revenue at split-off:	

	A	B	C

(c)		

(a)

1					1
2					2
3					3
4					4
5					5

(b)

	Retain Scanner	Replace Scanner	Net Income Increase (Decrease)	
6				6
7				7
8				8
9				9
10				10
11				11
12				12
13				13
14				14

(c)

15		15
16		16
17		17
18		18
19		19
20		20
21		21
22		22
23		23
24		24
25		25
26		26
27		27
28		28
29		29
30		30
31		31
32		32
33		33
34		34
35		35
36		36
37		37
38		38
39		39
40		40

E7-14

	Retain Machine	Replace Machine	Net Income Increase (Decrease)	
1				1
2				2
3				3
4				4
5				5
6				6
7				7
8				8
9				9
10				10

E7-15

	Continue	Eliminate	Net Income Increase (Decrease)	
1				1
2				2
3				3
4				4
5				5
6				6
7				7
8				8
9				9
10				10
11				11
12				12
13				13
14				14
15				15
16				16
17				17
18				18
19				19
20				20
21				21
22				22
23				23
24				24
25				25

Name

Section

Date

		Stunner	Double-Set	Total

1 (a)

4 (b)

14 (c)

Calculation of contribution margin per unit:	A	B	C
1			
2			
3			
4			
5 Fixed costs =			
6			
7			

Company profit with Products A and B:	A	B	Total
8			
9			
10			
11			
12			
13			
14			
15			
16			
17			

Company profit with Product A and C:	A	C	Total
18			
19			
20			
21			
22			
23			
24			
25			
26			
27			
28			
29			
30			
31			
32			
33			
34			
35			
36			
37			
38			
39			
40			

(a)

		Reject Order	Accept Order	Net Income Increase (Decrease)
1				
2				
3				
4				
5				
6				
7				
8				
9				
10				
11				
12				
13				
14				
15				
16				
17				
18				
19				
20				
21				
22				
23				
24				
25				
26 (b)				
27				
28				
29				
30				
31 (c)				
32				
33				
34				
35				
36 (d)				
37				
38				
39				
40				

(a)

		Make WISCO	Buy WISCO	Net Income Increase (Decrease)
1				
2				
3				
4				
5				
6				
7				
8				
9				
10				
11				
12				

(b)

| 13 |
| 14 |
| 15 |
| 16 |
| 17 |
| 18 |

(c)

| 19 |
| 20 |
| 21 |
| 22 |

		Make WISCO	Buy WISCO	Net Income Increase (Decrease)
23				
24				
25				
26				
27				
28				
29				
30				

| 31 |
| 32 |
| 33 |
| 34 |

(d)

| 35 |
| 36 |
| 37 |
| 38 |
| 39 |
| 40 |

(a)

	(1)	Table Cleaner Not Processed Further		

(2) Table Cleaner Processed Further

(3)

(b)

		Don't Process Table Cleaner Further	Process Table Cleaner Further	Net Income Increase (Decrease)

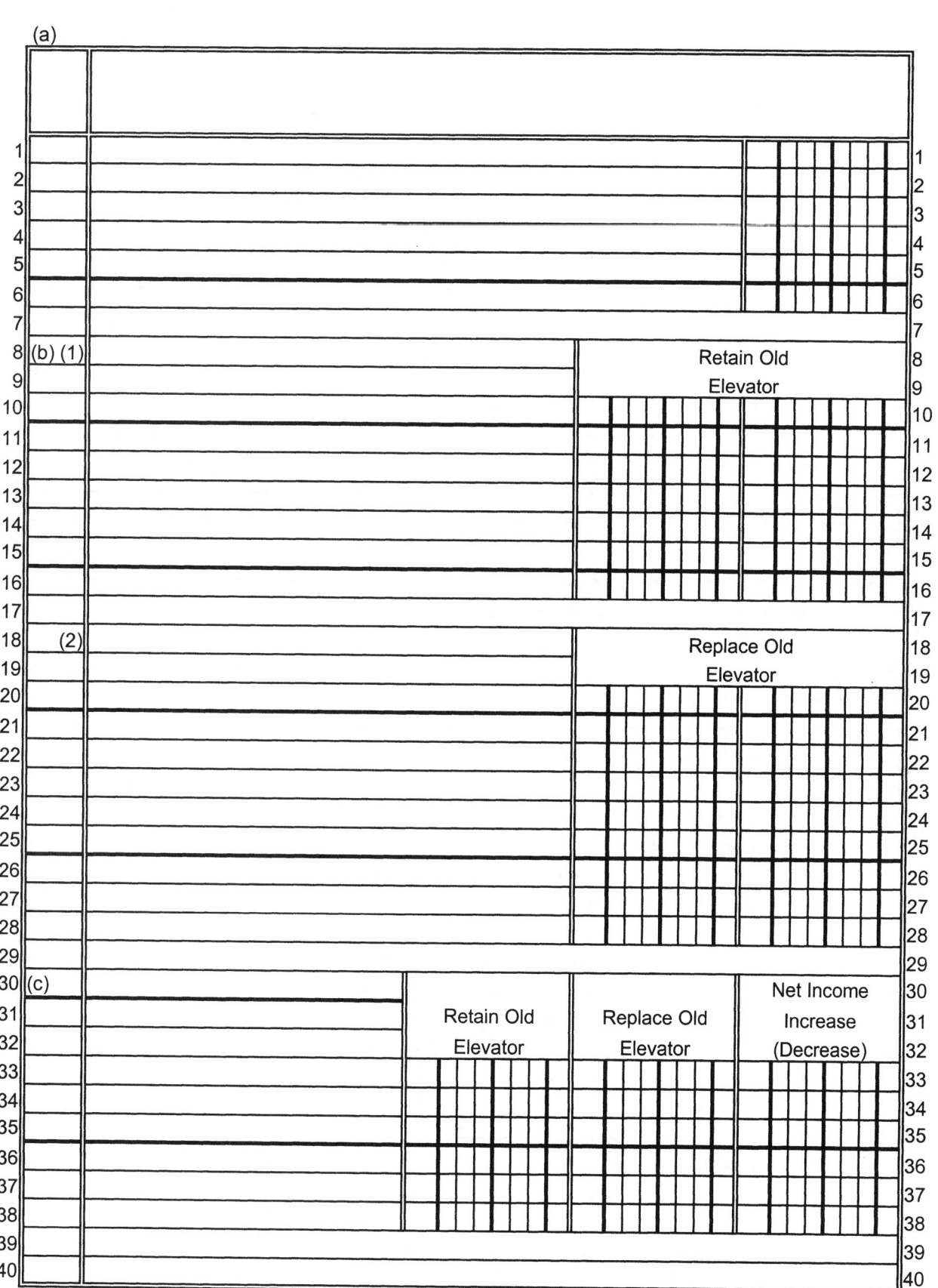

(a)

(b) (1)

Retain Old
Elevator

(2)

Replace Old
Elevator

(c)

	Retain Old Elevator	Replace Old Elevator	Net Income Increase (Decrease)

(d)

1	1
2	2
3	3
4	4
5	5
6	6
7	7
8	8
9	9
10	10
11	11
12	12
13	13
14	14
15	15
16	16
17	17
18	18
19	19
20	20
21	21
22	22
23	23
24	24
25	25
26	26
27	27
28	28
29	29
30	30
31	31
32	32
33	33
34	34
35	35
36	36
37	37
38	38
39	39
40	40

(a)

	Division I	Division II
1		
2		
3		
4		
5		
6		
7		

(b)

(1) Division I	Continue	Eliminate	Net Income Increase (Decrease)
1			
2			
3			
4			
5			
6			
7			
8			
9			
10 (2) Division II			
11			
12			
13			
14			
15			
16			
17			
18			
19			
20			
21			
22			
23			
24			
25			
26			
27			
28			

(c)

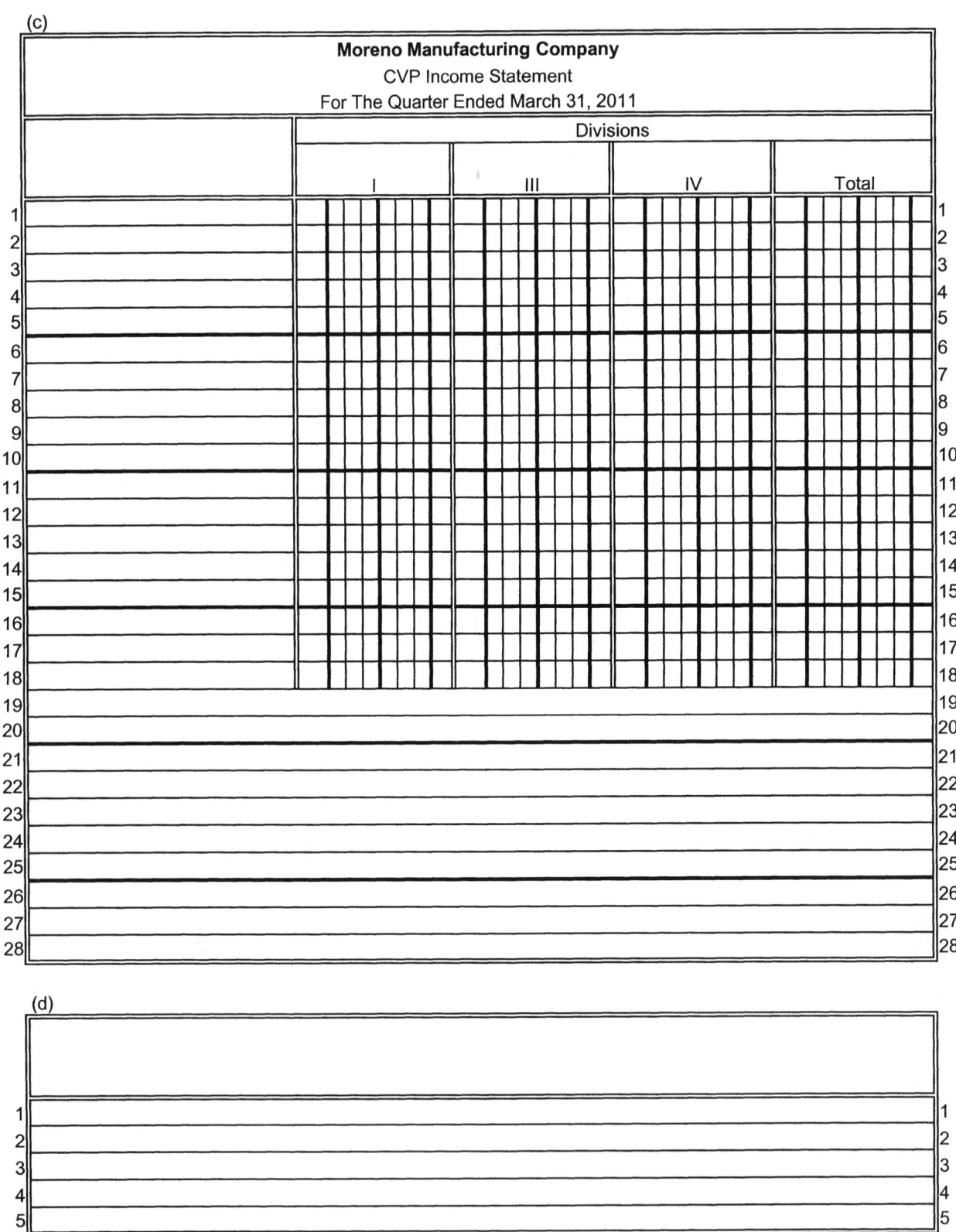

Moreno Manufacturing Company
CVP Income Statement
For The Quarter Ended March 31, 2011

(d)

(a)

	Reject Order	Accept Order	Net Income Increase (Decrease)
1			
2			
3			
4			
5			
6			
7			
8			
9			
10			
11			
12			
13			
14			
15			

(b), (c), and (d)

1	(b)
2	
3	
4	(c)
5	
6	
7	
8	(d)
9	
10	
11	
12	
13	
14	
15	
16	
17	
18	
19	
20	

(a)

		Make BIZBE	Buy BIZBE	Net Income Increase (Decrease)	
1					1
2					2
3					3
4					4
5					5
6					6
7					7
8					8
9					9
10					10
11					11
12					12
13					13

(b)

14	14
15	15
16	16
17	17
18	18

(c)

		Make BIZBE	Buy BIZBE	Net Income Increase (Decrease)	
19					19
20					20
21					21
22					22
23					23
24					24
25					25

26	26
27	27
28	28
29	29
30	30
31	31
32	32
33	33

(d)

34	34
35	35
36	36
37	37
38	38
39	39
40	40

(a)

	(1)	Cleaner Not Processed Further			

(2) General-Purpose Cleaner Processed Further

(3)

(b)

	Don't Process G-P Cleaner Further	Process G-P Cleaner Further	Net Income Increase (Decrease)

(a)

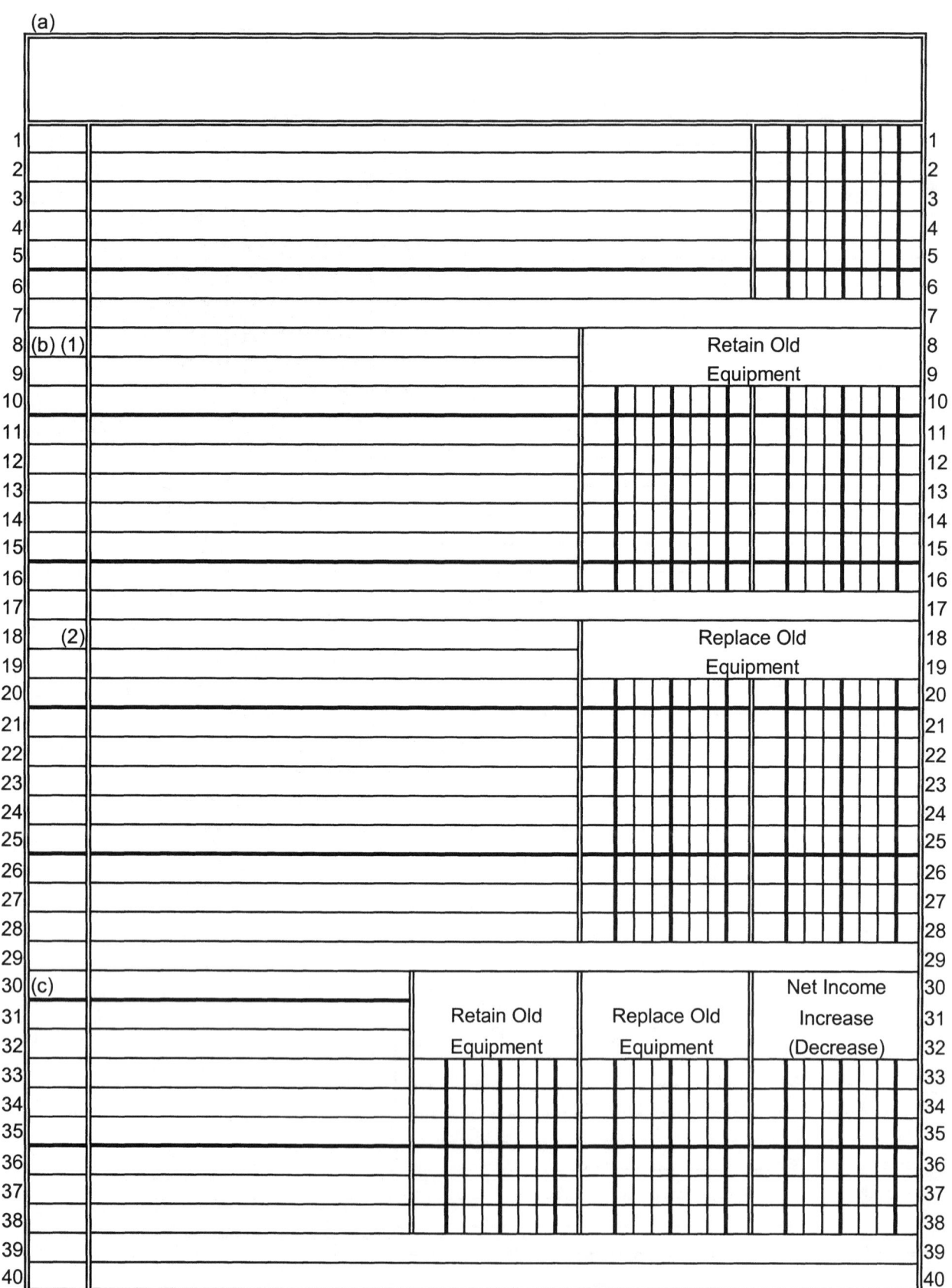

1		
2		
3		
4		
5		
6		
7		

(b) (1)

	Retain Old Equipment
8	
9	
10	
11	
12	
13	
14	
15	
16	
17	

(2)

	Replace Old Equipment
18	
19	
20	
21	
22	
23	
24	
25	
26	
27	
28	
29	

(c)

	Retain Old Equipment	Replace Old Equipment	Net Income Increase (Decrease)
30			
31			
32			
33			
34			
35			
36			
37			
38			
39			
40			

(d)

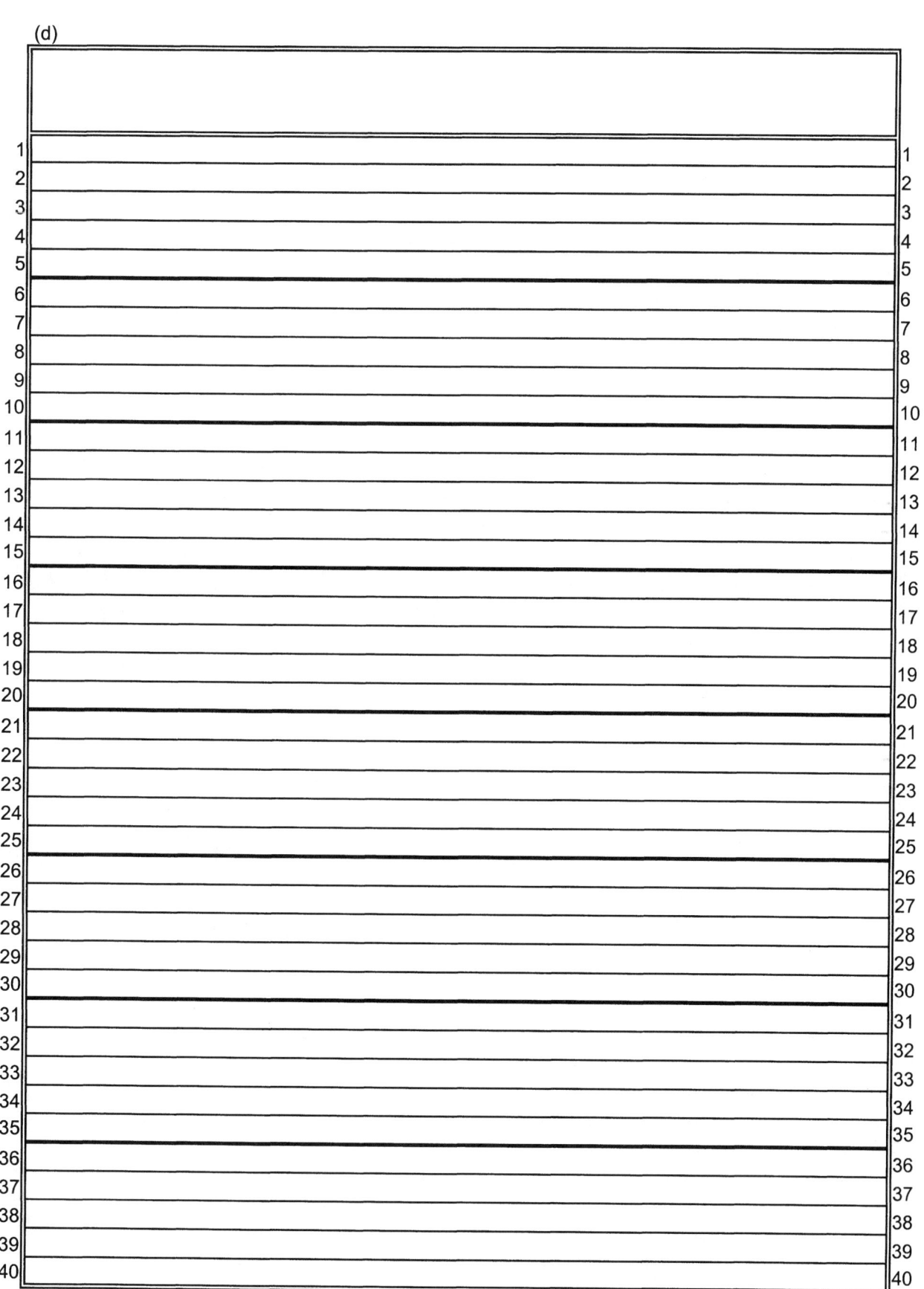

(a)

	Division III	Division IV
1		
2		
3		
4		
5		
6		
7		

(b)

(1) Division III	Continue	Eliminate	Net Income Increase (Decrease)
1			
2			
3			
4			
5			
6			
7			
8			
9			
10 (2) Division IV			
11			
12			
13			
14			
15			
16			
17			
18			
19			
20			
21			
22			
23			
24			
25			
26			
27			
28			

(c)

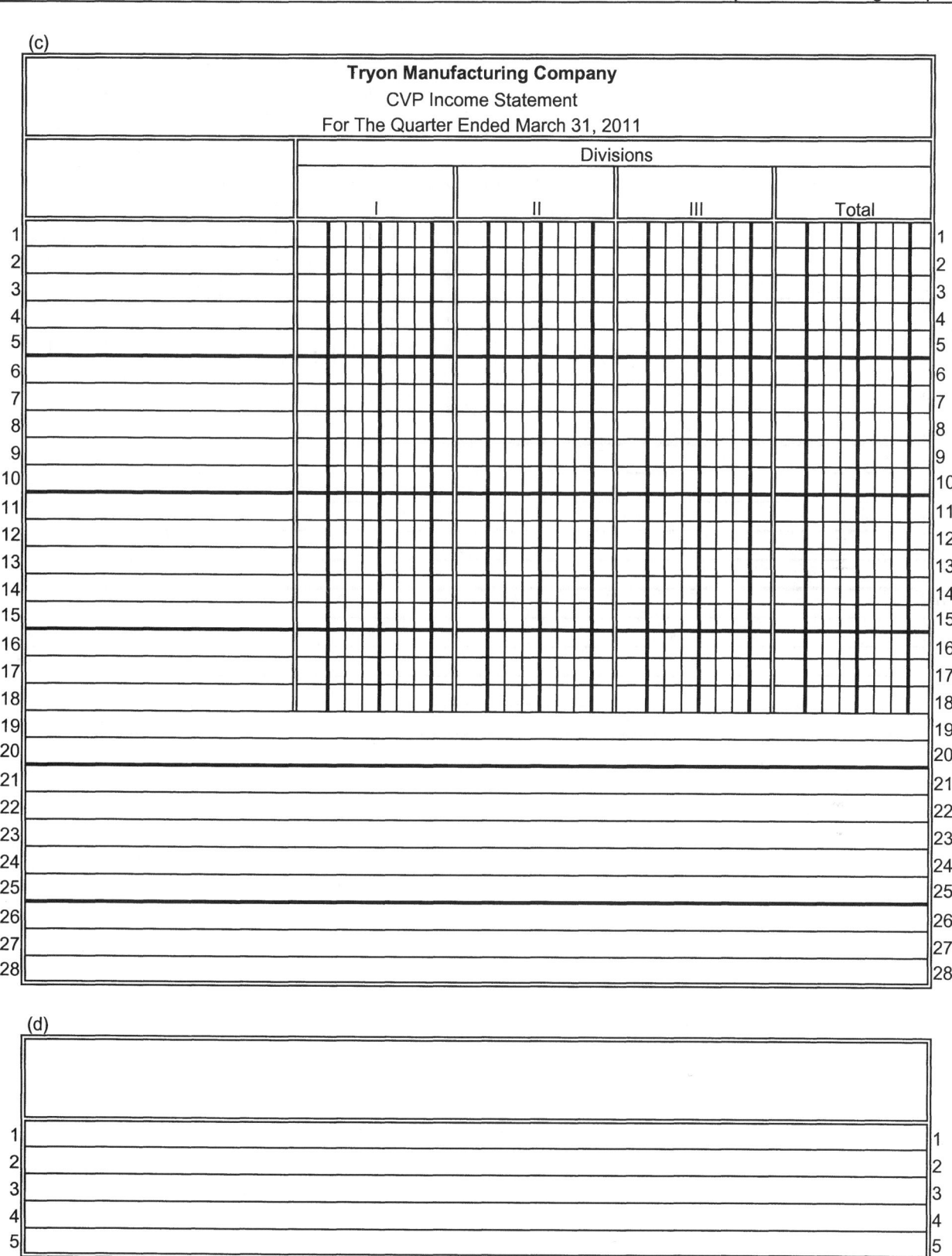

Tryon Manufacturing Company
CVP Income Statement
For The Quarter Ended March 31, 2011

	Divisions			
	I	II	III	Total
1				
2				
3				
4				
5				
6				
7				
8				
9				
10				
11				
12				
13				
14				
15				
16				
17				
18				
19				
20				
21				
22				
23				
24				
25				
26				
27				
28				

(d)

1	
2	
3	
4	
5	

	Retain Old Machine	Purchase New Machine	Net Income Increase (Decrease)
1			
2			
3			
4			
5			
6			
7			
8			
9			
10			
11			
12			
13			
14			
15			
16			
17			
18			
19			
20			
21			
22			

(a)

	Make	Buy Silver Star	Buy Alpha
1			
2			
3			
4			
5			
6			
7			
8			
9			
10			
11			
12			
13			
14			
15			

(b)

(c)

1		1
2		2
3		3
4		4
5		5
6		6
7		7
8		8
9		9
10		10

BE8-2

	1	2	3	4	5	6	7	
1								1
2								2
3								3
4								4
5								5
6								6
7								7
8								8
9								9
10								10
11								11
12								12
13								13
14								14
15								15
16								16
17								17
18								18
19								19
20								20
21								21
22								22
23								23
24								24
25								25
26								26
27								27
28								28
29								29
30								30
31								31
32								32
33								33
34								34
35								35
36								36
37								37
38								38
39								39
40								40

DO IT! 8-2

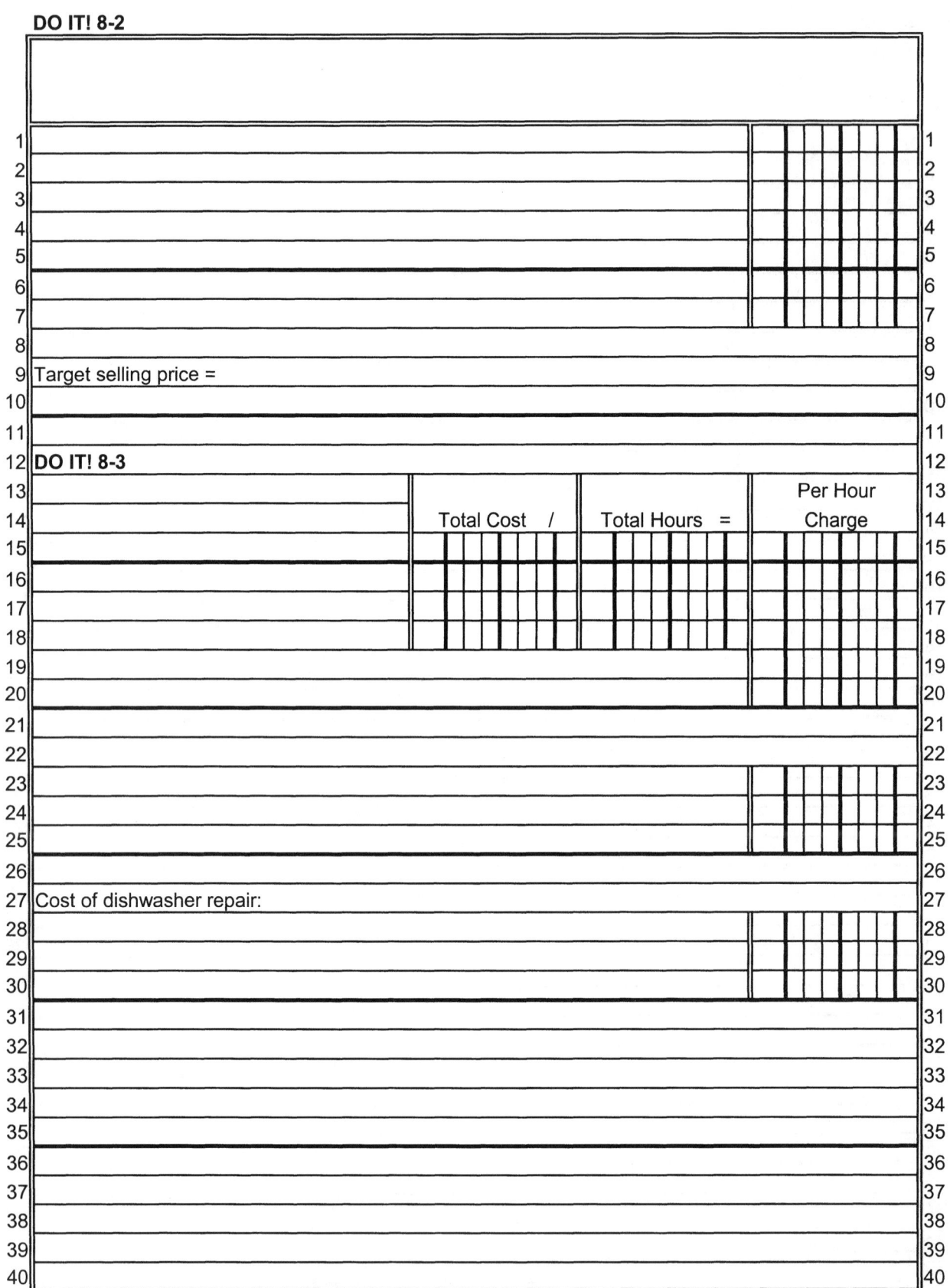

1			
2			
3			
4			
5			
6			
7			
8			
9	Target selling price =		
10			
11			

DO IT! 8-3

		Total Cost /	Total Hours =	Per Hour Charge

Cost of dishwasher repair:

	(a)							
1	Market price							1
2	Less: Desired profit							2
3	Target cost							3
4								4
5	(b)							5

E8-4

			Per Unit
	(a)	Total cost per unit:	
1			
2			
3			
4			
5			
6			
7			
8			
9		(b) Target selling price =	
10			
11			

E8-5

			Per Unit
	(a)	Total cost per unit:	
13			
14			
15			
16			
17			
18			
19			
20			
21			
22			
23		(b) Desired ROI per unit =	
24			
25			
26			
27			
28		(c) Markup percentage	
29		using toatl cost per unit =	
30			
31			
32			
33			
34		(d) Target selling price =	
35			
36			
37			
38			
39			
40			

E8-6

			Per Session	
	(a)	Total cost per session:		
1				1
2				2
3				3
4				4
5				5
6				6
7				7
8				8
9				9
10	(b)	Desired ROI per session =		10
11				11
12				12
13				13
	(c)	Markup percenatge on		14
15		Total cost per session:		15
16				16
17				17
18	(d)	Target price per session =		18
19				19
20				20

E8-7

	(a)	
1	Fixed manufacturing overhead per unit =	1
2		2
3	Fixed selling and administrative expenses per unit =	3
4		4
5	(b) Desired ROI per unit =	5
6		6
7		7
8		8
9		9
10		10
11		11
12		12
13		13
14		14
15		15

E8-7 (Continued)

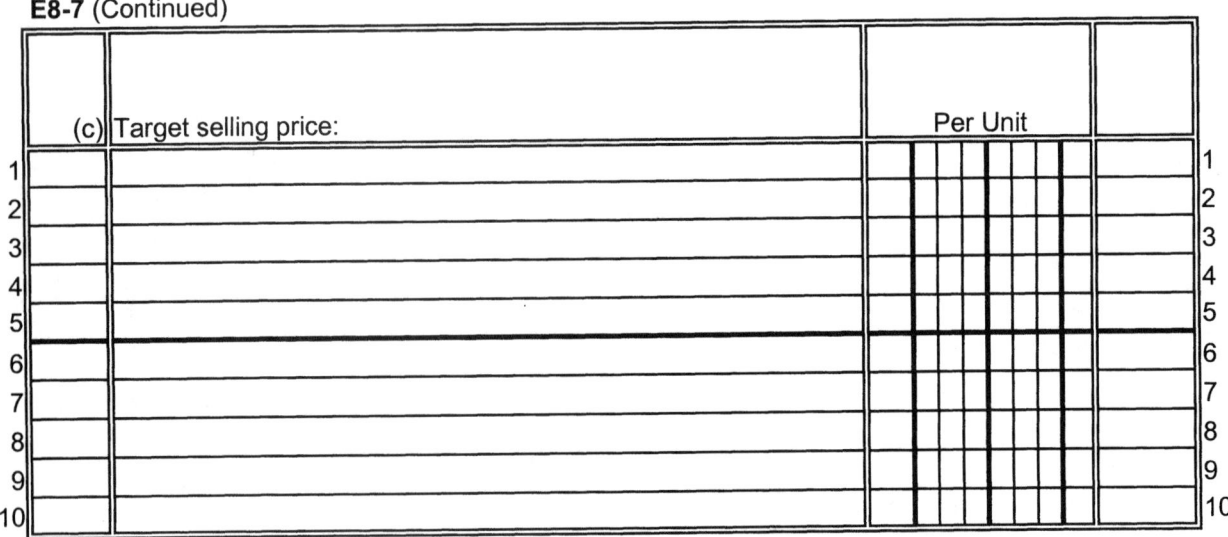

	(c) Target selling price:	Per Unit	
1			
2			
3			
4			
5			
6			
7			
8			
9			
10			

E8-8

	(a)	Total Cost /	Total Hours =	Per Hour Charge	
1	Hourly rate for repairs:				
2					
3	Overhead costs:				
4					
5					
6					
7					
8	Profit margin				
9	Rate charged per hour of labor				
10					
11	(b)	Material Loading Charges /	Total Invoice Cost, Parts and Materials =	Material Loading Percentage	
12					
13					
14					
15	Overhead costs:				
16					
17					
18					
19					
20					
21					
22	Profit margin				
23	Material loading percentage				
24					
25					

E8-8 (Continued)

(c)   Job: Sharrer Corporation - Rebuild spot welder

1 Labor charges:			
2			
3 Material charges:			
4			
5			
6 Total price of labor and material			
7			

E8-9

(a)

	Total Cost /	Total Hours =	Per Hour Charge	
1 Hourly labor rate for repairs:				
2				
3 Overhead costs:				
4				
5				
6				
7				
8 Profit margin				
9 Rate charged per hour of labor				
10				
11				

(b)

	Material Loading Charges /	Total Invoice Cost, Parts and Materials =	Material Loading Percentage	
16 Overhead costs:				
17				
18				
19				
20				
21				
22				
23 Profit margin				
24 Material loading percentage				
25				
26				
27				
28				

E8-9 Continued)

		(c)	
1	Job: Sublette Builders		1
2	Labor charges		2
3			3
4	Material charges:		4
5			5
6			6
7	Total price of labor and material		7
8			8
9			9
10			10

E8-10

		Total Cost /	Total Hours =	Hourly Charge		
1	Hourly labor rate:					1
2						2
3	Overhead costs:					3
4						4
5						5
6	Total hourly cost					6
7						7
8	Profit margin =					8
9						9
10	(b)	Material Loading Charges /	Total Invoice Costs, Parts & Materials =	Material Loading Percentage		10
11						11
12						12
13	Overhead costs:					13
14						14
15						15
16						16
17						17
18						18
19	Other overhead costs					19
20	Total					20
21						21
22	Material loading charge (with profit)					22
23	Material loading charge (without profit)					23
24	Profit margin on materials					24
25						25

E8-10 (Continued)

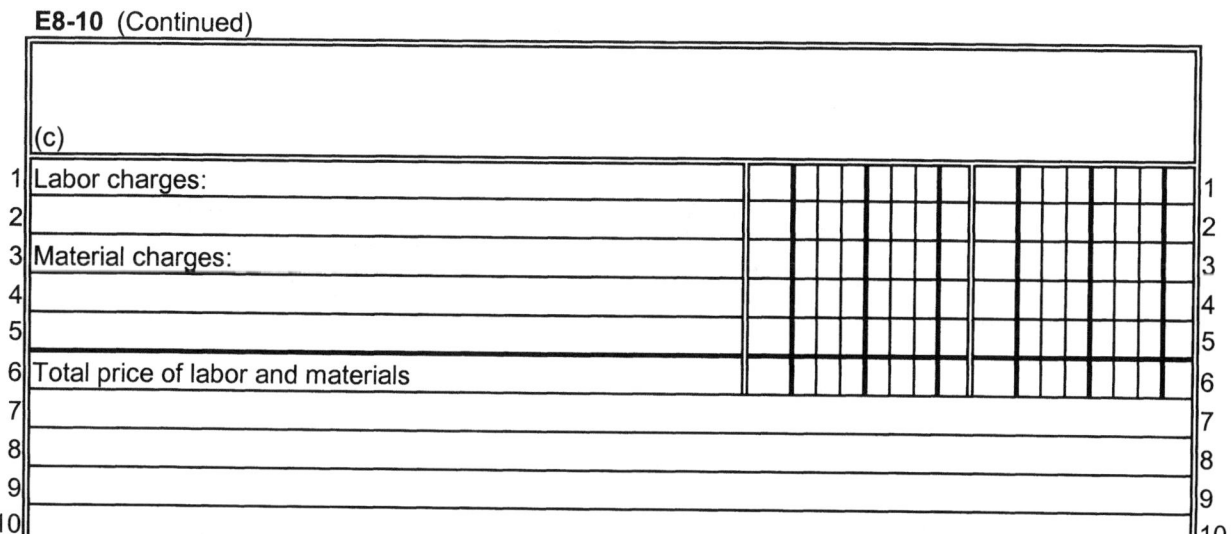

(c)

1 | Labor charges:
2 |
3 | Material charges:
4 |
5 |
6 | Total price of labor and materials
7 |
8 |
9 |
10 |

E8-13

(a)

1 | Minimum transfer price =
2 |
3 |
4 | (b)   The lost contribution margin per unit is:
5 |
6 |
7 |
8 |
9 | Total lost contribution margin =
10 |
11 |
12 | (c)
13 |
14 |
15 |
16 |
17 |
18 |
19 |
20 |

(a)

(1) The effect on Cycle Division is:

	Present Situation	Purchase from FrameBody
Selling price		
Variable cost of goods sold:		
Body frame		
Other variable costs		
Contribution margin		

(2) The effect on FrameBody is:

Selling price to Cycle Division	
Variable cost of goods sold:	

(3) The effect on Sarrel's net income is:

(b)

(1) The effect on Cycle Division is:

(2) The effect on FrameBody is:

Selling price lost	
Selling price to Cycle Division	
Lost contribution margin per cycle	
Number of cycles	
Lost contribution margin	

(3) The effect on Sarrel's net income is:

Cycle Division gain	
FrameBody loss	
Overall loss	

E8-17

	(a)		Division A	Division B	Total Company	
1						1
2						2
3						3
4						4
5						5
6						6
7						7
8	(b)					8
9						9
10						10
11						11
12	(c) (i)					12
13						13
14						14
15	(ii)					15
16						16
17						17
18	(iii)					18
19						19
20						20
21						21
22						22
23						23
24						24
25						25
26						26
27						27
28						28
29						29
30						30
31						31
32						32
33						33
34						34
35						35
36						36
37						37
38						38
39						39
40						40

*E8-18

(a)		Per Unit
1		
2		
3		
4		
5		
6		
7		
8		
9		
10	(b)	Desired ROI per unit =
11		
12		
13	(c)	Absorption cost pricing
14		markup percentage =
15		
16		
17	(d)	Variable cost pricing
18		markup percentage =

		Variable Cost Per Unit
(a)		
1		
2		
3		
4		
5		
6		

		Total Costs /	Budgeted Volume =	Cost Per Unit
7				
8				
9				
10				
11				
12				
13				

			Variable Cost Per Unit
14	Variable cost per unit		
15	Fixed cost per unit		
16	Total cost per unit		
17			
18	(b)	Totl cost per unit	
19		Markup	
20		Desired ROI per unit	
21			
22			
23	(c)	Total cost per unit	
24		Desired ROI per unit	
25		Target selling price	
26			
27			
28	(d)	Variable cost per unit	
29		Fixed cost per unit	
30		Total cost per unit	
31			
32			
33			
34			
35			
36			
37			
38			
39			
40			

	Variable Cost Per Unit
(a)	
1	
2	
3	
4	
5	
6	
7	
8	

	Total Costs /	Budgeted Volume =	Cost Per Unit
9			
10			
11			
12			
13			
14			
15			

	Amount
16	
17 Variable cost per unit	
18 Fixed cost per unit	
19 Total cost per unit	
20	
21	
22 Desired ROI per unit =	
23	
24	
25 Markup percentage =	
26	
27	
28 Total cost per unit	
29 Desired ROI per unit	
30 Target selling price	
31	
32	
33	
34	
35	
36	
37	
38	
39	
40	

(b)			Variable Cost Per Unit	
1				
2				
3				
4				
5				
6				
7				
8				

	Total Costs /	Budgeted Volume =	Cost Per Unit	
9				
10				
11				
12				
13				
14				
15				
16				
17				

18 Variable cost per unit		
19 Fixed cost per unit		
20 Total cost per unit		
21		
22		
23 Desired ROI per unit =		
24		
25		
26		
27 Markup percentage =		
28		
29		
30		
31 Total cost per unit		
32 Desired ROI per unit		
33 Target selling price		
34		
35		
36		
37		
38		
39		
40		

(a) Computation of time charge rate:	Total Cost /	Total Hours =	Per Hour Charge	
1 Hourly labor rate for repairs:				1
2				2
3 Overhead costs:				3
4				4
5				5
6				6
7				7
8 Rate charged per labor hour				8
9				9
10				10
11 (b)	Material Loading Charges /	Total Invoice Cost, Parts and Materials =	Material Loading Percentage	11
12				12
13 Computation of material loading charge:				13
14 Overhead costs:				14
15				15
16				16
17				17
18				18
19				19
20				20
21 Total				21
22				22
23 Material loading percentage				23
24				24
25 (c) Price quotation for time and material:				25
26				26
27	**Dave's Electronic Repair Shop**			27
28	Time and Material Price Quotation			28
29	January 5, 2011			29
30 Job: Rebuild big screen TV set:				30
31				31
32 Labor charges:				32
33				33
34 Material charges:				34
35				35
36				36
37 Total price of labor and material				37
38				38
39				39
40				40

1	(a)	1
2		2
3		3
4		4
5		5
6		6
7	(b)	7
8		8
9		9
10		10
11		11
12		12
13		13
14		14
15		15
16		16
17	(c)	17
18		18
19		19
20		20
21		21
22		22
23		23
24		24
25		25
26		26
27	(d)	27
28	The printing operation would lose:	28
29		29
30		30
31	Business Books would save:	31
32		32
33	Overall loss to the company as a whole	33
34		34
35		35
36		36
37		37
38		38
39		39
40		40

(a)			

(b)

Lost contribution margin by Board Division:

    Total lost contribution margin

Lost contribution margin by Chip Division:

    Total lost contribution margin

Overall lost contribution margin for the company

Name

Section

Date

*Problem 8-7A

Hansen Corporation

(a) Absorption cost pricing:

Computation of unit manufacturing cost and target selling price

(b) Variable cost pricing:

Computation of total variable cost and target selling price

Absorption Cost Pricing		
1 (a) Computation of unit manufacturing cost:		
2		
3		Per Unit
4		
5		
6		
7		
8		
9		
10		
11 Computation of markup percentage to provide a 30% ROI:		
12		
13 Markup		
14 Percentage =		
15		
16		
17 (b) Computation of target price:		
18		
19 Target price =		
20		
21 Proof of 30% ROI under absorption cost approach:		
22	**Swensen Windows Inc.**	
23	Budgeted Absorption Cost Approach Income Statement	
24	(Tinted Window)	
25		
26		
27		
28		
29		
30		
31		
32		
33 Desired ROI =		
34		
35		
36 Markup percenatge =		
37		
38		
39		
40		

	Variable Cost Pricing		Per Unit
1	(c) Computation of unit variable cost:		
2			
3			
4			
5			
6			
7			
8			
9			
10			
11			
12	Computation of markup percentage to provide a 30% ROI:		
13			
14	Markup		
15	Percentage =		
16			
17			
18	(d) Computation of target price:		
19			
20	Target price =		
21			
22	Proof of 30% ROI under variable cost pricing:		
23	**Swensen Windows Inc.**		
24	Budgeted Contribution Cost Approach Income Statement		
25	(Tinted Window)		
26			
27			
28			
29			
30			
31			
32			
33			
34			
35	Desired ROI =		
36			
37			
38	Markup percentage =		
39			
40			

(e)

		Variable Cost Per Unit
(a)		
1		
2		
3		
4		
5		
6		

	Total Costs /	Budgeted Volume =	Cost Per Unit
7			
8			
9			
10			
11			
12			
13			

		Cost Per Unit
14 Variable cost per unit		
15 Fixed cost per unit		
16 Total cost per unit		
17		
18 (b) Total cost per unit		
19 Markup		
20 Desired ROI per unit		
21		
22		
23 (c) Total cost per unit		
24 Desired ROI per unit		
25 Target selling price		
26		
27		

28 (d) Variable cost per unit		
29 Fixed cost per unit		
30 Total cost per unit		
31		
32		
33		
34		
35		
36		
37		
38		
39		
40		

(a)			Variable Cost Per Unit
1			
2			
3			
4			
5			
6			
7			
8			

	Total Costs /	Budgeted Volume =	Cost Per Unit
9			
10			
11			
12			
13			
14			
15			
16			

		Cost Per Unit
17	Variable cost per unit	
18	Fixed cost per unit	
19	Total cost per unit	
20		
21		
22	Desired ROI per unit =	
23		
24		
25	Markup percentage =	
26		
27		
28	Total cost per unit	
29	Desired ROI per unit	
30	Target selling price	
31		
32		
33		
34		
35		
36		
37		
38		
39		
40		

(b)			Variable Cost Per Unit
1			
2			
3			
4			
5			
6			
7			
8			

	Total Costs /	Budgeted Volume =	Cost Per Unit
9			
10			
11			
12			
13			
14			
15			
16			
17			
18 Variable cost per unit			
19 Fixed cost per unit			
20 Total cost per unit			
21			
22			
23 Desired ROI per unit =			
24			
25			
26			
27 Markup percentage =			
28			
29			
30			
31 Total cost per unit			
32 Desired ROI per unit			
33 Target selling price			
34			
35			
36			
37			
38			
39			
40			

(a) Computation of time charge rate:	Total Cost /	Total Hours =	Per Hour Charge	
1 Hourly labor rate for repairs:				1
2				2
3 Overhead costs:				3
4				4
5				5
6				6
7				7
8 Rate charged per hour of labor				8
9				9
10				10

(b) Computation of material loading charge:	Material Loading Charges	Total Invoice Cost, Parts and Materials	Material Loading Percentage	
11 (b)				11
12				12
13 Computation of material loading charge:				13
14 Overhead costs:				14
15				15
16				16
17				17
18				18
19				19
20				20
21 Total				21
22				22
23 Material loading percentage				23
24				24

(c) Price quotation for time and material:			
25 (c) Price quotation for time and material:			25
26			26
27	**Momentum Bike Repair Shop**		27
28	Time and Material Price Quotation		28
29	January 5, 2011		29
30 Job: Fix Giant Mountain bike			30
31			31
32 Labor charges:			32
33			33
34 Material charges:			34
35			35
36			36
37 Total price of labor and material			37
38			38
39			39
40			40

1	(a)	1
2		2
3		3
4		4
5		5
6		6
7	(b)	7
8		8
9		9
10		10
11		11
12		12
13		13
14		14
15		15
16		16
17	(c)	17
18		18
19		19
20		20
21		21
22		22
23		23
24		24
25		25
26		26
27	(d)	27
28	The printing operation would lose:	28
29		29
30		30
31	Superior! would save:	31
32		32
33	Overall loss to the company as a whole	33
34		34
35		35
36		36
37		37
38		38
39		39
40		40

1	(a)							
2								
3								
4								
5								
6								
7								
8								
9								
10								
11								
12	(b)							
13	Lost contribution margin by Soprano Division:							
14								
15								
16								
17								
18								
19								
20								
21	Total lost contribution margin							
22								
23	Lost contribution margin by Peg Division:							
24								
25								
26								
27								
28								
29								
30	Total lost contribution margin							
31								
32	Overall lost contribution margin for the company							
33								
34								
35								
36								
37								
38								
39								
40								

(a)   Absorption cost pricing:

Computation of unit manufacturing cost and target selling price

(b)   Variable cost pricing:

Computation of total variable cost and target selling price

	Absorption Cost Pricing	
1	(a) Computation of unit manufacturing cost:	
2		
3		Per Unit
4		
5		
6		
7		
8		
9		
10		
11	Computation of markup percentage to provide a 20% ROI:	
12		
13	Markup	
14	Percentage =	
15		
16		
17	(b) Computation of target price:	
18		
19	Target price =	
20		
21	Proof of 20% ROI under absorption cost approach:	
22	**Ben Paul Bikes Inc.**	
23	Budgeted Absorption-Cost Income Statement	
24	(Mountain Bike)	
25		
26		
27		
28		
29		
30		
31		
32		
33	Desired ROI =	
34		
35		
36	Markup percenatge =	
37		
38		
39		
40		

	Variable Cost Pricing	Per Unit
1	(c) Computation of unit variable cost:	
2		
3		
4		
5		
6		
7		
8		
9		
10		
11		
12	Computation of mark up percentage to provide a 20% ROI:	
13		
14	Markup	
15	Percentage =	
16		
17		
18	(d) Computation of target price:	
19		
20	Target price =	
21		
22	Proof of 20% ROI under variable cost pricing:	
23	**Ben Paul Bikes Inc.**	
24	Budgeted Variable-Cost Income Statement	
25	(Mountain Bike)	
26		
27		
28		
29		
30		
31		
32		
33		
34		
35	Desired ROI =	
36		
37		
38	Markup percentage =	
39		
40		

	(e)	
1		1
2		2
3		3
4		4
5		5
6		6
7		7
8		8
9		9
10		10
11		11
12		12
13		13
14		14
15		15
16		16
17		17
18		18
19		19
20		20
21		21
22		22
23		23
24		24
25		25
26		26
27		27
28		28
29		29
30		30
31		31
32		32
33		33
34		34
35		35
36		36
37		37
38		38
39		39
40		40

(a)

(b) Variable cost per unit:	Basic Wash	Deluxe Wash	Premium Wash

Fixed cost per unit:	Total Costs /	Budgeted Volume =	Cost Unit

Computation of selling price (45,000 units):	Basic	Deluxe	Premium

1	(c)	Revenues:	1
2			2
3			3
4			4
5			5
6		Variable expenses:	6
7			7
8			8
9			9
10			10
11		Fixed expenses	11
12		Net income	12
13			13
14			14
15		ROI =	15
16			16
17			17
18			18
19			19
20	(d)		20
21			21
22			22
23			23
24			24
25			25
26			26
27			27
28			28
29			29
30			30
31			31
32			32
33			33
34			34
35			35
36			36
37			37
38			38
39			39
40			40

BE9-2

Mussatto Company

Sales Budget

For the Year Ending December 31, 2011

	Quarter				Year
	1	2	3	4	

BE9-3

Mussatto Company

Production Budget

For the First Six Months Ending June 30, 2011

	Quarter		Six
	1	2	Months

BE9-4

Hannon Company	
Direct Materials Budget	
For the Month Ending January 31, 2012	

BE9-5

	Quarter		**Six**
	1	2	**Months**

Cobb Company
Direct Labor Budget
For the Six Months Ending June 30, 2011

BE9-6

Eckert Inc.

Manufacturing Overhead Budget

For the Year Ending December 31, 2011

	Quarter				Year
	1	2	3	4	
1					
2					
3					
4					
5					
6					
7					

BE9-7

Kaspar Company

Selling and Administrative Expense Budget

For the Year Ending December 31, 2011

	Quarter				Year
	1	2	3	4	
8					
9					
10					
11					
12					
13					
14					
15					
16					
17					
18					
19					
20					
21					
22					
23					

BE9-8

	Paige Company	
	Budgeted Income Statement	
	For the Year Ending December 31,2011	

	Collections from Customers		
BE9-9			
Credit Sales	January	February	March

BE9-10

DO IT! 9-2

	Wellstone Company			
	Production Budget			
	For the Six Months Ending June 30, 2011			
		Quarter		Six
		1	2	Months
1				
2				
3				
4				
5				
6				
7				
8				
9				

DO IT! 9-4

(a)   Total unit cost:

	Quantity	Unit Cost	Total

(b)

	Oak Creek Company
	Budgeted Income Statement
	For the Year Ending December 31, 2011

Name

Section

Date

Oak Creek Company

Oak Creek Company

Sales Budget

For the Year Ending December 31, 2011

	Quarter				Year
	1	2	3	4	

Oak Creek Company

Production Budget

For the Year Ending December 31, 2011

	Quarter				Year
	1	2	3	4	

Name

Section

Date   Oak Creek Company

Oak Creek Company

Direct Materials Budget

For the Year Ending December 31, 2011

	Quarter				Year
	1	2	3	4	

Name

Section

Date

Venetian Company

Cash Budget

April

You will find this working paper at the end of this booklet.

You will find this working paper at the end of this booklet.

Pletcher Company
Production Budget
For the Year Ending December 31, 2011

Product HD-240

	Quarter				Year
	1	2	3	4	
1					
2					
3					
4					
5					
6					
7					
8					
9					
10					
11					
12					
13					
14					
15					

E9-5

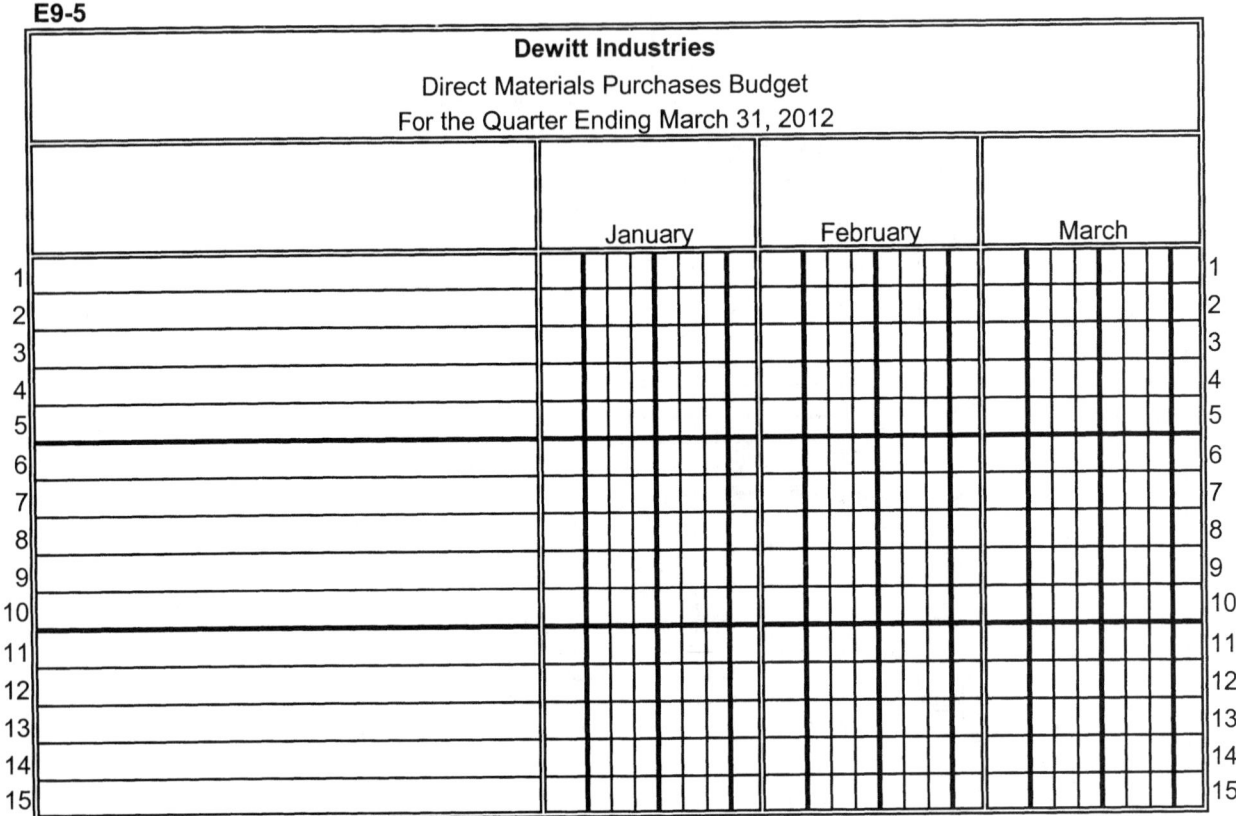

Dewitt Industries

Direct Materials Purchases Budget

For the Quarter Ending March 31, 2012

	January	February	March

E9-7

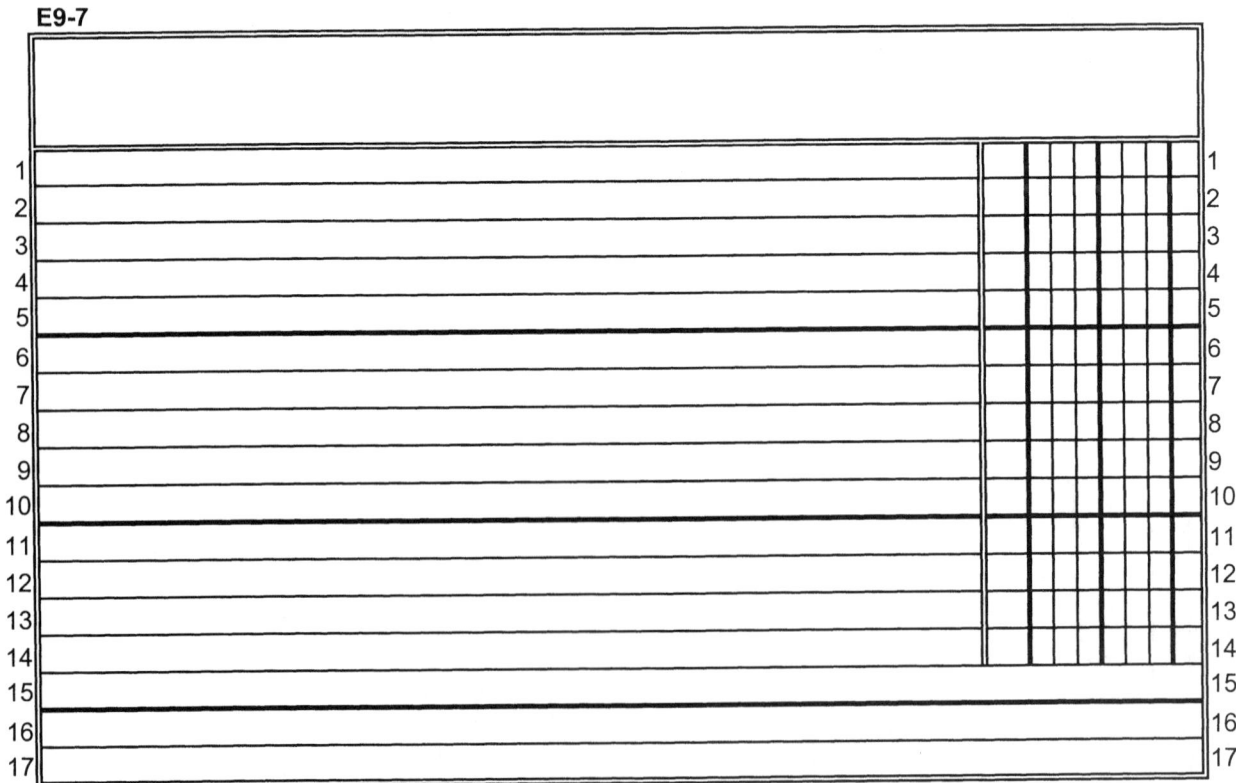

(a)

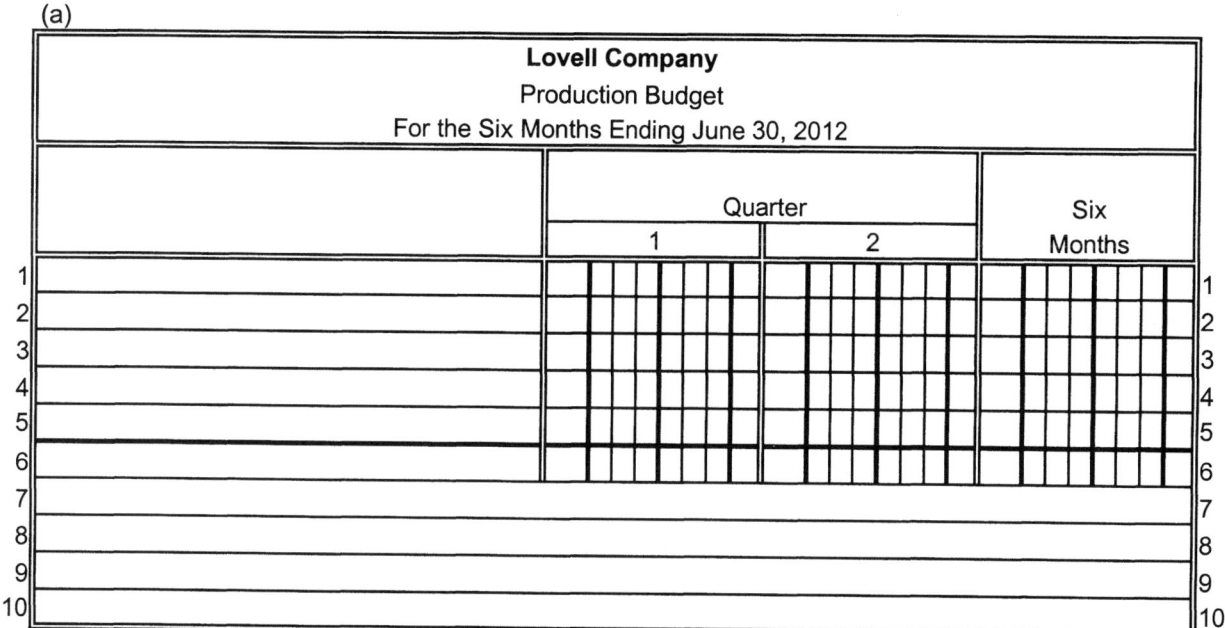

Lovell Company

Production Budget

For the Six Months Ending June 30, 2012

	Quarter		Six
	1	2	Months

(b)

Lovell Company

Direct Materials Budget

For the Six Months Ending June 30, 2012

	Quarter		Six
	1	2	Months

E9-8

Gonzales, Inc.

Direct Labor Budget

For the Year Ending December 31, 2011

	Quarter				Year
	1	2	3	4	
1					
2					
3					
4					
5					
6					
7					
8					
9					

E9-9

Choo-Foo Company

Production Budget

For the Quarter Ending March 31, 2011

	Jan	Feb	Mar	Total
1				
2				
3				
4				
5				
6				
8				

E9-9 (Concluded)

Choo-Foo Company
Direct Labor Budget
For the Quarter Ending March 31, 2011

	Jan			Feb			Mar			Total		
1												
2												
3												
4												
5												
6												
7												
8												

Frizell Company

Manufacturing Overhead Budget

For the Year Ending December 31, 2011

	Variable Overhead per DLH	Quarter				Year
		1	2	3	4	
1 Variable Costs						
2 Indirect materials						
3 Indirect labor						
4 Maintenenace						
5 Total variable						
6						
7						
8 Fixed costs						
9 Supervisory salaries						
10 Depreciation						
11 Maintenance						
12 Total fixed						
13 Total manufacturing overhead						
14						
15 Direct labor hours						
16 Manufacturing overhead rate						
17 per direct labor hour						
18						

	Medina Company		
	Selling and Administrative Expense Budget		
	For the Six Months Ending June 30, 2011		
	Quarter		Six Months
	1	2	
1			
2			
3			
4			
5			
6			
7			
8			
9			
10			
11			
12			
13			
14			
15			
16			
17			
18			
19			
20			
21			
22			
23			
24			
25			
26			
27			
28			
29			
30			

(a)

Ortiz Company

Production Budget

For the Two Months Ending February 28, 2011

	January	February
1		
2		
3		
4		
5		
6		
7		
8		
9		
10		

(b)

Ortiz Company

Direct Materials Budget

For the Month Ending January 31, 2011

	January
1	
2	
3	
4	
5	
6	
7	
8	
9	
10	
11	
12	
13	
14	
15	

(a)

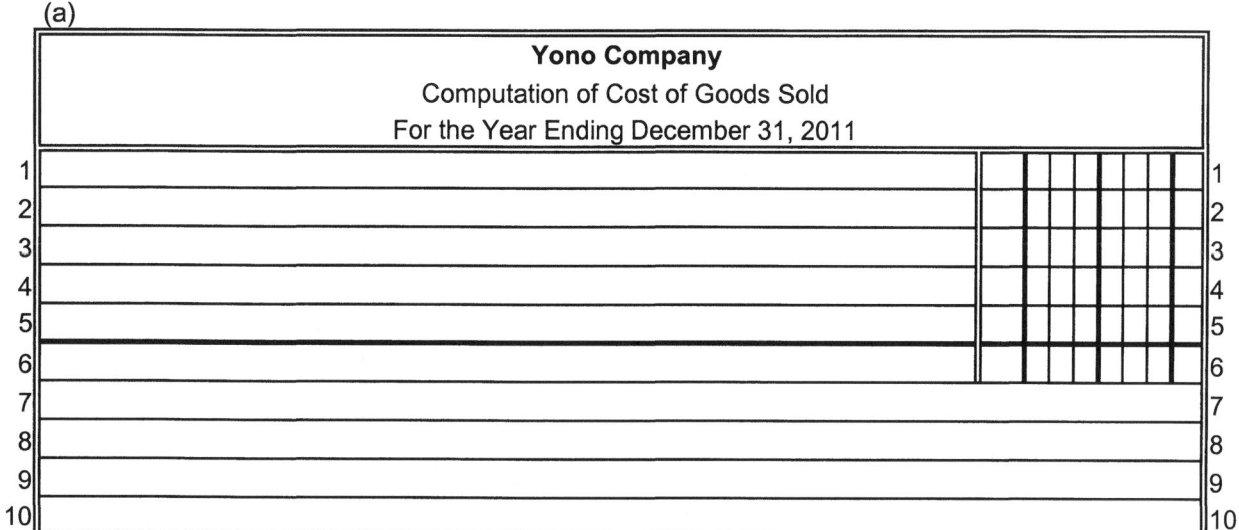

Yono Company

Computation of Cost of Goods Sold

For the Year Ending December 31, 2011

(b)

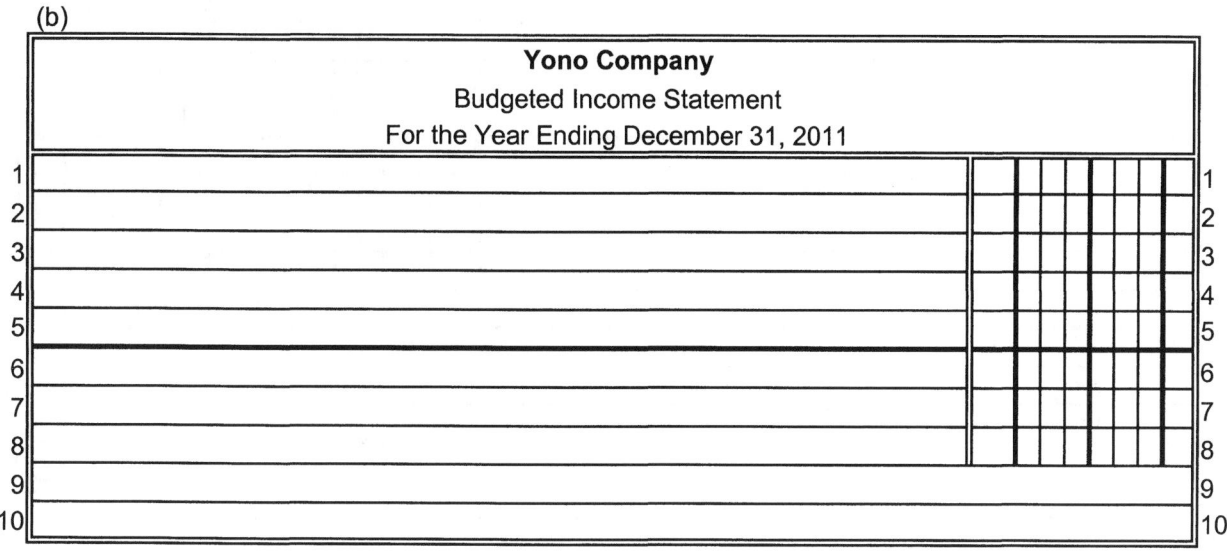

Yono Company

Budgeted Income Statement

For the Year Ending December 31, 2011

		January	Februrary	
1				1
2	Beginning Cash Balance	$ 46000		2
3				3
4				4
5				5
6				6
7				7
8				8
9				9
10				10
11				11
12				12
13				13
14				14
15				15
16				16
17				17
18				18
19				19
20				20
21				21
22				22
23				23
24				24
25				25
26				26
27				27
28				28
29				29
30				30

Malone Company
Cash Budget
For the Two Months Ending February 28, 2011

	Fultz Corporation									
	Cash Budget									
	For the Quarter Endingd March 31, 2011									
1	Beginning cash balance	$		3	1	0	0	0		1
2										2
3										3
4										4
5										5
6										6
7										7
8										8
9										9
10										10
11										11
12										12
13										13
14										14
15										15
16										16
17										17
18										18
19										19
20										20
21										21
22										22
23										23
24										24
25										25
26										26
27										27
28										28
29										29
30										30

(a)

Harrington Company

Cash Budget

For the Month Ending July 31, 2011

(b)

(a)

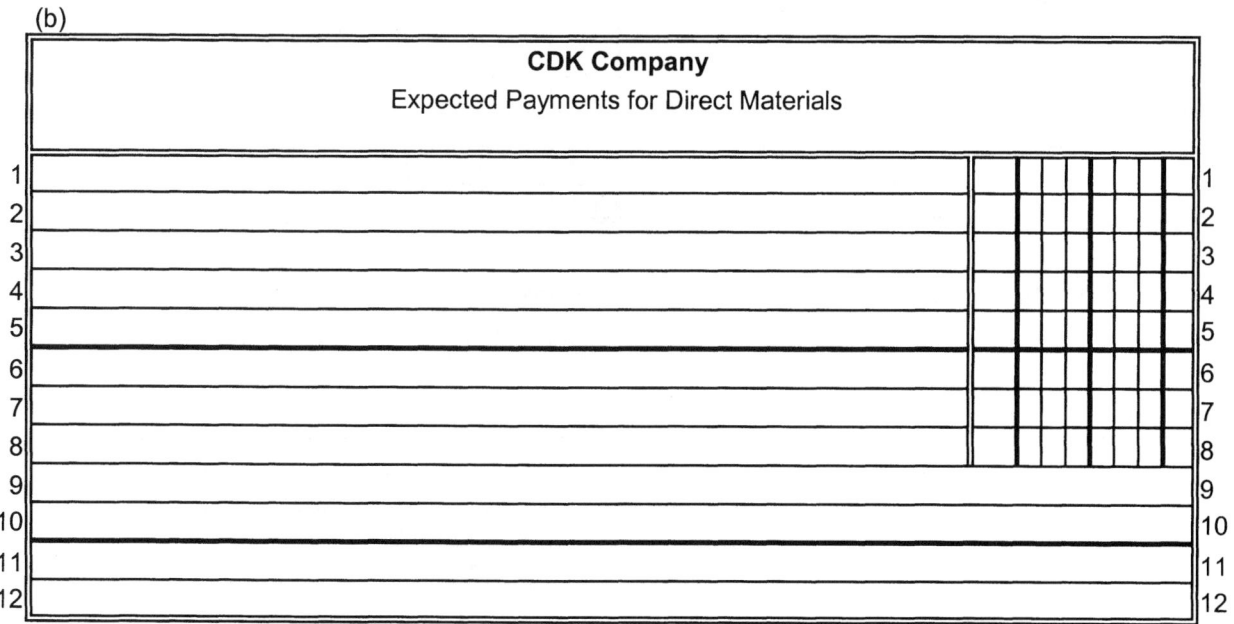

| **CDK Company** |
| Expected Collections from Customers |

(b)

| **CDK Company** |
| Expected Payments for Direct Materials |

(a) (1)

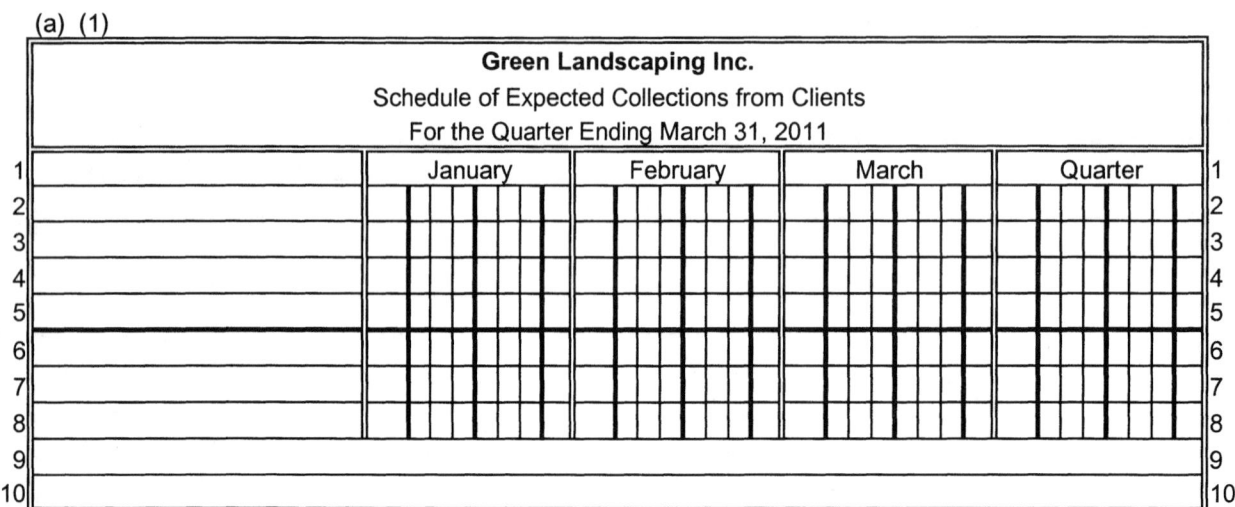

Green Landscaping Inc.

Schedule of Expected Collections from Clients

For the Quarter Ending March 31, 2011

	January	February	March	Quarter

(2)

Green Landscaping Inc.

Schedule of Expected Payments for Landscaping Supplies

For the Quarter Ending March 31, 2011

	January	February	March	Quarter

(b)

(1)

(2)

Deitz Dental Clinic Cash Budget For the Two Quarters Ending June 30, 2011	1st Quarter	2nd Quarter
Beginning Cash Balance	$ 30000	

(a)

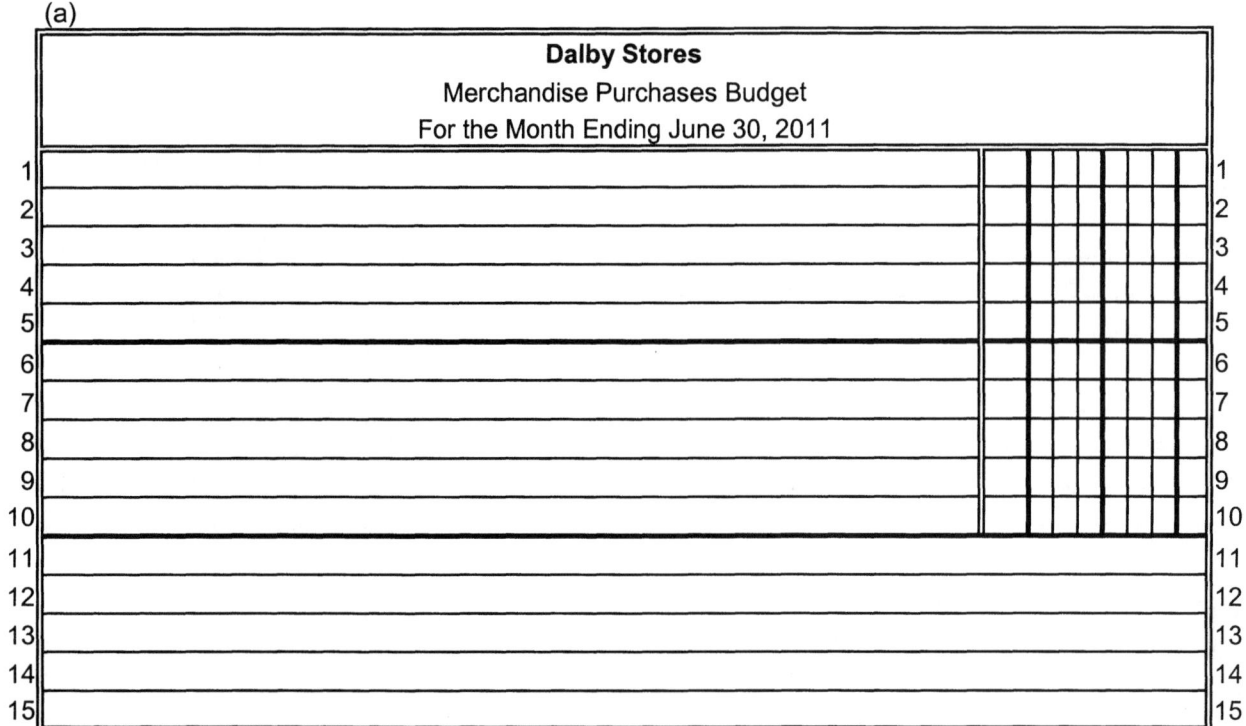

Dalby Stores

Merchandise Purchases Budget

For the Month Ending June 30, 2011

(b)

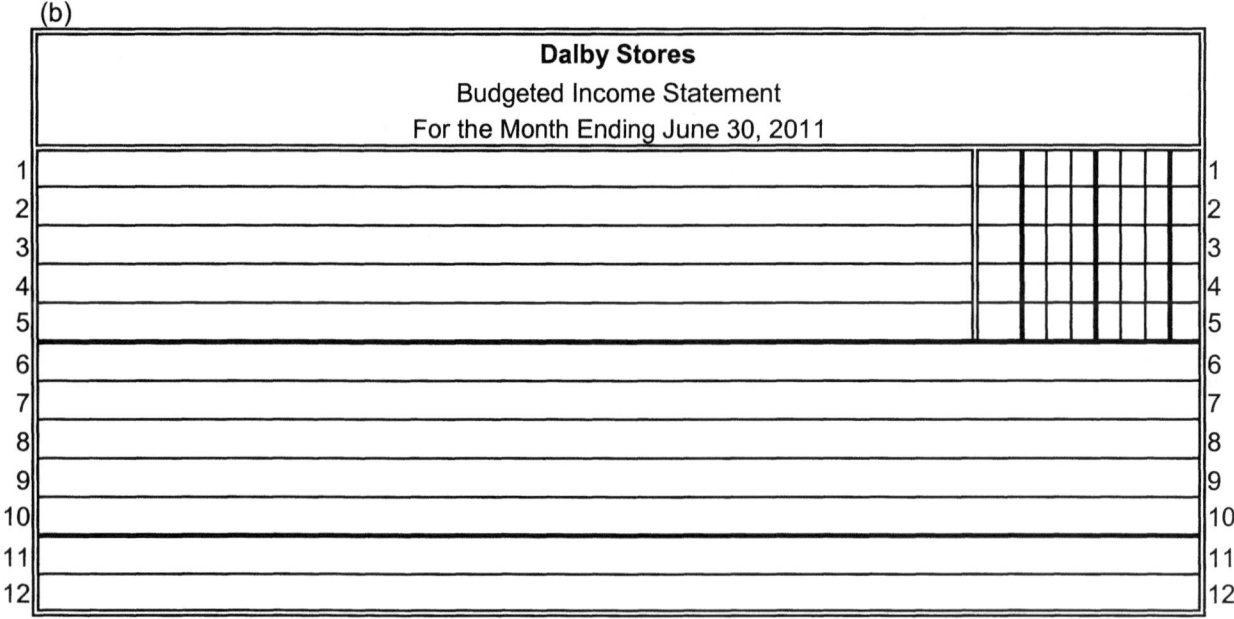

Dalby Stores

Budgeted Income Statement

For the Month Ending June 30, 2011

Zelmer Farm Supply Company

Sales Budget

For the Six Months Ending June 30, 2012

	Quarter		Six Months
	1	2	
1			
2			
3			
4			

Zelmer Farm Supply Company

Production Budget

For the Six Months Ending June 30, 2012

	Quarter		Six Months
	1	2	
1			
2			
3			
4			
5			
6			

Zelmer Farm Supply Company

Direct Materials Budget-Gumm

For the Six Months Ending June 30, 2012

	Quarter		Six Months
	1	2	
1			
2			
3			
4			
5			
6			
7			
8			
9			
10			
11			
12			
13			
14			

Zelmer Farm Supply Company
Direct Labor Budget
For the Six Months Ending June 30, 2012

	Quarter		Six Months
	1	2	
1			
2			
3			
4			
5			
6			
7			
8			
9			
10			

Zelmer Farm Supply Company
Selling and Administrative Expense Budget
For the Six Months Ending June 30, 2012

	Quarter		Six Months
	1	2	
1			
2			
3			
4			
5			

Zelmer Farm Supply Company

Budgeted Income Statement

For the Six Months Ending June 30, 2012

1	1
2	2
3	3
4	4
5	5
6	6
7	7
8	8
9	9
10	10

Zelmer Farm Supply Company

Schedule-Standard Cost Per Bag

Cost Element	Quantity	Unit Cost	Total	
1				1
2				2
3				3
4				4
5				5
6				6
7				7
8				8
9				9
10				10

(a)

Jantzen Inc. Sales Budget For the Year Ending December 31, 2012			
	JB 50	JB 60	Total
1			
2			
3			
4			

(b)

Jantzen Inc. Production Budget For the Year Ending December 31, 2012			
	JB 50	JB 60	Total
1			
2			
3			
4			
5			
6			
7			

(c)

Jantzen Inc. Direct Materials Budget For the Year Ending December 31, 2012			
	JB 50	JB 60	Total
1			
2			
3			
4			
5			
6			
7			
8			
9			
10			
11			
12			
13			
14			

(d)

Jantzen Inc. Direct Labor Budget For the Year Ending December 31, 2012	JB 50	JB 60	Total	
1				1
2				2
3				3
4				4
5				5
6				6
7				7
8				8
9				9
10				10

(e)

Jantzen Inc. Budgeted Income Statement For the Year Ending December 31, 2012	JB 50	JB 60	Total	
1				1
2				2
3				3
4				4
5				5
6				6
7				7
8				8
9				9
10				10
11				11
12				12
13				13
14				14
15				15
16				16
17				17
18				18
19				19
20				20

(a)

		Plan A	Plan B	
	Nieto Industries			
	Sales Budget			
	For the Year Ending December 31, 2012			
1				1
2				2
3				3

(b)

		Plan A	Plan B	
	Nieto Industries			
	Production Budget			
	For the Year Ending December 31, 2012			
1				1
2				2
3				3
4				4
5				5
6				6

(c) and (d)

		Plan A	Plan B	
1	(c) Total variable costs			1
2				2
3	Total fixed costs			3
4				4
5	Total costs			5
6				6
7	Total units			7
8	Cost per unit			8
9				9
10				10
11	(d) Gross profit			11
12				12
13				13
14				14
15				15
16				16
17				17
18				18

(a)

	January	February
(1) Expected collections from customers		
(2) Expected payments for direct materials		

(b)

Dinkle Company

Cash Budget

For the Two Months Ending February 29, 2012

	January	February
Beginning cash balance	$ 60000	

(a)

Hardesty Company - San Miguel Store
Merchandise Purchases Budget
For the Months of May and June, 2012

	May	June	
1			1
2			2
3			3
4			4
5			5
6			6
7			7
8			8

(b)

Hardesty Company - San Miguel Store
Budgeted Income Statement
For the Months of May and June, 2012

	May	June	
1			1
2			2
3			3
4			4
5			5
6			6
7			7
8			8
9			9
10			10
11			11
12			12
13			13
14			14
15			15
16			16
17			17
18			18
19			19
20			20
21			21
22			22
23			23
24			24
25			25

	Clarke Industries																			
	Budgeted Income Statement																			
	For the Year Ending December 31, 2012																			
1																				1
2																				2
3																				3
4																				4
5																				5
6																				6
7																				7
8																				8
9																				9
10																				10
11																				11
12																				12
13																				13
14																				14
15																				15
16																				16
17																				17
18																				18
19																				19
20																				20
21																				21
22																				22
23																				23
24																				24
25																				25

Clarke Industries									
Budgeted Balance Sheet									
December 31, 2012									
Assets									
Current assets									
Cash									
Accounts receivable									
Finished goods inventory									
Total current assets									
Property, plant, and equipment									
Equipment									
Less: Accumulated depreciation									
Total assets									
Liabilities and Stockholders' Equity									
Liabilities									
Notes payable									
Accounts payable									
Income taxes payable									
Total liabilities									
Stockholders' equity									
Common stock									
Retained earnings									
Total stockholders' equity									
Total liabilities and stockholders' equity									

Suppan Farm Supply Company

Sales Budget

For the Six Months Ending June 30, 2011

	Quarter		Six Months
	1	2	
1			
2			
3			
4			

Suppan Farm Supply Company

Production Budget

For the Six Months Ending June 30, 2011

	Quarter		Six Months
	1	2	
1			
2			
3			
4			
5			
6			

Suppan Farm Supply Company

Direct Materials Budget-Crup

For the Six Months Ending June 30, 2011

	Quarter		Six Months
	1	2	
1			
2			
3			
4			
5			
6			
7			
8			
9			
10			
11			
12			
13			
14			

Suppan Farm Supply Company Direct Labor Budget For the Six Months Ending June 30, 2011			
	Quarter		Six Months
	1	2	
1			
2			
3			
4			
5			
6			
7			
8			
9			
10			

Suppan Farm Supply Company Selling and Administrative Expense Budget For the Six Months Ending June 30, 2011			
	Quarter		Six Months
	1	2	
1			
2			
3			
4			
5			

Suppan Farm Supply Company
Budgeted Income Statement
For the Six Months Ending June 30, 2011

1													1
2													2
3													3
4													4
5													5
6													6
7													7
8													8
9													9
10													10

Suppan Farm Supply Company
Schedule-Standard Cost Per Bag

	Cost Element	Quantity	Unit Cost	Total	
1					1
2					2
3					3
4					4
5					5
6					6
7					7
8					8
9					9
10					10

(a)

Durham Inc.
Sales Budget
For the Year Ending December 31, 2011

	LN 35	LN 40	Total
1			
2			
3			
4			

(b)

Durham Inc.
Production Budget
For the Year Ending December 31, 2011

	LN 35	LN 40	Total
1			
2			
3			
4			
5			
6			
7			

(c)

Durham Inc.
Direct Materials Budget
For the Year Ending December 31, 2011

	LN 35	LN 40	Total
1			
2			
3			
4			
5			
6			
7			
8			
9			
10			
11			
12			
13			
14			

(d)

Durham Inc.

Direct Labor Budget

For the Year Ending December 31, 2011

	LN 35	LN 40	Total
1			
2			
3			
4			
5			
6			
7			
8			
9			
10			

(e)

Durham Inc.

Budgeted Income Statement

For the Year Ending December 31, 2011

	LN 35	LN 40	Total
1			
2			
3			
4			
5			
6			
7			
8			
9			
10			
11			
12			
13			
14			
15			
16			
17			
18			
19			
20			

(a)

Speier Industries
Sales Budget
For the Year Ending December 31, 2012

	Plan A	Plan B
1		
2		
3		

(b)

Speier Industries
Production Budget
For the Year Ending December 31, 2012

	Plan A	Plan B
1		
2		
3		
4		
5		
6		

(c) and (d)

	Plan A	Plan B
1 (c) Total variable costs		
2		
3 Total fixed costs		
4		
5 Total costs		
6		
7 Total units		
8 Cost per unit		
9		
10		
11 (d) Gross profit		
12		
13		
14		
15		
16		
17		

(a)

	January	February
1 (1) Expected collections from customers		
2		
3		
4		
5		
6		
7 (2) Expected payments for direct materials		
8		
9		
10		
11		

(b)

Vidro Company

Cash Budget

For the Two Months Ending February 29, 2012

	January	February
1 Beginning cash balance	$ 50000	
2		
3		
4		
5		
6		
7		
8		
9		
10		
11		
12		
13		
14		
15		
16		
17		
18		
19		
20		
21		
22		
23		

(a)

Guzman Company - Westwood Store		
Merchandise Purchases Budget		
For the Months of July and August, 2011		
	July	August
1		
2		
3		
4		
5		
6		
7		
8		

(b)

Guzman Company - Westwood Store		
Budgeted Income Statement		
For the Months of July and August, 2011		
	July	August
1		
2		
3		
4		
5		
6		
7		
8		
9		
10		
11		
12		
13		
14		
15		
16		
17		
18		
19		
20		
21		
22		
23		
24		
25		

1																1
2																2
3																3
4																4
5																5
6																6
7																7
8																8
9																9
10																10
11																11
12																12
13																13
14																14
15																15
16																16
17																17
18																18
19																19
20																20
21																21
22																22
23																23
24																24
25																25
26																26
27																27
28																28
29																29
30																30
31																31
32																32
33																33
34																34
35																35
36																36
37																37
38																38
39																39
40																40

BE10-1

Noble Company

Sales Budget Report

For the Quarter Ended March 31, 2011

Product line	Budget	Actual	Difference	
1				
2				
3				
4				
5				

BE10-2

Noble Company

Sales Budget Report

For the Quarter Ended June 30, 2011

Product Line	Second Quarter			Year to Date		
	Budget	Actual	Difference	Budget	Actual	Difference
6						
7						
8						
9						
10						
11						
12						
13						
14						

BE10-3 (a)

Goody Company			
Static Direct Labor Budget Report			
For the Month Ended January 31, 2011			
	Budget	Actual	Difference

(b)

Goody Company			
Flexible Direct Labor Budget Report			
For the Month Ended January 31, 2011			
	Budget	Actual	Difference

BE10-4

Ortiz Company
Monthly Flexible Manufacturing Budget
For the Year 2011

1 Activity level					
2 Finished units	80000	100000	120000		

BE10-5

	Budget	Actual	Difference	
			Favorable	F
Units produced	100000	100000	Unfavorable	U

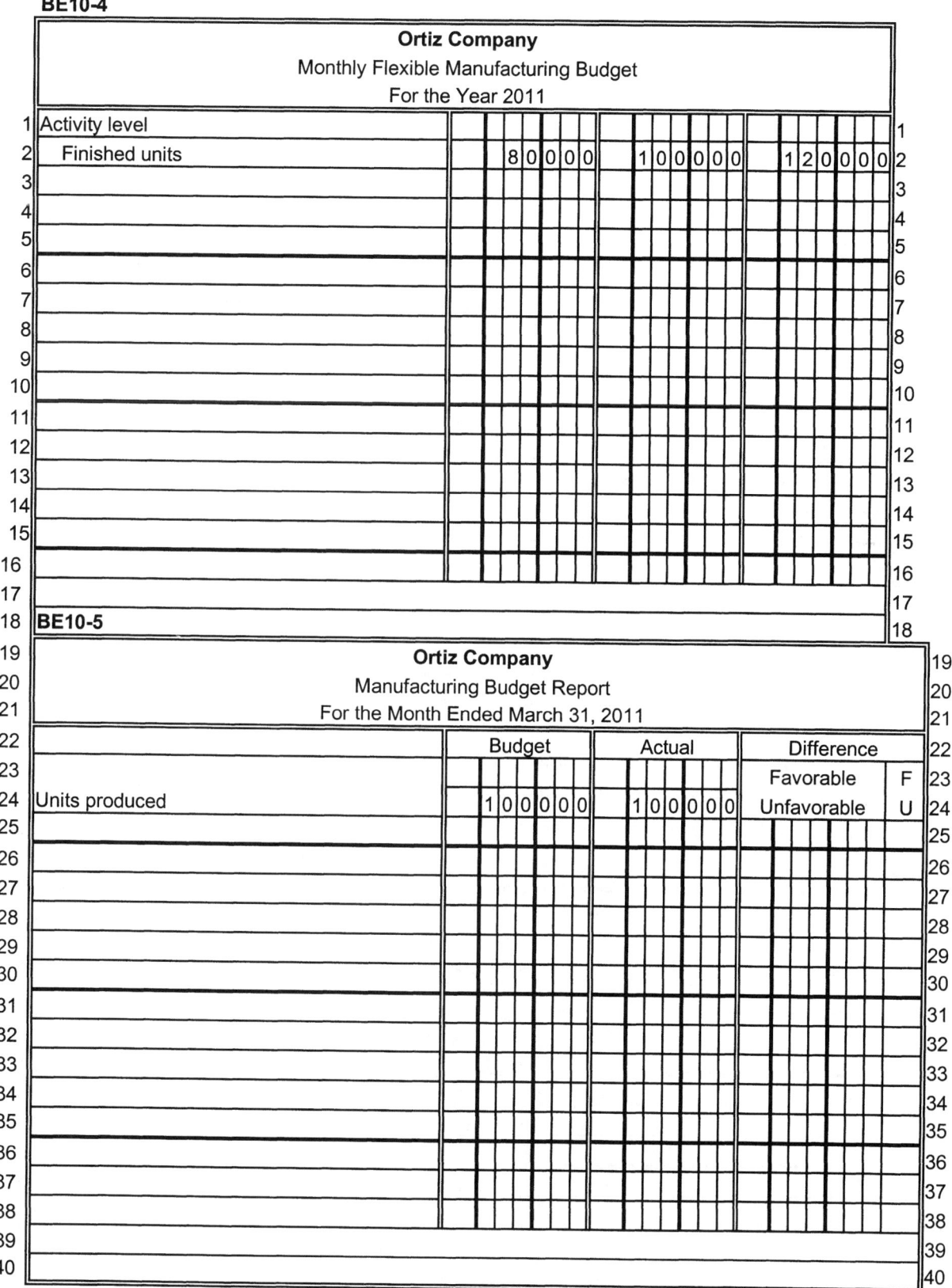

BE10-6

Everly Company
Assembly Department
Manufacturing Overhead Cost Responsibility Report
For the Month Ended April 30, 2011

Controllable Cost	Budget	Actual	Difference	
			Favorable	F
			Unfavorable	U

BE10-7

Justus Manufacturing Company
Water Division
Responsibility Report
For the Year Ended December 31, 2011

	Budget	Actual	Difference	
			Favorable	F
			Unfavorable	U

BE10-8

Mize Company - Plastics Division
Management Responsibility Report
For the Year Ended December 31, 2011

	Budget	Actual	Difference	
			Favorable	F
			Unfavorable	U

Units produced	Budget at 6,000 units	Actual 6,000 units	Difference Favorable (F) Unfavorable (U)	
1				1
2				2
3				3
4				4
5				5
6				6
7				7
8				8
9				9
10				10
11				11
12				12
13				13
14				14
15				15
16				16
17				17
18				18
19				19
20				20
21				21
22				22
23				23
24				24
25				25

	Deep South Division Responsibility Report For the Year Ended December 31, 2011			Difference		
		Budget	Actual	Favorable (F) Unfavorable (U)		
1						1
2						2
3						3
4						4
5						5
6						6
7						7
8						8
9						9
10						10

(a)   Return on investment for 2011:

(b)   Expected return on investment for alternative 1:

Expected return on investment for alternative 2:

Exercise 10-2

Bruno Company

(a)

Bruno Company

Selling Expense Report

For the Quarter Ended March 31

	By Month			Year to Date		
Month	Budget	Actual	Difference	Budget	Actual	Difference
January						
February						
March						

(b) and (c)

(b)

(c)

E10-3

	Roche Company				
	Monthly Flexible Manufacturing Overhead Budget				
	For the Year 2011				
1	Activity level					
2	Direct labor hours	7000	8000	9000	10000
3					
4					
5					
6					
7					
8					
9					
10					
11					
12					
13					
14					
15					

E10-4 (a)

	Roche Company			
	Manufacturing Overhead Flexible Budget Report			
	For the Month Ended July 31, 2011			
		Budget at	Actual Costs	Difference
				Favorable (F)
3	Direct labor hours (DLH)	9,000 DLH	9,000 DLH	Unfavorable (U)
4				
5				
6				
7				
8				
9				
10				
11				
12				
13				
14				
15				
16				
17				
18				
19				
20				

(b)

Roche Company Manufacturing Overhead Flexible Budget Report For the Month Ended July 31, 2011			
Direct labor hours (DLH)	Budget at 8,500	Actual Costs 8,500	Difference Favorable (F) Unfavorable (U)

(c)

E10-5

	Zeller Company				
	Monthly Flexible Selling Expense Budget				
	For the Year 2011				
1	Activity level				
2	Sales	$170,000	$180,000	$190,000	$200,000
3					
4					
5					
6					
7					
8					
9					
10					
11					
12					
13					
14					
15					

E10-6 (a)

	Zeller Company			
	Selling Expense Flexible Budget Report			
	For the Month Ended March 31, 2011			
		Budget at $170,000	Actual Costs $170,000	Difference Favorable (F) Unfavorable (U)
3	Sales			
4				
5				
6				
7				
8				
9				
10				
11				
12				
13				
14				
15				
16				
17				
18				
19				
20				

(b)

	Zeller Company				
	Selling Expense Flexible Budget Report				
	For the Month Ended March 31, 2011				
				Difference	
				Favorable F	
		Budget	Actual Costs	Unfavorable U	
4 Sales		$ 1 8 0 0 0 0	$ 1 8 0 0 0 0		4
5					5
6					6
7					7
8					8
9					9
10					10
11					11
12					12
13					13
14					14
15					15
16					16
17					17
18					18

(c)

(a)

Kitchen Care Inc. Flexible Production Cost Budget			
Activity level:			
Production levels	90000	100000	110000

(b)

(a)

	Doggone Groomers Flexible Budget			
Activity level:				
Direct labor hours	550	600	700	

(b)

(c)

(d)

(a)

	Turney Company		
	Manufacturing Overhead Flexible Budget Report		
	For the Quarter Ended March 31, 2011		
	Budget	Actual Costs	Difference Favorable F Unfavorable U

(b)

	Turney Company		
	Manufacturing Overhead Responsibility Report		
	For the Quarter Ended March 31, 2011		
Controllable Costs	Budget	Actual Costs	Difference Favorable F Unfavorable U

(a)

Garza Company - Clothing Department				
Selling Expense Flexible Budget Report				
For the Month Ended October 31, 2011				
		Budget	Actual Costs	Difference Favorable F Unfavorable U
Sales in units		10000	10000	

(b)

(a)

Edington Plumbing Company
Home Plumbing Services Segment
Responsibility Report
For the Quarter Ended March 31, 2011

	Budget	Actual	Difference Favorable F Unfavorable U
Service revenue	$ 25000	$ 26000	$

(b)

(a)

To Dallas Department Manager - Finishing				Month: July
Controllable Costs	Budget	Actual	Fav/Unfav	

(b)

To Assembly Plant Manager - Dallas				Month: July
Controllable Costs	Budget	Actual	Fav/Unfav	

(c)

To Vice President - Production				Month: July
Controllable Costs	Budget	Actual	Fav/Unfav	

E10-14 (a)

Hardin Company Mixing Department Responsibility Report For the Month Ended January 31, 2011			
Controllable Cost	Budget	Actual	Difference Favorable F Unfavorable U

(b)

E10-15 (a)

(1)	
(2)	
(3)	
(4)	
(5)	
(6)	

E10-15 (b)

Fuqua Manufacturing Inc. Women's Shoe Division Responsibility Report For the Month Ended June 30, 2011			
	Budget	Actual	Difference Favorable F Unfavorable U

E10-16

Duncan Donnegal Company Sports Equipment Division Responsibility Report 2011			
		Budget	Actual	Difference Favorable F Unfavorable U
(a)			
(b)			

(a)

Danner and LaRussa Dental Clinic				
Preventive Services				
Responsibility Report				
For the Month Ended May 31, 2011				
			Difference	
	Budget	Actual	Favorable F Unfavorable U	
Service revenue				

(b)

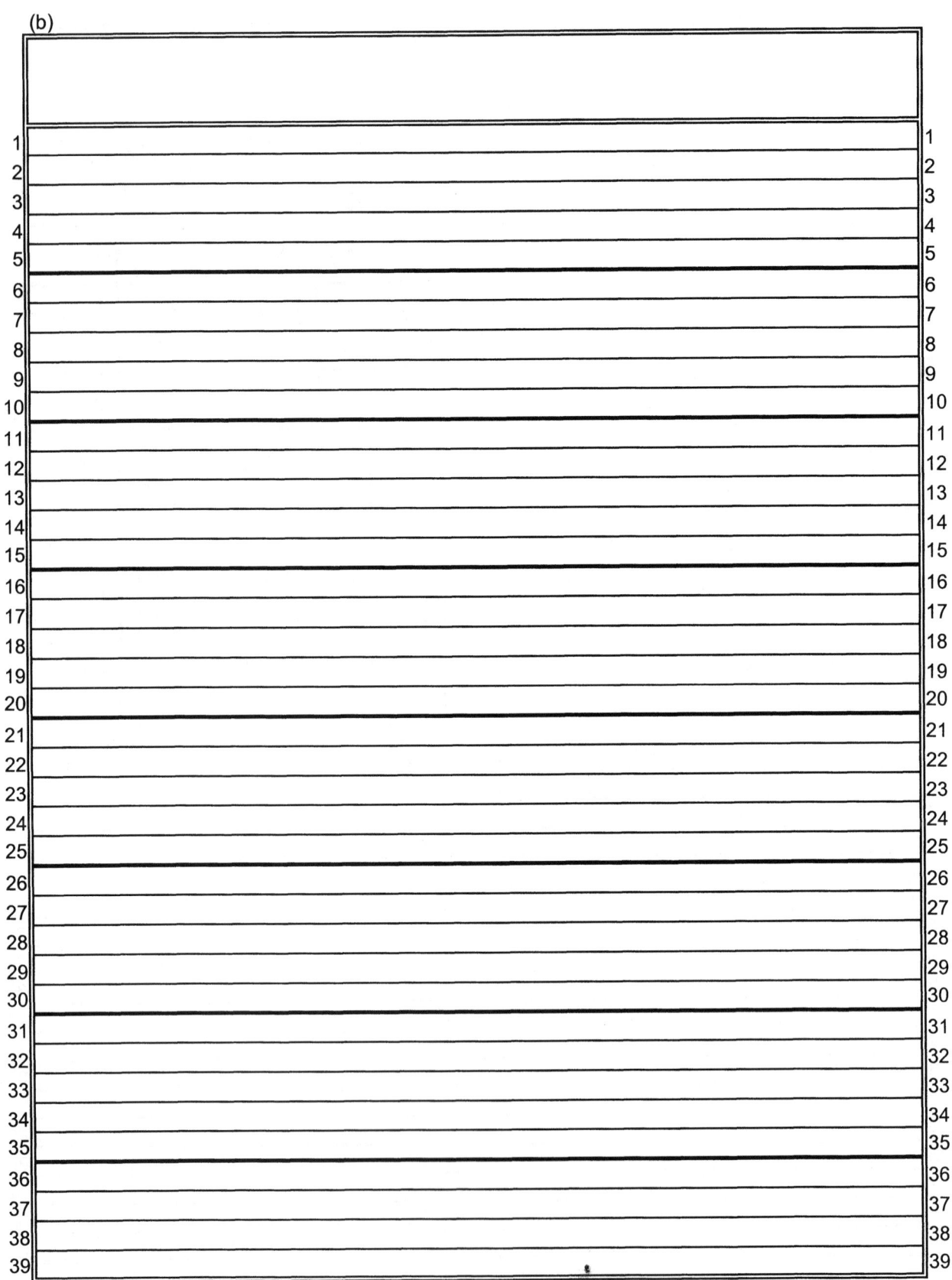

(a)

Hass Company Packaging Department Monthly Manufacturing Overhead Flexible Budget For the Year 2011					
Activity level Direct labor hours		27000	30000	33000	36000
1					
2					
3					
4					
5					
6					
7					
8					
9					
10					
11					
12					
13					
14					
15					
16					
17					
18					

(b)

		Budget at 27,000 DLH	Actual Costs 27,000 DLH	Difference Favorable F Unfavorable U	
Direct labor hours (DLH)					
1					1
2					2
3					3
4					4
5					5
6					6
7					7
8					8
9					9
10					10
11					11
12					12
13					13
14					14
15					15
16					16
17					17

Hass Company
Packaging Department
Manufacturing Overhead Flexible Budget Report
For the Month Ended October 31, 2011

(c)

1		1
2		2
3		3
4		4
5		5

(a)

Deleon Company

Monthly Manufacturing Overhead Flexible Budget

Ironing Department

For the Year 2008

Activity level Direct labor hours	35,000	40,000	45,000	50,000
1				
2				
3				
4				
5				
6				
7				
8				
9				
10				
11				
12				
13				
14				

(b)

Deleon Company

Ironing Department

Manufacturing Overhead Flexible Budget Report

For the Month Ended June 30, 2011

Direct labor hours (DLH)	Budget at 42,000 DLH	Actual Costs 42,000 DLH	Difference Favorable F Unfavorable U	
1				
2				
3				
4				
5				
6				
7				
8				
9				
10				
11				
12				
13				
14				

1	(c)	1
2		2
3		3
4		4
5		5
6	(d)	6
7		7
8		8
9		9
10		10

(e)

1	Costs (in thousands)	1
2		2
3		3
4		4
5		5
6		6
7		7
8		8
9		9
10		10
11		11
12		12
13		13
14		14
15		15
16		16
17		17
18		18
19		19
20		20
21		21
22		22
23		23
24		24
25	Direct Labor Hours (in thousands)	25

(a)

1		1
2		2

(b)

Colt Company

Assembling Department

Flexible Budget Report

For the Month Ended August 31, 2011

Units	Budget at _____ Units	Actual Costs _____ Units	Difference Favorable F Unfavorable U		
1					1
2					2
3					3
4					4
5					5
6					6
7					7
8					8
9					9
10					10
11					11
12					12
13					13
14					14
15					15
16					16
17					17
18					18
19					19
20					20
21					21
22					22
23					23
24					24
25					25
26					26
27					27
28					28
29					29

Name

Section

Date

(c)

Colt Company				
Assembling Department				
Flexible Budget Report				
For the Month Ended September 30, 2011				
			Difference	
	Budget at	Actual Costs	Favorable F	
Units	64,000 Units	64,000 Units	Unfavorable U	

(a)

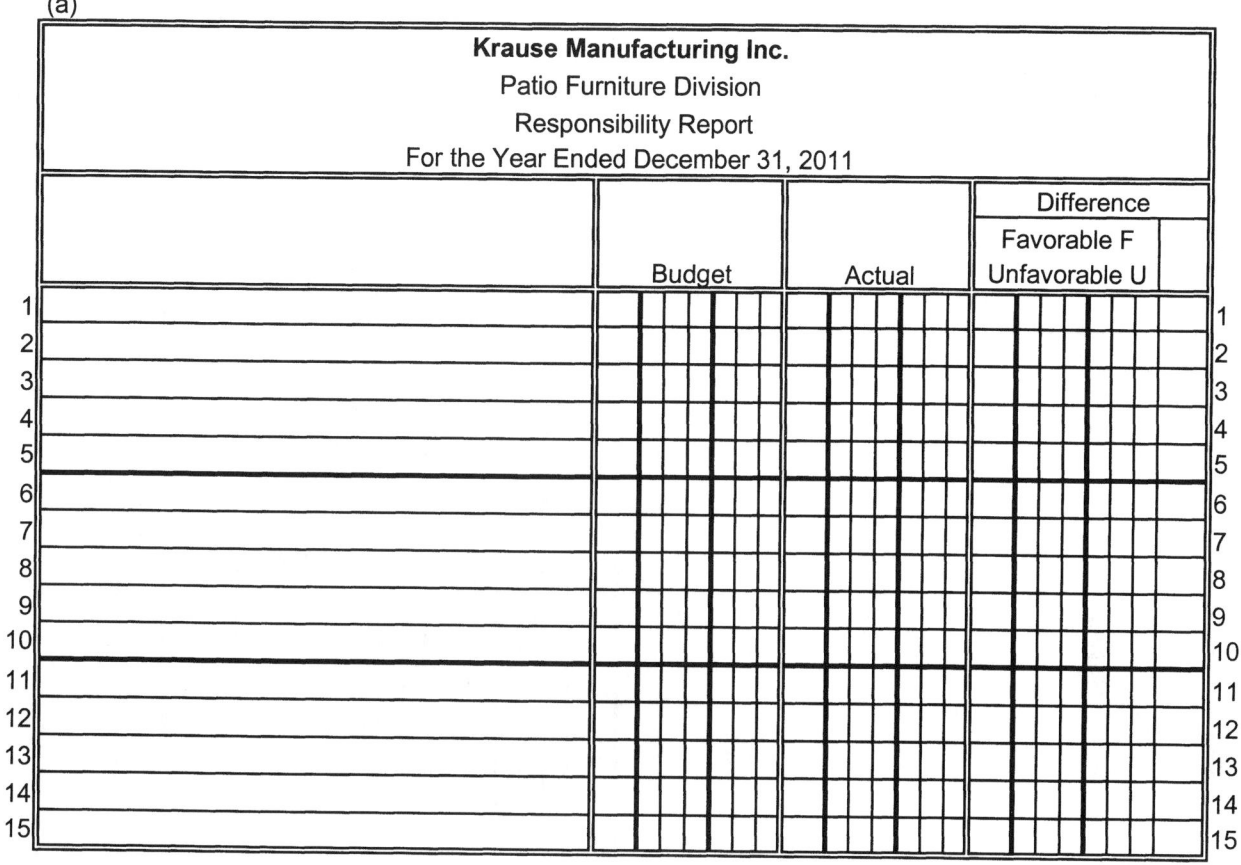

Krause Manufacturing Inc. Patio Furniture Division Responsibility Report For the Year Ended December 31, 2011				
	Budget	Actual	Difference Favorable F Unfavorable U	
1				1
2				2
3				3
4				4
5				5
6				6
7				7
8				8
9				9
10				10
11				11
12				12
13				13
14				14
15				15

(b)

(c)

(a)

Mercer Manufacturing Company
Home Division
Responsibility Report (in thousands of dollars)
For the Year Ended December 31, 2011

	Budget	Actual	Difference Favorable F Unfavorable U	
1				1
2				2
3				3
4				4
5				5
6				6
7				7
8				8
9				9
10				10
11				11
12				12
13				13
14				14
15				15

(b)

1	1
2	2
3	3
4	4
5	5
6	6
7	7
8	8
9	9
10	10
11	11
12	12
13	13
14	14
15	15
16	16

(c)

1	1.	1
2		2
3		3
4		4
5	2.	5
6		6
7		7
8		8
9		9
10	3.	10
11		11
12		12
13		13
14		14
15		15
16		16

Section _____

Date _____

(a)

No. 1

To Cutting Department Manager - Seattle Division	Month: January		
Controllable Costs	Budget	Actual	Fav/Unfav
1				1
2				2
3				3
4				4
5				5
6				6
7				7
8				8
9				9

No. 2

To Division Production Manager - Seattle	Month: January		
Controllable Costs	Budget	Actual	Fav/Unfav
1				1
2				2
3				3
4				4
5				5
6				6
7				7
8				8
9				9
10				10

No. 3

To Vice - President - Production	Month: January		
Controllable Costs	Budget	Actual	Fav/Unfav
1				1
2				2
3				3
4				4
5				5
6				6
7				7
8				8
9				9
10				10

(a) (Continued)

No. 4

To President		Month: January
Controllable Costs	Budget	Actual	Fav/Unfav

(b)

1.

2.

3.

(a)

Ogleby Company Assembly Department Flexible Monthly Manufacturing Overhead Budget For the Year 2011				
Activity level Direct labor hours	18,000	20,000	22,000	24,000
1				
2				
3				
4				
5				
6				
7				
8				
9				
10				
11				
12				
13				
14				
15				
16				
17				
18				

(b)

Ogleby Company			
Assembly Department			
Manufacturing Overhead Budget Report (Flexible)			
For the Month Ended January 31, 2011			
Direct labor hours (DLH)	Budget at 20,000 DLH	Actual Costs 20,000 DLH	Difference Favorable F Unfavorable U

(c)

(a)

Parcells Manufacturing Company Flexible Monthly Manufacturing Overhead Budget Assembly Department For the Year 2011				
Activity level Direct labor hours	22,500	25,000	27,500	30,000
1				
2				
3				
4				
5				
6				
7				
8				
9				
10				
11				
12				
13				
14				

(b)

Parcells Manufacturing Company Assembly Department Manufacturing Overhead Budget Report (Flexible) For the Month Ended July 31, 2011			Difference	
Direct labor hours (DLH)	Budget at 27,500 DLH	Actual Costs 27,500 DLH	Favorable F Unfavorable U	
1				
2				
3				
4				
5				
6				
7				
8				
9				
10				
11				
12				
13				
14				

(c)

1

2

3

4

5

(d)

6

7

8

9

10

(e)

Costs (in thousands)

Direct Labor Hours (in thousands)

(a)

(b)

Fernetti Company

Packaging Department

Budget Report (Flexible)

For the Month Ended May 31, 2011

	Budget at _____ Units	Actual Costs _____ Units	Difference Favorable F Unfavorable U	
1				
2				
3				
4				
5				
6				
7				
8				
9				
10				
11				
12				
13				
14				
15				
16				
17				
18				
19				
20				
21				
22				
23				
24				
25				
26				
27				
28				

(c)

	Fernetti Company Packaging Department Budget Report (Flexible) For the Month Ended June 30, 2011				
Units		Budget at 40,000 Units	Actual Costs 40,000 Units	Difference Favorable F Unfavorable U	
1					
2					
3					
4					
5					
6					
7					
8					
9					
10					
11					
12					
13					
14					
15					
16					
17					
18					
19					
20					
21					
22					
23					
24					
25					
26					
27					
28					
29					
30					
31					
32					
33					
34					
35					
36					

(a)

Widnet Manufacturing Inc. Home Appliance Division Responsibility Report For the Year Ended December 31, 2011				
	Budget	Actual	Difference Favorable F Unfavorable U	
1				
2				
3				
4				
5				
6				
7				
8				
9				
10				
11				
12				
13				
14				

(b)

(c)

(a)

Schwinn Manufacturing Company Lawnmower Division Responsibility Performance Report (in thousands of dollars) For the Year Ended December 31, 2011			
	Budget	Actual	Difference Favorable F Unfavorable U
1			
2			
3			
4			
5			
6			
7			
8			
9			
10			
11			
12			
13			

(b)

1
2
3
4
5
6
7
8
9
10

(c)

(1)

(2)

(3)

(a)   No. 1

To Cutting Department Manager - Phoenix Division		Budget	Actual	Fav/Unfav	
	Controllable Costs				
1					1
2					2
3					3
4					4
5					5
6					6
7					7
8					8
9					9

Month: January

No. 2

To Division Production Manager - Phoenix		Budget	Actual	Fav/Unfav	
	Controllable Costs				
1					1
2					2
3					3
4					4
5					5
6					6
7					7
8					8
9					9
10					10

Month: January

No. 3

To Vice - President - Production		Budget	Actual	Fav/Unfav	
	Controllable Costs				
1					1
2					2
3					3
4					4
5					5
6					6
7					7
8					8
9					9
10					10

Month: January

(a) (Continued)   No. 4

To President		Month: January	
Controllable Costs	Budget	Actual	Fav/Unfav
1			
2			
3			
4			
5			
6			
7			
8			
9			
10			

(b)

1.

2.

3.

(a)

1	(1)	1
2		2
3		3
4		4
5		5
6		6
7		7
8		8
9		9
10		10
11	(2)	11
12		12
13		13
14		14
15		15
16		16
17		17
18		18
19		19
20		20
21		21
22		22
23		23
24		24
25		25
26	(3)	26
27		27
28		28
29		29
30		30
31		31
32		32
33		33
34		34
35		35
36		36
37		37
38		38
39		39
40		40

(b)

G-Bar Pastures Income Statement Flexible Budget Report For the Year Ended December 31, 2011				
Boarding days (BD)	Budget at 18,980 BD	Actual Costs at 18,980 BD	Difference Favorable F Unfavorable U	
1				
2				
3				
4				
5				
6				
7				
8				
9				
10				
11				
12				
13				
14				
15				
16				
17				
18				
19				
20				
21				
22				
23				
24				
25				

(c)

1 (1)
2
3
4
5
6
7
8
9
10 (2)
11
12
13
14
15
16 (3)
17
18
19
20
21 (d)
22
23
24
25
26
27
28
29
30
31
32
33
34
35
36
37
38
39
40

1	(a)
2	
3	
4	
5	
6	(b)
7	
8	
9	
10	
11	

(c)

Edmonds Company

Production Department

Manufacturing Overhead Flexible Budget Report

For the Month Ended _____

	Budget at 1,500 Units	Actual at 1,500 Units	Difference Favorable F Unfavorable U	
1				
2				
3				
4				
5				
6				
7				
8				
9				
10				
11				
12				
13				
14				
15				
16				
17				
18				
19				
20				

Name

Section

Date

Edmonds Company

(d)

1				1
2				2
3				3
4				4
5				5
6				6

Edmonds Company

Production Department

Manufacturing Overhead Responsibility Report

For The Month Ended _____

Controllable Cost	Budget	Actual	Difference Favorable F Unfavorable U

*BE11-8

	Account Titles	Debit	Credit	
1	(a)			1
2				2
3				3
4				4
5				5
6	(b)			6
7				7
8				8
9				9
10				10
11				11
12				12

13	***BE11-9**			13

	Account Titles	Debit	Credit	
14				14
15				15
16				16
17	(a)			17
18				18
19				19
20				20
21				21
22	(b)			22
23				23
24				24
25				25
26				26
27				27
28				28
29				29
30				30
31				31
32				32
33				33
34				34
35				35
36				36
37				37
38				38
39				39
40				40

Manufacturing Cost Element	Standard Quantity x	Standard Price =	Standard Cost
1			
2			
3			
4			
5			
6			
7			
8			
9			
10			
11			
12			
13			
14			
15			
16			
17			
18			
19			
20			
21			
22			
23			
24			
25			
26			
27			
28			
29			
30			
31			
32			
33			
34			
35			
36			
37			
38			
39			
40			

		1	2	3	4	5	6		
1	(a)								1
2									2
3									3
4									4
5									5
6									6
7	(b)								7
8									8
9									9
10									10
11									11
12									12
13	(c)								13
14									14
15									15
16									16
17									17
18									18
19									19
20									20
21									21
22									22
23									23
24									24
25									25
26									26
27									27
28									28
29									29
30									30
31									31
32									32
33									33
34									34
35									35
36									36
37									37
38									38
39									39
40									40

E11-2

Ingredient	Amount Per Gallon	Standard Waste	Standard Usage	Standard Price	Standard Cost Per Gallon
1 Grape concentrate					
2 Sugar					
3 Lemons					
4 Yeast					
5 Nutrient					
6 Water					
7					
8					
9					
10					

E11-3

1 Direct materials:		
2		
3		
4		
5		
6 Direct labor:		
7		
8		
9		
10 Manufacturing overhead:		
11		
12		
13		
14		
15		
16		
17		
18		
19		
20		
21		
22		
23		
24		
25		

	(a)	
1	(a)	
2		
3		
4		
5		
6	(b)	
7		
8		
9		
10		
11	(c)	Standard direct labor cost
12		per oil change =
13		
14	(d)	Direct labor quantity variance =

You will find this working paper at the end of this booklet.

(a)

Donohue Landscaping

Variance Report - Purchasing Department

For the Current Month

Project	Actual Pounds Purchased	(1) Actual Price	(2) Standard Price	Price Variance	Explanation	
Macintosh						1
						2
						3
Chang						4
						5
Kahn						6
						7
						8
						9
						10

(b)

Donohue Landscaping

Variance Report - Production Department

For the Current Month

Project	Actual Pounds	Standard Pounds	Standard Price	Quantity Variance	Explanation	
Macintosh						1
						2
Chang						3
Kahn						4
						5
						6
						7
						8

Peters Corporation
Variance Report - Purchasing Department
For the Week Ended January 9, 2012

Type of Materials	Quantity Purchased	Actual Price	Standard Price	Price Variance		Explanation
Rogue 11		$ 5 20	$ 5 00	$ 52 00		Price increase
Storm 17			3 25	10 50	U	Rush order
Beast 29		0 45		4 40	F	Bought larger quantity

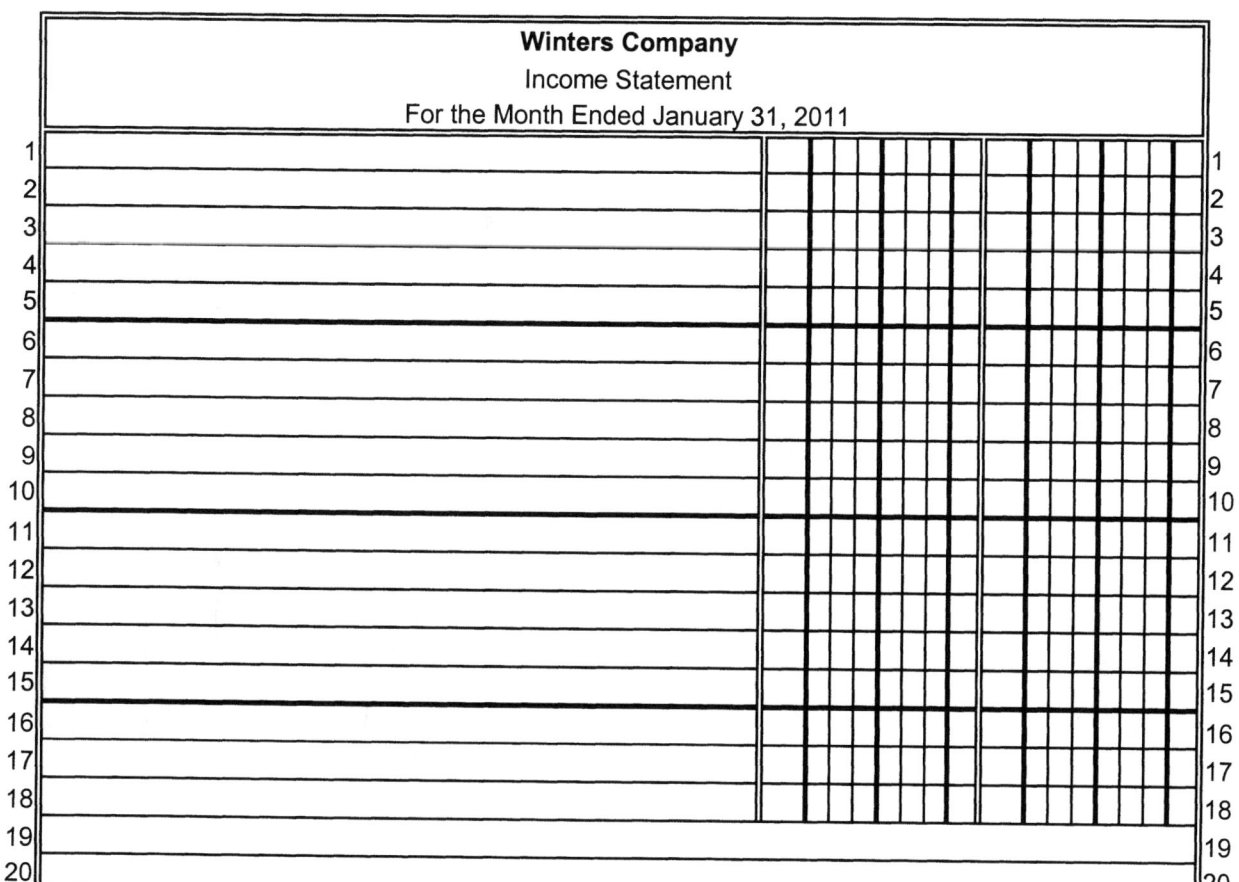

Winters Company
Income Statement
For the Month Ended January 31, 2011

		Account Titles	Debit	Credit	
1	1.				1
2					2
3					3
4					4
5	2.				5
6					6
7					7
8					8
9	3.				9
10					10
11					11
12					12
13	4.				13
14					14
15					15
16					16
17	5.				17
18					18
19					19
20					20
21					21
22					22
23					23
24					24
25					25
26					26
27					27
28					28
29					29
30					30
31					31
32					32
33					33
34					34
35					35
36					36
37					37
38					38
39					39
40					40

		Account Titles	Debit	Credit	
1					1
2					2
3					3
4					4
5					5
6					6
7					7
8					8
9					9
10					10
11					11
12					12
13					13
14					14
15					15
16					16
17					17
18					18
19					19
20					20
21					21
22					22
23					23
24					24
25					25

(a) Item	Amount	Hours	Rate	
1				1
2				2
3				3

(b)

			F	5
Total overhead variance:			U	6
				7
				8
				9
				10
Overhead controllable variance:				11
				12
				13
				14
				15
Overhead volume variance:				16
				17
				18
				19
				20

(c)

(a)

	F U
(1) Total materials variance:	
Materials price variance:	
Materials quantity variance:	
(2) Total labor variance:	
Labor price variance:	
Labor quantity variance:	
(b)	
Total overhead variance:	

(c)

Peterson Manufacturing Corporation

Income Statement

For the Month Ended June 30, 2011

1		
2		
3		
4		
5		
6		
7		
8		
9		
10		
11		
12		
13		
14		
15		
16		
17		
18		
19		
20		
21		
22		
23		
24		
25		
26		
27		
28		
29		
30		
31		
32		
33		
34		
35		
36		
37		
38		
39		
40		

(a)

	F U
1 Materials price variance:	1
2	2
3	3
4	4
5 Materials quantity variance:	5
6	6
7	7
8	8
9 Labor price variance:	9
10	10
11	11
12	12
13 Labor quantity variance:	13
14	14
15	15
16	16
17 (b)	17
18 Total overhead variance:	18
19	19
20	20
21	21
22	22
23	23
24	24
25	25
26	26
27	27
28	28
29	29
30	30
31	31
32	32
33	33
34	34
35	35
36	36
37	37
38	38
39	39
40	40

(c)

Farming Labs, Inc.

Income Statement

For the Month Ended November 30, 2011

(d)

(a)

		Account Titles	Debit	Credit	
1	1.				1
2					2
3					3
4					4
5	2.				5
6					6
7					7
8					8
9	3.				9
10					10
11					11
12					12
13	4.				13
14					14
15					15
16					16
17	5.				17
18					18
19					19
20	6.				20
21					21
22					22
23	7.				23
24					24
25					25
26	8.				26
27					27
28					28
29					29
30					30
31					31
32					32
33					33
34	9.				34
35					35
36					36
37					37
38					38
39					39
40					40

(b)

Raw Materials	Work in Process
Inventory	Inventory

Materials	Materials
Price Variance	Quantity Variance

Factory	Manufacturing
Labor	Overhead

Labor	Labor
Price Variance	Quantity Variance

Finished Goods	Cost of
Inventory	Goods Sold

(c)

	Account Titles	Debit	Credit	
1				1
2				2
3				3
4				4
5				5
6				6
7				7
8				8
9				9
10				10
11				11
12				12
13				13
14				14
15				15

(d)

Johnson Corporation

Income Statement

For the Month Ended January 31, 2011

1				1
2				2
3				3
4				4
5				5
6				6
7				7
8				8
9				9
10				10
11				11
12				12
13				13
14				14
15				15
16				16
17				17
18				18
19				19
20				20

(a)

	F U
(1) Total materials variance:	
Materials price variance:	
Materials quantity variance:	
(2) Total labor variance:	
Labor price variance:	
Labor quantity variance:	
(b)	
Total overhead variance:	

(c)

Sanchez Manufacturing Company
Income Statement
For the Month Ended July 31, 2011

(a)

	F U
Materials price variance:	
Materials quantity variance:	
Labor price variance:	
Labor quantity variance:	
(b)	
Total overhead variance:	

(c)

Moran Labs

Income Statement

For the Month Ended May 31, 2011

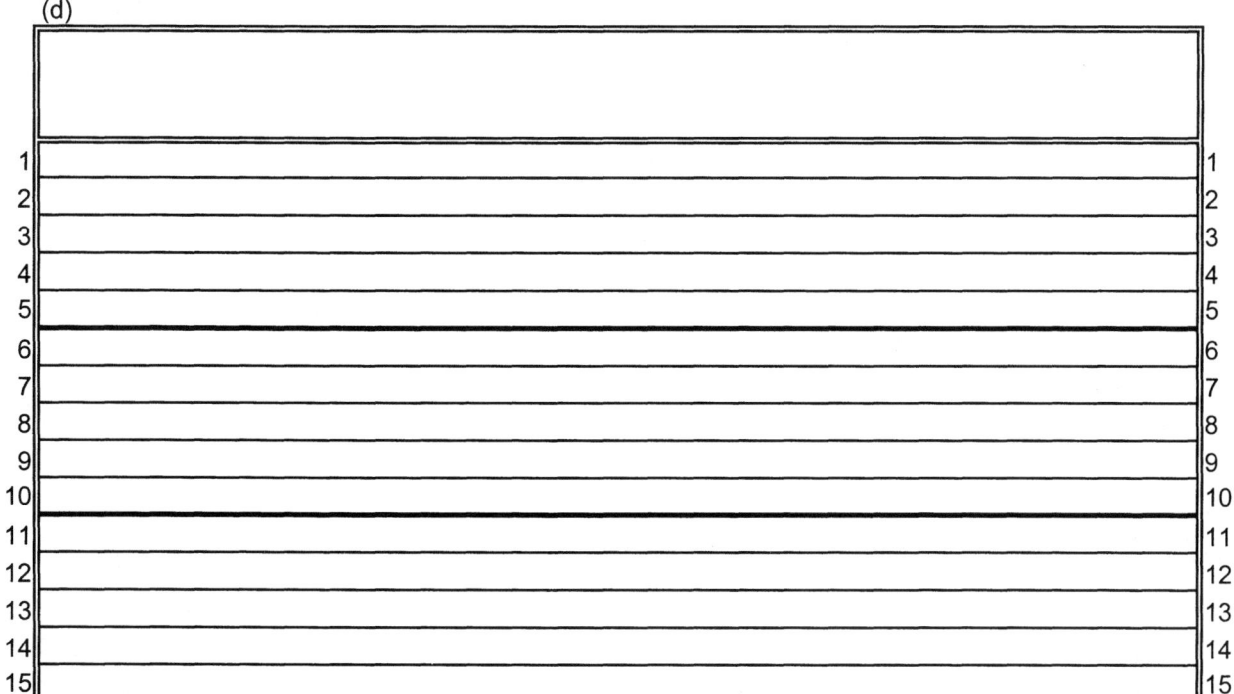

(d)

(a)

	Account Titles	Debit	Credit	
1	1.			1
2				2
3				3
4				4
5	2.			5
6				6
7				7
8				8
9	3.			9
10				10
11				11
12				12
13	4.			13
14				14
15				15
16				16
17	5.			17
18				18
19				19
20	6.			20
21				21
22				22
23	7.			23
24				24
25				25
26	8.			26
27				27
28				28
29				29
30				30
31				31
32	9.			32
33				33
34				34
35				35
36				36
37				37
38				38
39				39
40				40

(b)

Raw Materials Inventory	Work in Process Inventory

Materials Price Variance	Materials Quantity Variance

Factory Labor	Manufacturing Overhead

Labor Price Variance	Labor Quantity Variance

Finished Goods Inventory	Cost of Goods Sold

(c)

	Account Titles	Debit	Credit	
1				1
2				2
3				3
4				4
5				5
6				6
7				7
8				8
9				9
10				10
11				11
12				12
13				13
14				14
15				15

(d)

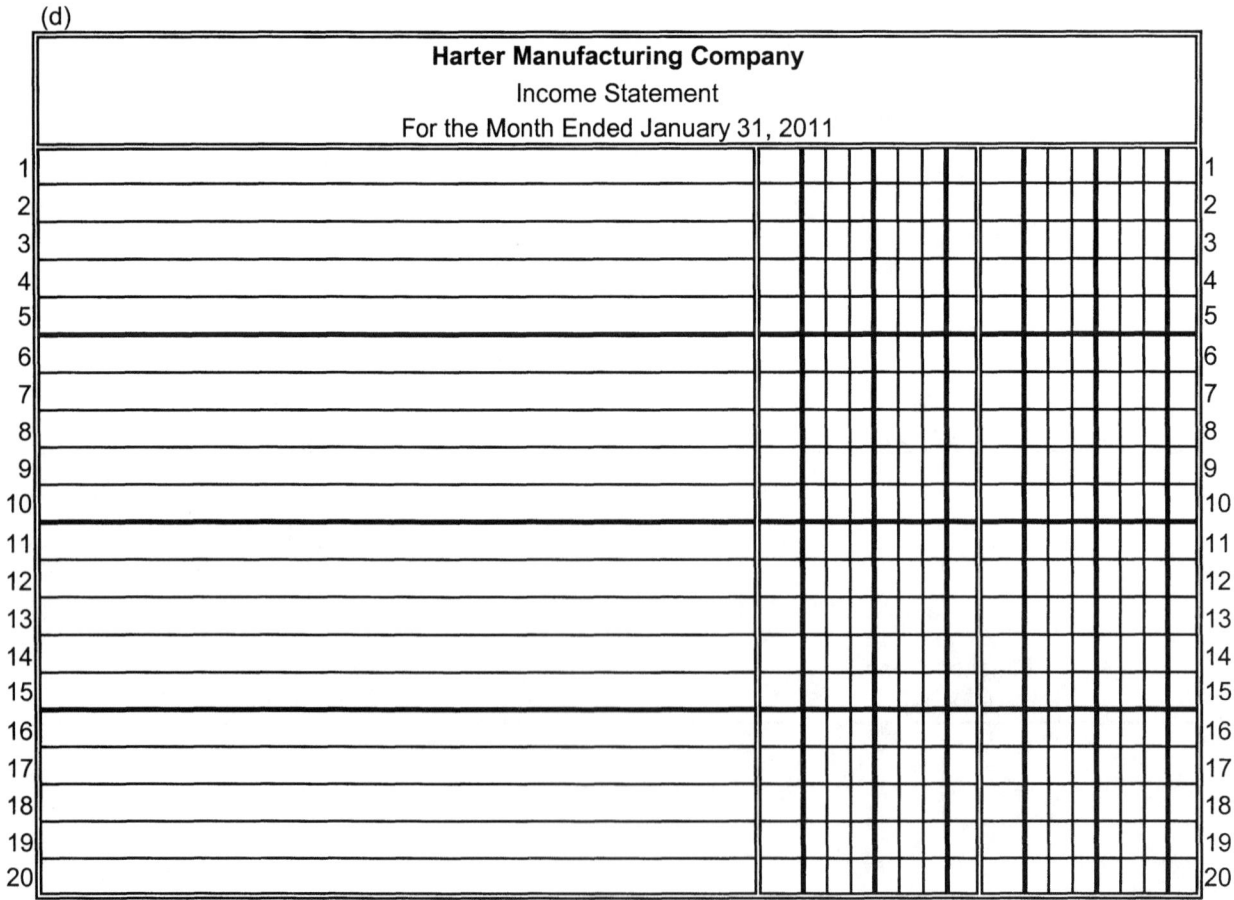

Harter Manufacturing Company
Income Statement
For the Month Ended January 31, 2011

1				1
2				2
3				3
4				4
5				5
6				6
7				7
8				8
9				9
10				10
11				11
12				12
13				13
14				14
15				15
16				16
17				17
18				18
19				19
20				20

(a)

(b)

(c)

(d)

(e)

BE12-2

	Cash Flows	Discount Factor	Present Value
1			
2			
3			
4			
5			
6			

BE12-3

	Cash Flows	10% Discount Factor	Present Value
7			
8			
9			
10			
11			
12			
13			
14			
15			

BE12-4

	Cash Flows	9% Discount Factor	Present Value
16			
17			
18			
19			
20			
21			
22			
23			
24			

BE12 Project A

	Cash Flows	9% Discount Factor	Present Value
25			
26			
27			
28			
29			
30			
31			
32			
33 Profitability index =			
34			
35			
36			
37			
38			
39			
40			

BE12 (Continued)

Project B	Cash Flows	9% Discount Factor	Present Value	
1				1
2				2
3				3
4				4
5				5
6				6
7 Profitability index =				7
8				8
9				9
10				10
11				11
12				12
13				13
14				14

BE12 Original estimate	Cash Flows	10% Discount Factor	Present Value	
15				15
16				16
17				17
18				18
19				19
20				20
21				21
22				22

Revised estimate	Cash Flows	10% Discount Factor	Present Value	
23				23
24				24
25				25
26				26
27				27
28				28
29				29
30				30
31				31
32				32
33				33
34				34
35				35
36				36
37				37
38				38
39				39
40				40

BE12-8

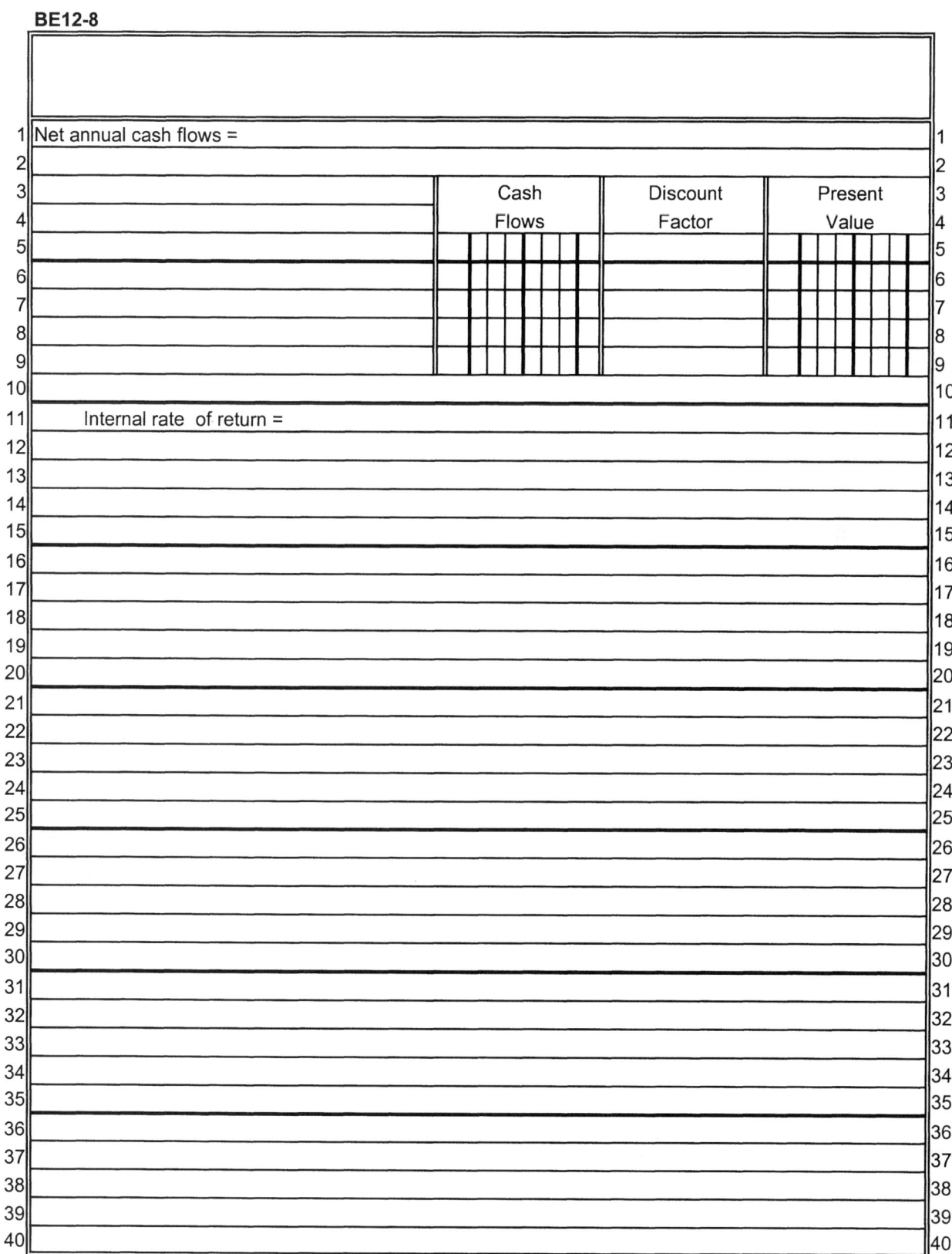

	Cash Flows	Discount Factor	Present Value
Net annual cash flows =			
Internal rate of return =			

DO IT! 12-1

1									1
2									2
3									3
4									4
5									5
6	Cash payback period =								6
7									7
8									8

DO IT! 12-2

		Cash	12% Discount	Present	
9					9
10					10
11					11
12					12
13					13
14					14
15		Cash	12% Discount	Present	15
16		Flow	Factor	Value	16
17					17
18					18
19					19
20					20
21					21
22					22
23					23
24					24

DO IT! 12-3

25				25
26				26
27				27
28				28
29				29
30	Internal rate of return =			30
31				31
32				32
33				33
34				34
35				35
36				36
37				37
38				38
39				39
40				40

1				1
2				2
3				3
4				4
5				5
6				6
7				7
8	Average investment =			8
9				9
10	Annual rate of return =			10
11				11
12				12
13				13
14				14
15				15
16				16
17				17
18				18
19				19
20				20
21				21
22				22
23				23
24				24
25				25
26				26
27				27
28				28
29				29
30				30
31				31
32				32
33				33
34				34
35				35
36				36
37				37
38				38
39				39
40				40

E12-1

			Cash Flows	8% Discount Factor	Present Value	
1	(a)	Cash payback period =				1
2						2
3						3
4		Net present value is:	Cash	8% Discount	Present	4
5			Flows	Factor	Value	5
6						6
7						7
8						8
9						9
10						10
11						11
12						12
13	(b)					13
14						14
15						15
16						16
17						17
18						18
19						19
20						20
21						21
22						22
23						23
24						24
25						25
26						26
27						27
28						28
29						29
30						30
31						31
32						32
33						33
34						34
35						35
36						36
37						37
38						38
39						39
40						40

(a) Computation of each project's payback period:

	AA		BB		CC	
Year	Net Annual Cash Inflow	Cumulative Cash Flow	Net Annual Cash Inflow	Cumulative Cash Flow	Net Annual Cash Inflow	Cumulative Cash Flow
1						
2						
3						
Payback Period =			Payback Period =		Payback Period =	

Most desirable project is:

Least desirable project is:

(b) Computation of each project's net present value:

	AA			BB			CC	
Year	Discount Factor	Cash Inflow	Present Value		Cash Inflow	Present Value		Cash Inflow	Present Value
1									
2									
3									
Total present value									
Investment									
Net present value									

Most desirable product is:

Least desirable project is:

	Cash Flows	Year	9% Discount Factor	Amount	Present Value
1					
2					
3					
4					
5					
6					
7					
8					
9					
10					
11					
12					
13					
14					
15					
16					
17					
18					
19					
20					
21					
22					
23					
24					
25					

Machine A	Cash Flows	9% Discount Factor	Present Value
1			
2			
3			
4			
5			
6			
7			
8 Profitability index =			
9			
10			
11			

Machine B	Cash Flows	9% Discount Factor	Present Value
14			
15			
16			
17			
18			
19			
20			
21 Profitability index =			

(a)	Total net investment =
	Annual net cash flow =
	Payback period =

(b)

Item	Amount	Years	PV Factor	Present Value

(c)

(a)

Project	Capital Investment	Net Annual Cash Inflows		Internal Rate of Return Factor	Closest Discount Factor	Internal Rate of Return
		Annual Income +	Depreciation Expense			
22A						
23A						
24A						

(b)

E12-9

	(a)	
1	Cost of hoist:	
2	Net cash flows:	
3		
4		
5		
6		
7		
8	Cash payback period =	
9		
10		
11	(b)	
12	Average investment =	
13		
14	Annual depreciation =	
15		
16	Annual net income =	
17		
18	Annual rate of return =	
19		
20		

E12-10

	(a)
1	(1) Cash payback period =
2	
3	
4	(2) Annual rate of return =
5	
6	
7	(b)

Item	Amount	Years	15% Discount Factor	Present Value

(a)

	Cash Flows	Year	Net Annual Cash Flow	Cumulative Cash Flow	
1					1
2					2
3					3
4					4
5					5
6	Payback period =				6
7					7
8					8

(b)

9	Average annual net income =	9
10		10
11		11
12	Average investment =	12
13		13
14		14
15	Annual rate of return =	15
16		16
17		17
18		18
19		19

(c)

	Net Cash Flows	Year	15% Discount Factor	Amount	Present Value	
20						20
21						21
22						22
23						23
24						24
25						25
26						26
27						27
28						28
29						29
30						30
31						31
32						32
33						33
34						34
35						35
36						36
37						37
38						38
39						39
40						40

(a)

	Project Granada						
1							
2	Payback period =						
3							
4							
5			Project Jackson				
6						Cumulative	
7				Cash		Cash	
8		Year		Flow		Flow	
9		1					
10		2					
11		3					
12		4					
13		5					
14							
15	Payback period =						
16							
17							
18							
19							
20			Project Dorantes				
21						Cumulative	
22				Cash		Cash	
23		Year		Flow		Flow	
24		1					
25		2					
26		3					
27		4					
28		5					
29							
30							
31	Payback period =						
32							
33							
34							
35							
36							
37							
38							
39							
40							

Name _____

Section _____

Date _____

Dinkel Company

(b)

Project Granada

Item	Amount	Years	PV Factor	Present Value	
					1
					2
					3
					4

Project Jackson

Project Dorantes

Year	Discount Factor	Cash Inflow	PV	Cash Inflow	PV	
1						1
2						2
3						3
4						4
5						5
6 Totals						6
7 Capital investment						7
8 Positive (negative) net present value						8
9						9
10						10
11						11
12						12
13						13
14						14

(c) and (d)

(c)   Annual Rate of Return

Project Granada =

Project Jackson =

Project Dorantes =

(d)

Project	Cash Payback	Net Present Value	Annual Rate of Return
Granada			
Jackson			
Dorantes			

(a)

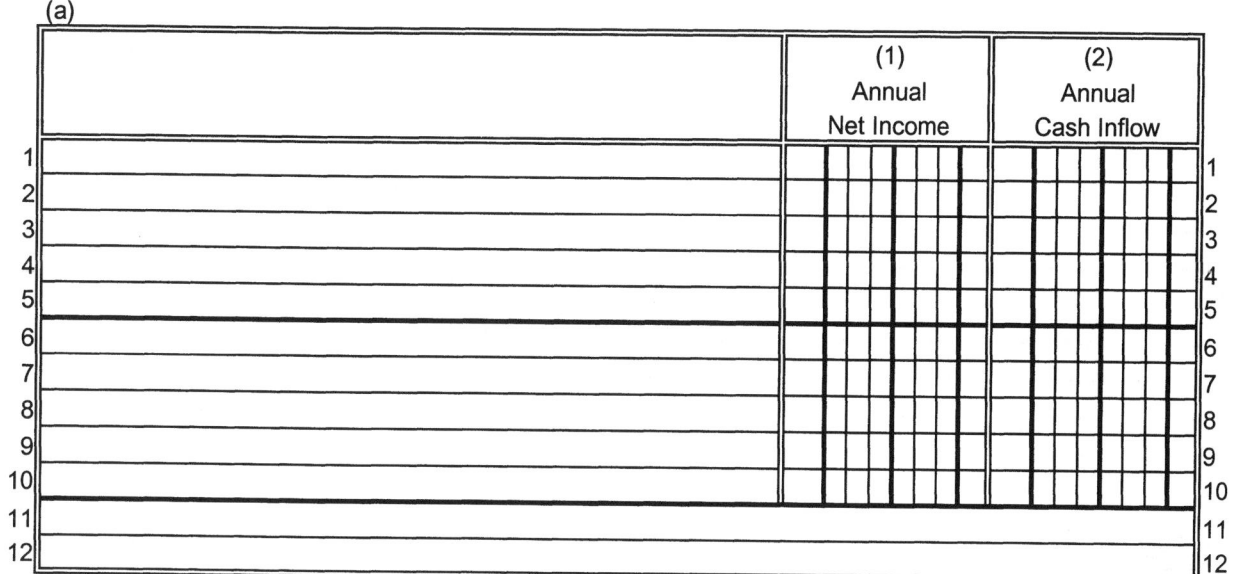

	(1) Annual Net Income	(2) Annual Cash Inflow
1		
2		
3		
4		
5		
6		
7		
8		
9		
10		
11		
12		

(b), (c), and (d)

		Cash Flow	8% Discount Factor	Present Value	
1	(b) (1) Cash payback period =				1
2					2
3					3
4					4
5	(2) Annual rate of return =				5
6					6
7					7
8					8
9	(c)				9
10					10
11					11
12					12
13					13
14					14
15					15
16	(d)				16
17					17
18					18
19					19
20					20
21					21
22					22
23					23

(a)

(1) Option A	Cash Flows	11% Discount Factor	Present Value
1			
2			
3			
4			
5			
6			
7			
8			

(2) Profitability index =

(3)	Cash Flows	Discount Factor	Present Value

Internal rate of return =

(1) Option B	Cash Flows	11% Discount Factor	Present Value

(2) Profitability index =

(a)   (Continued)

(3)

	Cash Flows	Discount Factor	Present Value
1			
2			
3			
4			
5			
6			
7			
8			
9	Internal rate of return =		
10			
11			
12			
13			
14			
15			

(b)

(a)

Original estimates	Cash Flows	9% Discount Factor	Present Value
1			
2			
3			
4			
5			
6			
7			
8			
9			
10			

(b)

Revised estimates	Cash Flows	9% Discount Factor	Present Value
12			
13			
14			
15			
16			
17			
18			
19			
20			
21			
22			
23			
24			
25			

(c)

| 26 |
| 27 |
| 28 |
| 29 |
| 30 |
| 31 |
| 32 |
| 33 |
| 34 |
| 35 |
| 36 |
| 37 |
| 38 |
| 39 |
| 40 |

(a)

Original estimates		Cash Flows	8% Discount Factor	Present Value	
1					1
2					2
3					3
4					4
5					5
6					6
7					7
8					8
9					9
10					10

(b)

Revised estimates		Cash Flows	8% Discount Factor	Present Value	
11					11
12					12
13					13
14					14
15					15
16					16
17					17
18					18
19					19
20					20
21					21
22					22
23					23
24					24

(c)

Original estimates at 11%		Cash Flows	11% Discount Factor	Present Value	
25					25
26					26
27					27
28					28
29					29
30					30
31					31
32					32
33					33
34					34
35					35
36					36
37					37
38					38
39					39
40					40

(d)

	Cash Flows	Discount Factor	Present Value
1			
2			
3			
4			
5			
6			
7			
8			
9			
10 Internal rate of return =			
11			
12			
13			
14			
15			
16			
17			
18			
19			
20			
21			
22			
23			
24			
25			
26			
27			
28			
29			
30			
31			
32			
33			
34			
35			
36			
37			
38			
39			
40			

(a)

Project Amanda								

1

2 Payback period =

3

4

5 Project Debbie

	Year			Cash Flow			Cumulative Cash Flow		
	1								
	2								
	3								
	4								
	5								

14

15 Payback period =

16

17

18

19

20 Project Penelope

	Year			Cash Flow			Cumulative Cash Flow		
	1								
	2								
	3								
	4								
	5								

29

30

31 Payback period =

32

33

34

35

36

37

38

39

40

Name

Section

Date

(b)

Project Amanda

Item	Amount	Years	PV Factor	Present Value

	Discount Factor	Project Debbie		Project Penelope	
Year		Cash Inflow	PV	Cash Inflow	PV
1					
2					
3					
4					
5					
Totals					
Capital investment					
Positive (negative) net present value					

(c) and (d)

(c)	Annual Rate of Return
Project Amanda =	
Project Debbie =	
Project Penelope =	

(d)

	Project	Cash Payback	Net Present Value	Annual Rate of Return
	Amanda			
	Debbie			
	Penelope			

(a)

	(1) Annual Net Income	(2) Annual Cash Inflow
1		
2		
3		
4		
5		
6		
7		
8		
9		
10		
11		
12		

(b), (c), and (d)

1	(b) (1) Cash payback period =			
2				
3				
4				
5	(2) Annual rate of return =			
6				
7				
8				
9	(c)	Cash Flow	15% Discount Factor	Present Value
10				
11				
12				
13				
14				
15				
16	(d)			
17				
18				
19				
20				
21				
22				
23				

(a)

(1) Option A	Cash Flows	11% Discount Factor	Present Value
1			
2			
3			
4			
5			
6			
7			
8			
(2) Profitability index =			

(3)	Cash Flows	Discount Factor	Present Value
Internal rate of return =			

(1) Option B	Cash Flows	11% Discount Factor	Present Value
(2) Profitability index =			

(a)   (Continued)

(3)

	Cash Flows	Discount Factor	Present Value	
1				1
2				2
3				3
4				4
5				5
6				6
7				7
8				8
9	Internal rate of return =			9
10				10
11				11
12				12
13				13
14				14
15				15

(b)

1		1
2		2
3		3
4		4
5		5
6		6
7		7
8		8
9		9
10		10
11		11
12		12
13		13
14		14
15		15
16		16
17		17
18		18
19		19
20		20

(a)

Original estimates	Cash Flows	10% Discount Factor	Present Value
1			
2			
3			
4			
5			
6			
7			
8			
9			
10			

(b)

Revised estimates	Cash Flows	10% Discount Factor	Present Value
13			
14			
15			
16			
17			
18			
19			
20			
21			
22			
23			
24			
25			

(c)

27	
28	
29	
30	
31	
32	
33	
34	
35	
36	
37	
38	
39	
40	

(a)

Original estimates	Cash Flows	12% Discount Factor	Present Value
1			
2			
3			
4			
5			
6			
7			
8			
9			
10			

(b)

Revised estimates	Cash Flows	12% Discount Factor	Present Value
12			
13			
14			
15			
16			
17			
18			
19			
20			
21			
22			
23			
24			

(c)

Original estimates at 15%	Cash Flows	15% Discount Factor	Present Value
26			
27			
28			
29			
30			
31			
32			
33			
34			
35			
36			
37			
38			
39			
40			

(d)

	Cash Flows	Discount Factor	Present Value
1			
2			
3			
4			
5			
6			
7			
8			
9			
10 Internal rate of return =			
11			
12			
13			
14			
15			
16			
17			
18			
19			
20			
21			
22			
23			
24			
25			
26			
27			
28			
29			
30			
31			
32			
33			
34			
35			
36			
37			
38			
39			
40			

Migami Corporation Income Statement Pro Forma	Purchase New Machine
1	1
2	2
3	3
4	4
5	5
6	6
7	7
8	8
9	9
10	10
11	11
12	12
13	13
14	14
15	15

	Cash Flows	15% Discount Factor	Present Value
1 (a) Annual rate of return =			
2			
3			
4			
5 (b) Cash payback period =			
6			
7			
8			
9 (c)			
10			
11			
12			
13			
14			
15 (d)			
16			
17			
18			
19			
20			

(a)

Original estimates	Cash Flows	11% Discount Factor	Present Value
1			
2			
3			
4			
5			
6			
7			
8			
9			
10			

(b)

Revised estimates	Cash Flows	11% Discount Factor	Present Value
13			
14			
15			
16			
17			
18			
19			
20			
21			
22			
23			
24			

(c)

Original estimates at 9%	Cash Flows	9% Discount Factor	Present Value
27			
28			
29			
30			
31			
32			
33			
34			
35			
36			
37			
38			
39			
40			

(d)

1	1
2	2
3	3
4	4
5	5
6	6
7	7
8	8
9	9
10	10
11	11
12	12
13	13
14	14
15	15
16	16
17	17
18	18
19	19
20	20
21	21
22	22
23	23
24	24
25	25
26	26
27	27
28	28
29	29
30	30
31	31
32	32
33	33
34	34
35	35
36	36
37	37
38	38
39	39
40	40

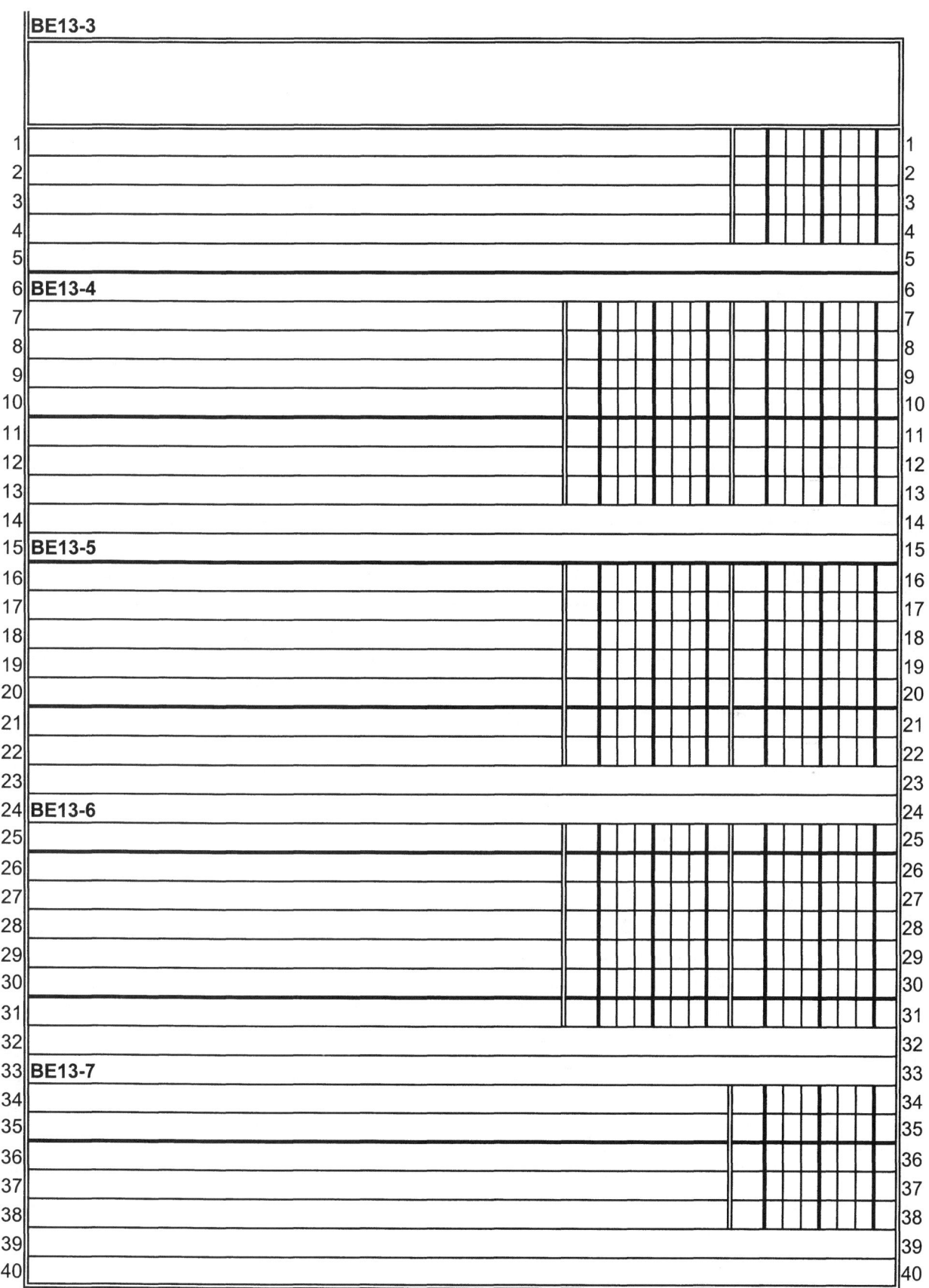

BE13-3

BE13-4

BE13-5

BE13-6

BE13-7

*BE13-12

	Balance 1/1/11	Reconciling Items Debit	Reconciling Items Credit	Balance 12/31/11	
1	Balance Sheet Accounts					1
2	Prepaid expenses	1 8 6 0 0				2
3	Accrued expenses payable	8 2 0 0				3
4						4
5						5
6	Statement of Cash Flow					6
7	Effects					7
8						8
9						9
10						10

	Account Titles	Debit	Credit	
1	1.(a)			1
2				2
3				3
4				4
5	(b)			5
6				6
7				7
8	2.(a)			8
9				9
10				10
11	(b)			11
12				12
13				13
14	3.(a)			14
15				15
16				16
17	(b)			17
18				18
19				19
20	4.(a)			20
21				21
22				22
23	(b)			23
24				24
25				25
26				26
27				27
28				28
29				29
30				30
31				31
32				32

E13-3 (Continued)

	Account Titles	Debit	Credit	
1	5. (a)			1
2				2
3				3
4				4
5	(b)			5
6				6
7				7
8				8
9				9
10	6.(a)			10
11				11
12				12
13				13
14				14
15	(b)			15
16				16
17				17
18				18
19				19
20				20

E13-4

	Nordstrom Company			
	Partial Statement of Cash Flows			
	For the Year Ended December 31, 2011			
1				1
2				2
3				3
4				4
5				5
6				6
7				7
8				8
9				9
10				10
11				11
12				12
13				13
14				14
15				15

Name

Section

Date

E13-5 Indirect

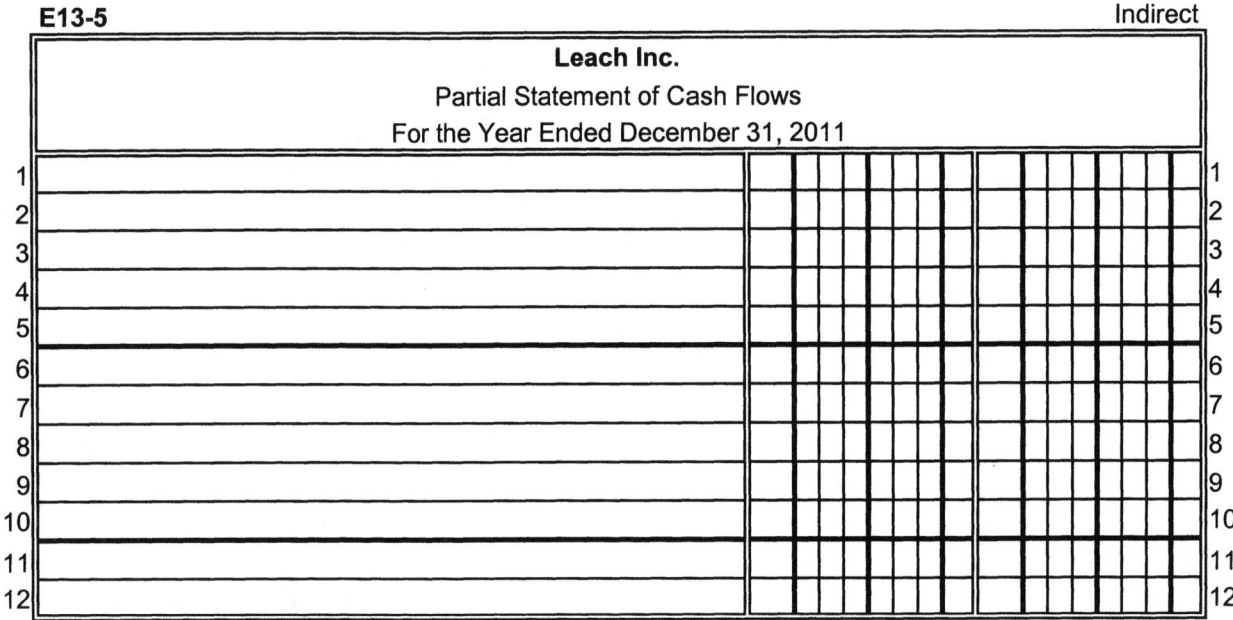

Leach Inc.
Partial Statement of Cash Flows
For the Year Ended December 31, 2011

E13-6 Indirect

Bennis Corp.
Partial Statement of Cash Flows
Foe the Year Ended December 31, 2011

Cash proceeds from sale of equipment calculations:

(a)   Indirect

Willingham Corporation

Statement of Cash Flows

For the Year Ended December 31, 2011

1		
2		
3		
4		
5		
6		
7		
8		
9		
10		
11		
12		
13		
14		
15		
16		
17		
18		
19		
20		
21		
22		
23		
24		
25		
26		
27		
28		
29		
30		

(b)   Free cash flow:

Indirect

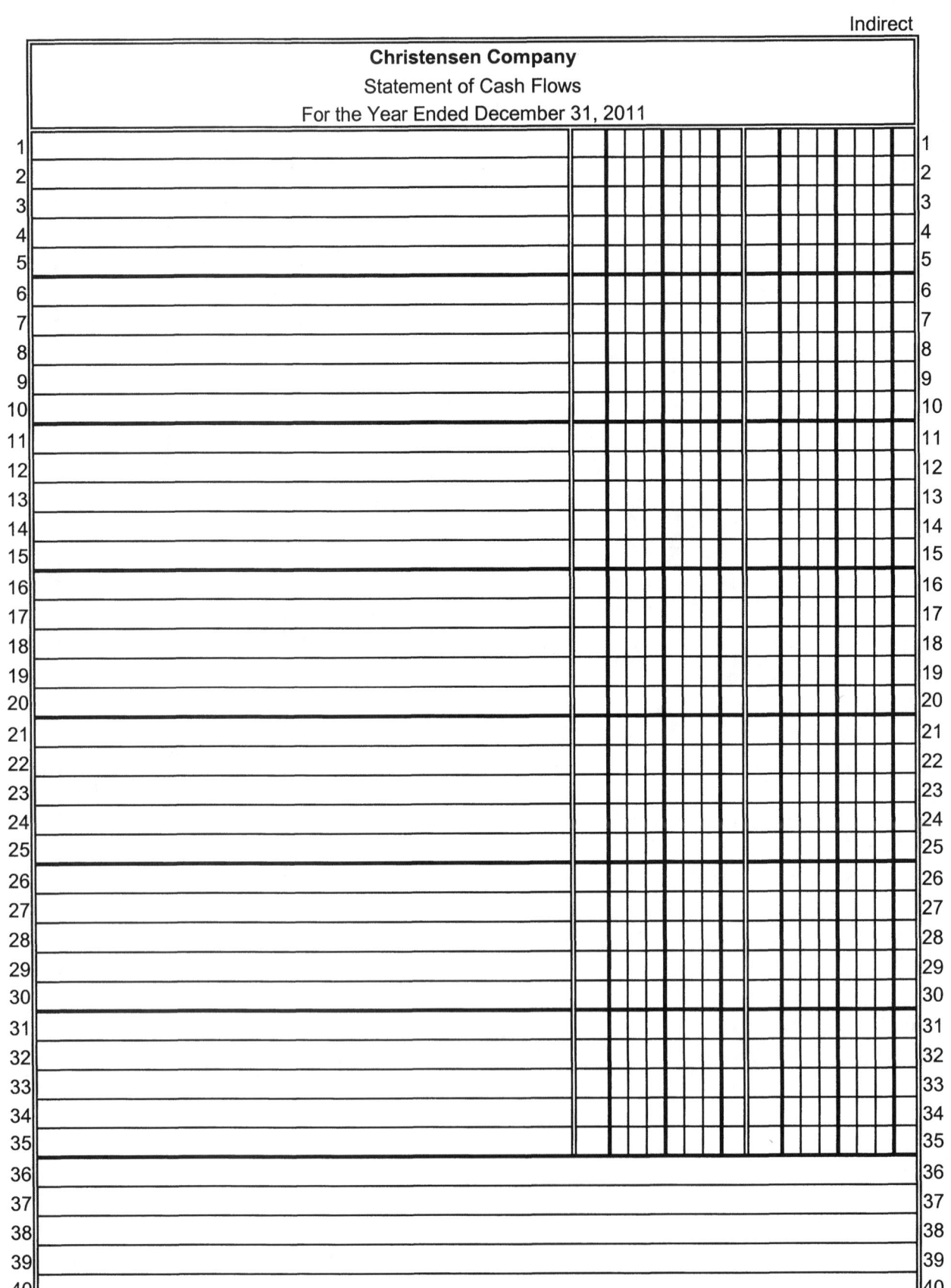

Christensen Company
Statement of Cash Flows
For the Year Ended December 31, 2011

(a)   Indirect

Rees Corporation
Statement of Cash Flows
For the Year Ended December 31, 2011

1				1
2				2
3				3
4				4
5				5
6				6
7				7
8				8
9				9
10				10
11				11
12				12
13				13
14				14
15				15
16				16
17				17
18				18
19				19
20				20
21				21
22				22
23				23
24				24
25				25
26				26
27				27
28				28
29				29
30				30
31				31
32				32
33				33
34				34
35	(b) Free cash flow:			35
36				36
37				37
38				38
39				39
40				40

	Molini Company						
	Worksheet - Statement of Cash Flows						
	For the Year Ended December 31, 2011						
			Reconciling Items				
Balance Sheet Accounts	Balance 12/31/10		Debit		Credit		Balance 12/31/11
1 Debits							1
2 Cash	2 2 0 0 0						6 3 0 0 0	2
3 Accounts receivable	7 6 0 0 0						8 5 0 0 0	3
4 Inventories	1 8 9 0 0 0						1 8 0 0 0 0	4
5 Land	1 0 0 0 0 0						7 5 0 0 0	5
6 Equipment	2 0 0 0 0 0						2 6 0 0 0 0	6
7 Totals	5 8 7 0 0 0						6 6 3 0 0 0	7
8							8
9 Credits							9
10 Accumulated depr. - equip.	4 2 0 0 0						6 6 0 0 0	10
11 Accounts payable	4 7 0 0 0						3 4 0 0 0	11
12 Bonds payable	2 0 0 0 0 0						1 5 0 0 0 0	12
13 Common stock	1 6 4 0 0 0						2 1 4 0 0 0	13
14 Retained earnings	1 3 4 0 0 0						1 9 9 0 0 0	14
15 Totals	5 8 7 0 0 0						6 6 3 0 0 0	15
16							16
17 Statement of Cash Flow							17
18 Effects							18
19							19
20							20
21							21
22							22
23							23
24							24
25							25
26							26
27							27
28							28
29							29
30							30
31							31
32							32
33							33
34							34
35							35
36							36
37							37
38							38

*E13-11
Direct

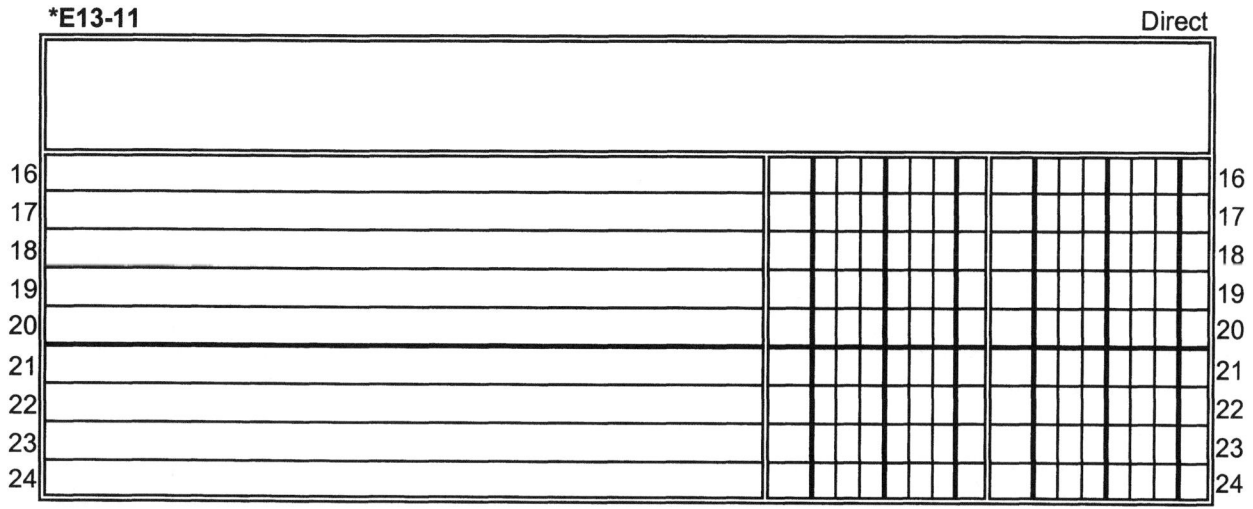

		16
16		16
17		17
18		18
19		19
20		20
21		21
22		22
23		23
24		24

Helpful T-accounts:

Accounts Receivable

Accounts Payable

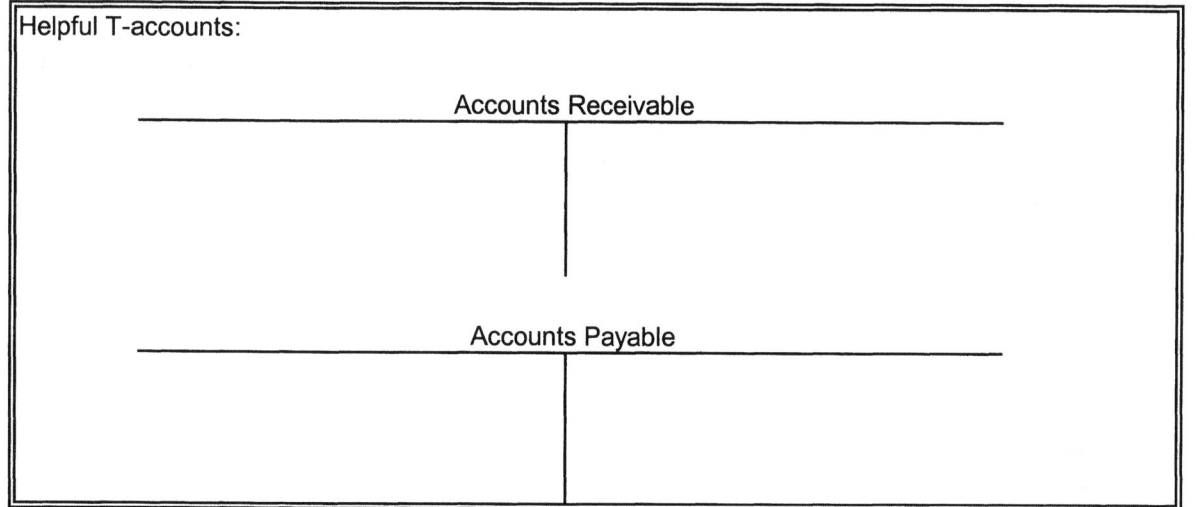

*E13-13
Direct

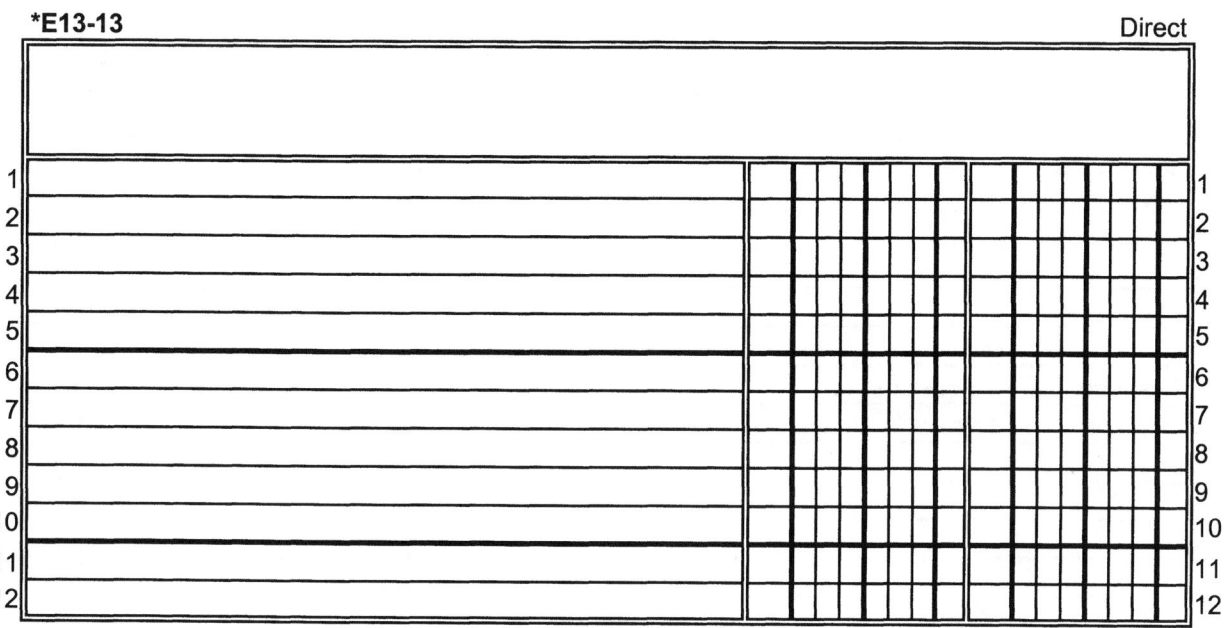

1		1
2		2
3		3
4		4
5		5
6		6
7		7
8		8
9		9
10		10
11		11
12		12

*E13-12   Direct

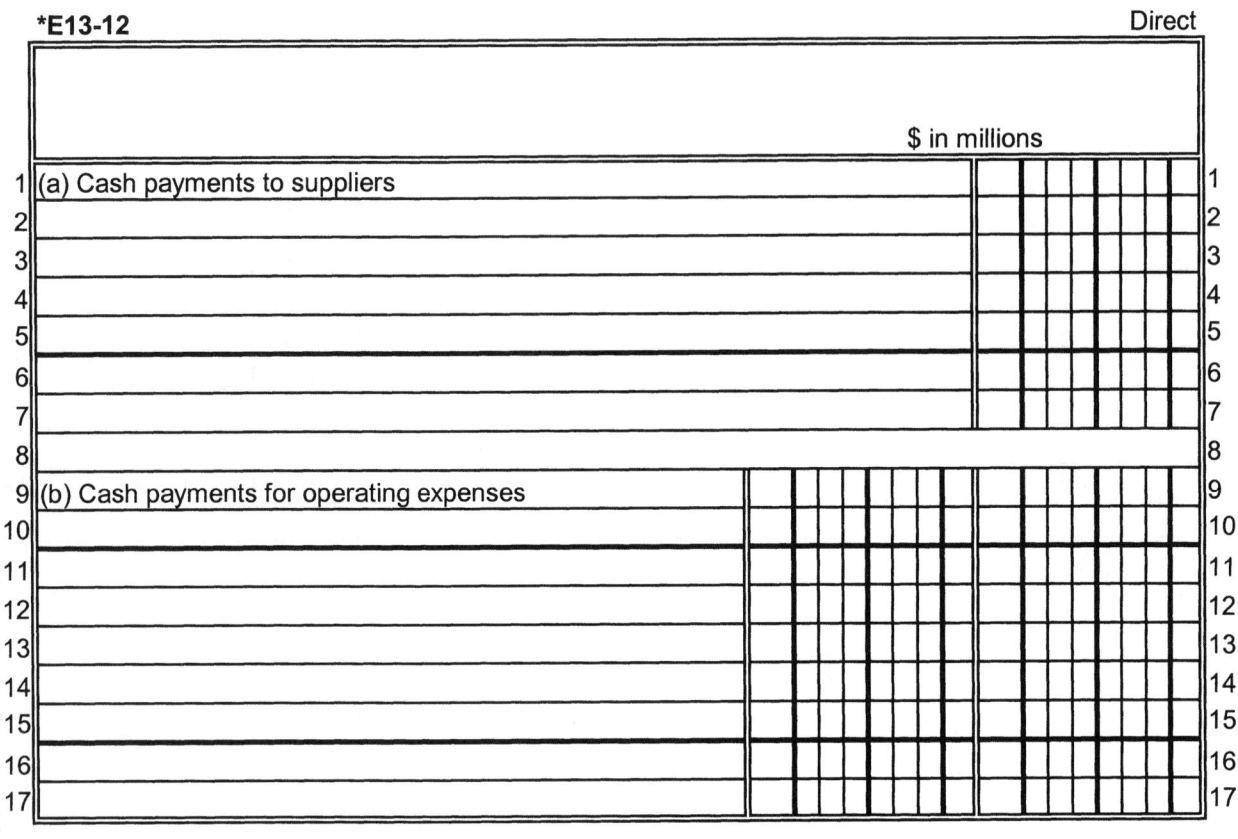

		$ in millions	
1	(a) Cash payments to suppliers		1
2			2
3			3
4			4
5			5
6			6
7			7
8			8
9	(b) Cash payments for operating expenses		9
10			10
11			11
12			12
13			13
14			14
15			15
16			16
17			17

*E13-14   Direct

1	Cash payments for rentals:	1
2		2
3		3
4		4
5		5
6	Cash payments for salaries:	6
7		7
8		8
9		9
10		10
11	Cash receipts from customers:	11
12		12
13		13
14		14
15		15
16		16
17		17

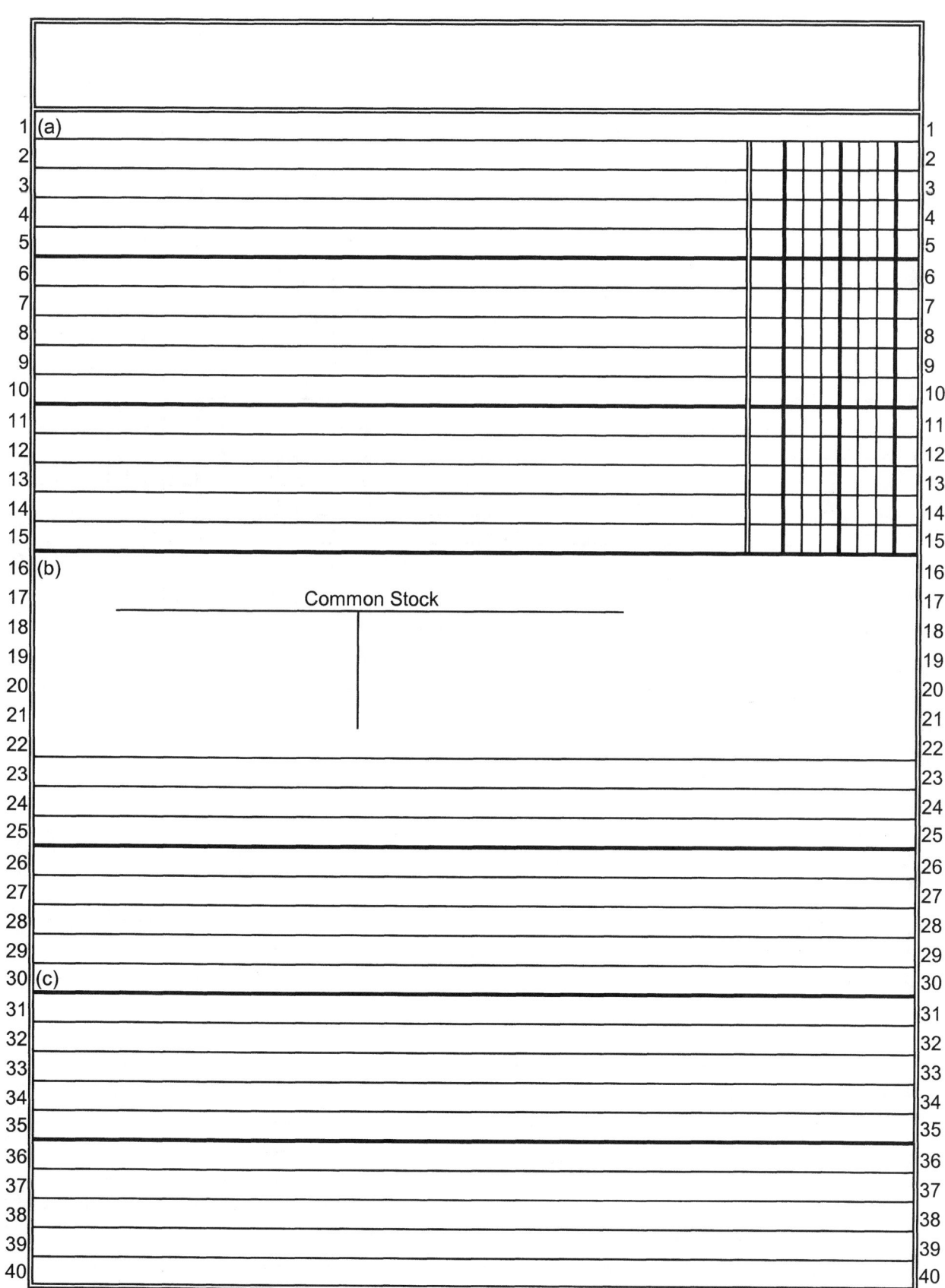

(a)

(b)

Common Stock

(c)

Indirect

Dillon Company
Partial Statement of Cash Flows
For the Year Ended November 30, 2011

1	Cash flows from operating activities	
2		
3		
4		
5		
6		
7		
8		
9		
10		
11		
12		
13		
14		
15		
16		
17		
18		
19		
20		
21		
22		
23		
24		
25		
26		
27		
28		
29		
30		
31		
32		
33		
34		
35		
36		
37		
38		
39		
40		

Direct

Dillon Company				
Partial Statement of Cash Flows				
For the Year Ended November 30, 2011				
1	Cash flows from operating activities				1
2					2
3					3
4					4
5					5
6					6
7					7
8					8
9	Computations-				9
10	(1) Cash receipts from customers:				10
11					11
12					12
13					13
14					14
15	(2) Cash payments to suppliers:				15
16					16
17					17
18					18
19					19
20					20
21					21
22	(3) Cash payments for operating expenses:				22
23					23
24					24
25					25
26					26
27					27
28					28
29					29
30					30
31					31
32					32
33					33
34					34
35					35
36					36
37					37
38					38
39					39
40					40

Indirect

Cotte Company				
Partial Statement of Cash Flows				
For the Year Ended December 31, 2011				

1	Cash flows from operating activities			
2				
3				
4				
5				
6				
7				
8				
9				
10				
11				
12				
13				
14				
15				
16				
17				
18				
19				
20				
21				
22				
23				
24				
25				
26				
27				
28				
29				
30				
31				
32				
33				
34				
35				
36				
37				
38				
39				
40				

Direct

Cotte Company				
Partial Statement of Cash Flows				
For the Year Ended December 31, 2011				
1 Cash flows from operating activities				
2				
3				
4				
5				
6				
7				
8 Computations-				
9 (1) Cash receipts from customers:				
10				
11				
12				
13				
14				
15 (2) Cash payments for operating expenses:				
16				
17				
18				
19				
20				
21				
22				
23 (3) Cash payments for income taxes:				
24				
25				
26				
27				
28				
29				
30				
31				
32				
33				
34				
35				
36				
37				
38				
39				
40				

Indirect

Cheaney Company Statement of Cash Flows For the Year Ended December 31, 2011		
1 Cash flows from operating activities		
2		
3		
4		
5		
6		
7		
8		
9		
10		
11		
12		
13		
14		
15		
16		
17		
18		
19		
20		
21		
22		
23		
24		
25		
26		
27		
28		
29		
30		
31		
32 (b) Free cash flow:		
33		
34		
35		
36		
37		
38		
39		
40		

(a)   Direct

Cheaney Company			
Statement of Cash Flows			
For the Year Ended December 31, 2011			

1	Cash flows from operating activities		
2			
3			
4			
5			
6			
7			
8			
9			
10			
11			
12			
13			
14			
15			
16			
17			
18			
19			
20			
21			
22			
23			
24			
25			
26			
27			
28			
29			
30	Computations:		
31	(1) Cash receipts from customers:		
32			
33			
34			
35			
36			
37			
38			
39			
40			

(a) (Continued)

	Cheaney Company					
	Statement of Cash Flows					
	For the Year Ended December 31, 2011					
1	Computations (continued):					
2	(2) Cash payments to suppliers:					
3						
4						
5						
6						
7						
8						
9						
10	(3) Cash payment for operating expenses:					
11						
12						
13						
14						
15						
16	(4) Cash payments for income taxes:					
17						
18						
19						
20						
21						

(b)

1	Free cash flow:	
2		
3		
4		
5		

Indirect

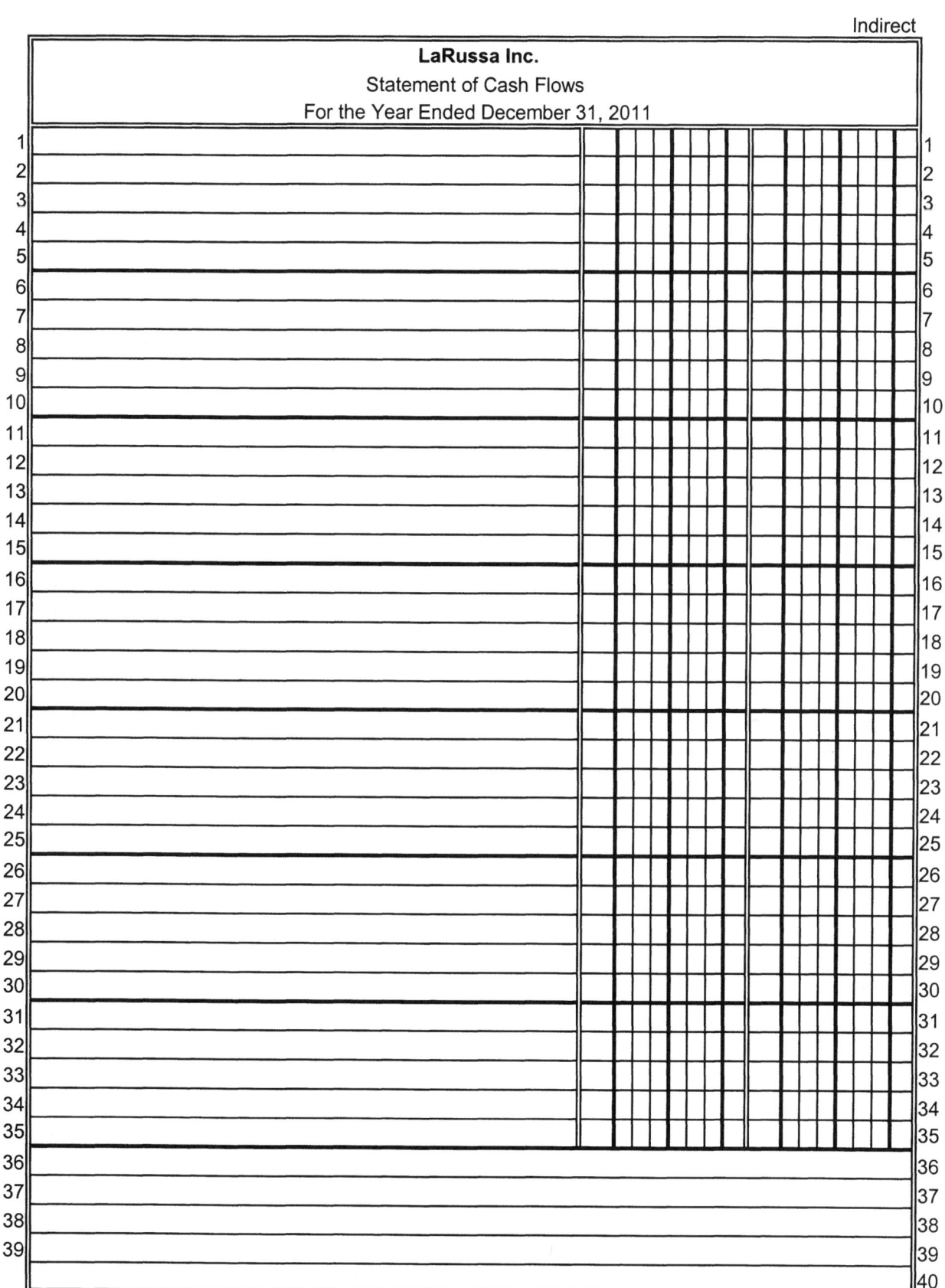

LaRussa Inc.			
Statement of Cash Flows			
For the Year Ended December 31, 2011			

Direct

LaRussa Inc. Statement of Cash Flows For the Year Ended December 31, 2011		
1		
2		
3		
4		
5		
6		
7		
8		
9		
10		
11		
12		
13		
14		
15		
16		
17		
18		
19		
20		
21		
22		
23		
24		
25		
26		
27		
28		
29		
30 Computations:		
31 (1) Cash receipts from customers:		
32		
33		
34		
35		
36		
37		
38		
39		
40		

LaRussa Inc.		
Statement of Cash Flows		
For the Year Ended December 31, 2011		
1	Computations (continued):	
2	(2) Cash payments to suppliers:	
3		
4		
5		
6		
7		
8		
9		
10	(3) Cash payment for operating expenses:	
11		
12		
13		
14		
15		
16		
17		
18		
19		
20		
21		

Indirect

Gould Company		
Statement of Cash Flows		
For the Year Ended December 31, 2011		

Biber Company
Worksheet - Statement of Cash Flows
For the Year Ended December 31, 2011

	Balance Sheet Accounts	Balance 12/31/10	Reconciling Items Debit	Reconciling Items Credit	Balance 12/31/11	
1	Debits					1
2	Cash	47250			92700	2
3	Accounts receivable	57000			90800	3
4	Inventories	102650			121900	4
5	Investments	87000			84500	5
6	Plant assets	205000			250000	6
7	Totals	498900			639900	7
8						8
9	Credits					9
10	Accum. Depr. - plant assets	40000			49500	10
11	Accounts payable	48280			57700	11
12	Accrued expenses payable	18830			12100	12
13	Bonds payable	70000			100000	13
14	Common stock	200000			250000	14
15	Retained Earnings	121790			170600	15
16	Totals	498900			639900	16
17						17
18	Stmt. of Cash Flows Effects					18
19						19
20						20
21						21
22						22
23						23
24						24
25						25
26						26
27						27
28						28
29						29
30						30
31						31
32						32
33						33
34						34
35						35
36						36
37						37
38						38

	(a)			
1	(a)			
2				
3				
4				
5				
6				
7				
8				
9				
10				
11				
12				
13				
14				
15				

Accumulated Depreciation - Equipment

Optional journal entries:

Account Titles	Debit	Credit

(b)	Cash Flow	Activity Classification-Inflow (Outflow)

Indirect

Marcessa Company					
Partial Statement of Cash Flows					
For the Year Ended December 31, 2011					
1	Cash flows from operating activities				1
2					2
3					3
4					4
5					5
6					6
7					7
8					8
9					9
10					10
11					11
12					12
13					13
14					14
15					15
16					16
17					17
18					18
19					19
20					20
21					21
22					22
23					23
24					24
25					25
26					26
27					27
28					28
29					29
30					30
31					31
32					32
33					33
34					34
35					35
36					36
37					37
38					38
39					39
40					40

Direct

Marcessa Company

Partial Statement of Cash Flows

For the Year Ended December 31, 2011

1	Cash flows from operating activities		
2			
3			
4			
5			
6			
7			
8			
9	Computations-		
10	(1) Cash receipts from customers:		
11			
12			
13			
14			
15	(2) Cash payments to suppliers:		
16			
17			
18			
19			
20			
21			
22	(3) Cash payments for operating expenses:		
23			
24			
25			
26			
27			
28			
29			
30			
31			
32			
33			
34			
35			
36			
37			
38			
39			
40			

Indirect

	Maxine Inc. Partial Statement of Cash Flows For the Year Ended December 31, 2011					
1	Cash flows from operating activities					1
2						2
3						3
4						4
5						5
6						6
7						7
8						8
9						9
10						10
11						11
12						12
13						13
14						14
15						15
16						16
17						17
18						18
19						19
20						20
21						21
22						22
23						23
24						24
25						25
26						26
27						27
28						28
29						29
30						30
31						31
32						32
33						33
34						34
35						35
36						36
37						37
38						38
39						39
40						40

Direct

Maxine Inc. Partial Statement of Cash Flows For the Year Ended December 31, 2011		
1	Cash flows from operating activities			1
2				2
3				3
4				4
5				5
6				6
7				7
8	Computations-			8
9	(1) Cash receipts from customers:			9
10				10
11				11
12				12
13				13
14				14
15	(2) Cash payments for operating expenses:			15
16				16
17				17
18				18
19				19
20				20
21				21
22				22
23	(3) Cash payments for income taxes:			23
24				24
25				25
26				26
27				27
28				28
29				29
30				30
31				31
32				32
33				33
34				34
35				35
36				36
37				37
38				38
39				39
40				40

(a)   Indirect

Tomas Company			
Statement of Cash Flows			
For the Year Ended December 31, 2011			

1 | Cash flows from operating activities

(b)   Free cash flow:

(a)   Direct

Tomas Company Statement of Cash Flows For the Year Ended December 31, 2011		
1 Cash flows from operating activities		
2		
3		
4		
5		
6		
7		
8		
9		
10		
11		
12		
13		
14		
15		
16		
17		
18		
19		
20		
21		
22		
23		
24		
25		
26		
27		
28		
29		
30 Computations:		
31 (1) Cash receipts from customers:		
32		
33		
34		
35		
36		
37		
38		
39		
40		

(a) (Continued)

	Tomas Company									
	Statement of Cash Flows									
	For the Year Ended December 31, 2011									
1	Computations (continued):									1
2	(2) Cash payments to suppliers:									2
3										3
4										4
5										5
6										6
7										7
8										8
9										9
10	(3) Cash payments for income taxes:									10
11										11
12										12
13										13
14										14
15										15
16										16
17										17
18										18
19										19
20										20
21										21

(b)

1	Free cash flow:	1
2		2
3		3
4		4
5		5

Indirect

	Armstrong Company
	Statement of Cash Flows
	For the Year Ended December 31, 2011

1									1
2									2
3									3
4									4
5									5
6									6
7									7
8									8
9									9
10									10
11									11
12									12
13									13
14									14
15									15
16									16
17									17
18									18
19									19
20									20
21									21
22									22
23									23
24									24
25									25
26									26
27									27
28									28
29									29
30									30
31									31
32									32
33									33
34									34
35									35
36									36
37									37
38									38
39									39
									40

Direct

	Armstrong Company		
	Statement of Cash Flows		
	For the Year Ended December 31, 2011		

1			
2			
3			
4			
5			
6			
7			
8			
9			
10			
11			
12			
13			
14			
15			
16			
17			
18			
19			
20			
21			
22			
23			
24			
25			
26			
27			
28			
29			
30	Computations:		
31	(1) Cash receipts from customers:		
32			
33			
34			
35			
36			
37			
38			
39			
40			

Armstrong Company								
Statement of Cash Flows								
For the Year Ended December 31, 2011								
1	Computations (continued):								1
2	(2) Cash payments to suppliers:								2
3									3
4									4
5									5
6									6
7									7
8									8
9									9
10	(3) Cash payment for operating expenses:								10
11									11
12									12
13									13
14									14
15									15
16									16
17									17
18									18
19									19
20									20
21									21

Indirect

Martin Company

Statement of Cash Flows

For the Year Ended December 31, 2011

	$ Amounts in millions	
	2008	2007
(a) Net cash provided by operating activities		
(b) Increase (decrease) in cash and cash equivalents		
(c)		
(d)		
(e)		
(f)		

	PepsiCo	Coca-Cola
1		
2 (a) Free cash flow (in millions):		
3		
4		
5		
6		
7		
8		
9		
10		
11		
12 (b)		
13		
14		
15		
16		
17		
18		
19		
20		
21		
22		
23		
24		
25		
26		
27		
28		
29		
30		
31		
32		
33		
34		
35		
36		
37		
38		
39		
40		

(a)   Indirect

Carpino Company
Statement of Cash Flows
For the Year Ended January 31, 2011

1		
2		
3		
4		
5		
6		
7		
8		
9		
10		
11		
12		
13		
14		
15		
16		
17		
18		
19		
20		
21		
22		
23		
24		
25		
26		
27		
28		
29		
30	Computation of net income (loss):	
31		
32		
33		
34		
35		
36		
37		
38		
39		
40		

(b)

1	1
2	2
3	3
4	4
5	5
6	6
7	7
8	8
9	9
10	10
11	11
12	12
13	13
14	14
15	15
16	16
17	17
18	18
19	19
20	20
21	21
22	22
23	23
24	24
25	25
26	26
27	27
28	28
29	29
30	30
31	31
32	32
33	33
34	34
35	35
36	36
37	37
38	38
39	39
40	40

BE14-3   Horizontal Analysis

		Dec. 31, 2012	Dec. 31, 2011	Increase or (Decrease)	
				Amount	Percentage
1	Accounts receivable				
2	Inventory				
3	Total assets				
4					

BE14-4   Vertical Analysis

		Dec. 31, 2012		Dec. 31, 2011	
		Amount	Percentage	Amount	Percentage
13	Accounts receivable				
14	Inventory				
15	Total assets				

BE14-5

		2012	2011	2010
25	Net income			

			Increase (Decrease)	
			Amount	Percentage
31	(a)	2010 - 2011		
32	(b)	2011 - 2012		

BE14-6

	2012	2011	Increase	
1				1
2 Net income	$ 585000		30%	2
3				3
4				4
5				5
6				6
7				7
8				8
9				9
10				10

BE14-7

11 **BE14-7**			11
12			12
13			13
14			14
15			15
16			16

BE14-8

	2012	2011	2010	
17 **BE14-8**				17
18 Sales	100.0	100.0	100.0	18
19 Cost of goods sold	59.2	62.4	64.5	19
20 Expenses	25.0	25.6	27.5	20
21				21
22				22
23				23
24				24
25				25
26				26

BE48-9

27 **BE48-9**		27
28 (a) Working capital		28
29		29
30		30
31		31
32		32
33 (b) Current ratio		33
34		34
35		35
36 (c) Acid-test ratio		36
37		37
38		38
39		39
40		40

BE14-14

Ming Corporation
Partial Income Statement

BE48-15

Reeves Corporation
Partial Income Statement

DO IT! 14-1

	Increase (Decrease) in 2012		Percent calculation	
	Amount	Percent		
1 Current assets				1
2 Plant assets				2
3 Total assets				3
4				4
5				5

DO IT! 14-3

Supply Corporation
Income Statement (Partial)

E14-1 Horizontal Analysis

Blevins Inc.
Condensed Balance Sheet
December 31,

		2012		2011	Increase or (Decrease) Amount	Percent	
1					Increase or (Decrease)		1
2	Assets	2012		2011	Amount	Percent	2
3	Current assets	$ 125000		$ 100000			3
4	Plant assets (net)	396000		330000			4
5	Total assets						5
6							6
7	Liabilities						7
8	Current liabilities	$ 91000		$ 70000			8
9	Long-term liabilities	133000		95000			9
10	Total liabilities						10
11							11
12	holders' Equity						12
13	Common stock, $1 par	161000		115000			13
14	Retained earnings	136000		150000			14
15	Total stockholders' equity						15
16	Total liabilities and						16
17	stockholders' equity						17
18							18
19							19

E14-2 Vertical Analysis

Gallup Corporation
Condensed Income Statement
For the Years Ended December 31,

		2012 Amount	Percent	2011 Amount	Percent	
24		2012		2011		24
25		Amount	Percent	Amount	Percent	25
26	Sales	$ 750000		$ 600000		26
27	Cost of goods sold	465000		390000		27
28	Gross profit					28
29	Selling expenses	120000		72000		29
30	Administrative expenses	60000		54000		30
31	Total operating expenses					31
32	Income before income taxes					32
33	Income tax expense	33000		24000		33
34	Net income					34
35						35
36						36
37						37
38						38
39						39
40						40

(a)   Horizontal Analysis

Conard Corporation

Comparative Balance Sheet

December 31,

		2012				2011			Increase (Decrease)	% Change from 2011	
1											1
2	Assets										2
3	Current assets	$	7 4 0 0 0		$	8 0 0 0 0					3
4	Property, plant, & equip. (net)		9 9 0 0 0			9 0 0 0 0					4
5	Intangibles		2 7 0 0 0			4 0 0 0 0					5
6	Total assets	$	2 0 0 0 0 0		$	2 1 0 0 0 0					6
7											7
8	Liabilities & Stockholders'										8
9	Equity										9
10	Current liabilities	$	4 2 0 0 0		$	4 8 0 0 0					10
11	Long-term liabilities		1 4 3 0 0 0			1 5 0 0 0 0					11
12	Stockholders' equity		1 5 0 0 0			1 2 0 0 0					12
13	Total liabilities and										13
14	stockholders' equity	$	2 0 0 0 0 0		$	2 1 0 0 0 0					14
15											15
16											16
17											17
18											18
19											19
20											20

(b)   Vertical Analysis

Conard Corporation

Condensed Balance Sheet

December 31, 2012

			Amount		Percent	
1	Assets					1
2	Current assets	$	7 4 0 0 0			2
3	Property, plant, and equipment (net)		9 9 0 0 0			3
4	Intangibles		2 7 0 0 0			4
5	Total assets	$	2 0 0 0 0 0			5
6						6
7	Stockholders' Equity					7
8	Current liabilities	$	4 2 0 0 0			8
9	Long-term liabilities		1 4 3 0 0 0			9
10	Stockholders' equity		1 5 0 0 0			10
11	Total liabilities and stockholders' equity	$	2 0 0 0 0 0			11
12						12
13						13
14						14
15						15

Hendi Corporation						
Condensed Income Statements						
For the Years Ended December 31,						
(a) Horizontal Analysis			Increase or (Decrease) During 2011			
	2012	2011	Amount	Percent		
Net sales	$ 600000	$ 500000				
Cost of goods sold	483000	420000				
Gross profit	117000	80000				
Operating expenses	57200	44000				
Net income	$ 59800	$ 36000				
(b) Vertical Analysis						
	2012			2011		
	Amount	Percent		Amount	Percent	
Net sales	$ 600000			$ 500000		
Cost of goods sold	483000			420000		
Gross profit	117000			80000		
Operating expenses	57200			44000		
Net income	$ 59800			$ 36000		

Exercise 14-6

Leach Incorporated

	Quick Assets +	Inventory +	Prepaid Expenses =	Total Current Assets	Total Current Liabilities	(a) Current Ratio	(b) Acid-test Ratio
1 Feb 1 Bal		$ 15000 0	$ 2000 0	$ 13000 00	$ 5000 00		
2							
3 Feb 3							
4							
5 Bal							
6							
7 Feb 7							
8							
9 Bal							
10							
11 Feb 11							
12							
13 Bal							
14							
15 Feb 14							
16							
17 Bal							
18							
19 Feb 18							
20							
21 Bal							
22							
23							

(a)

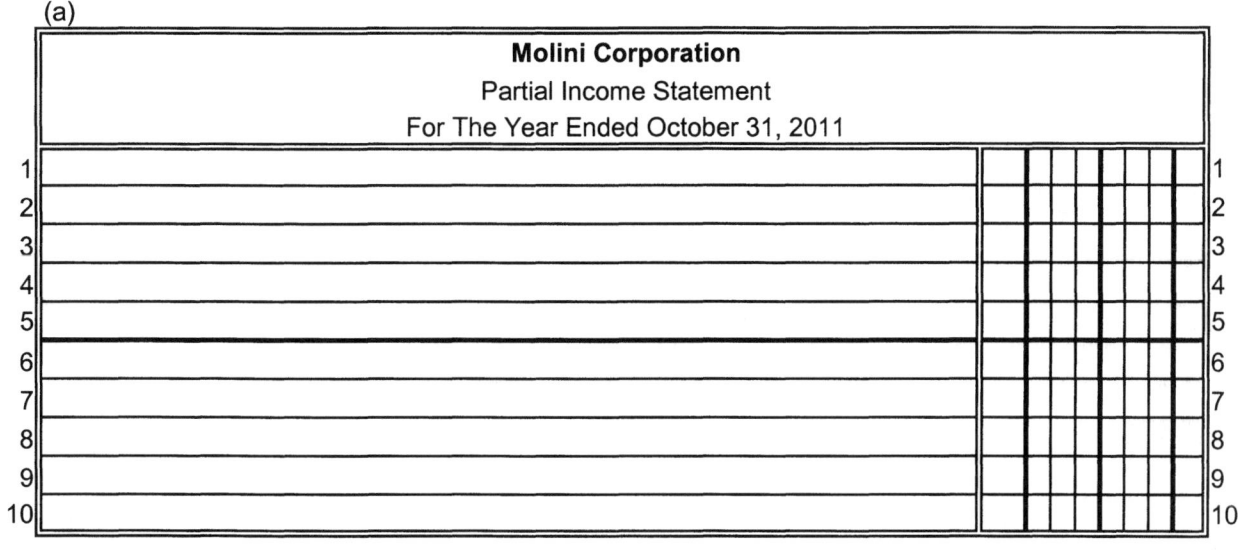

Molini Corporation

Partial Income Statement

For The Year Ended October 31, 2011

(b)

(a)

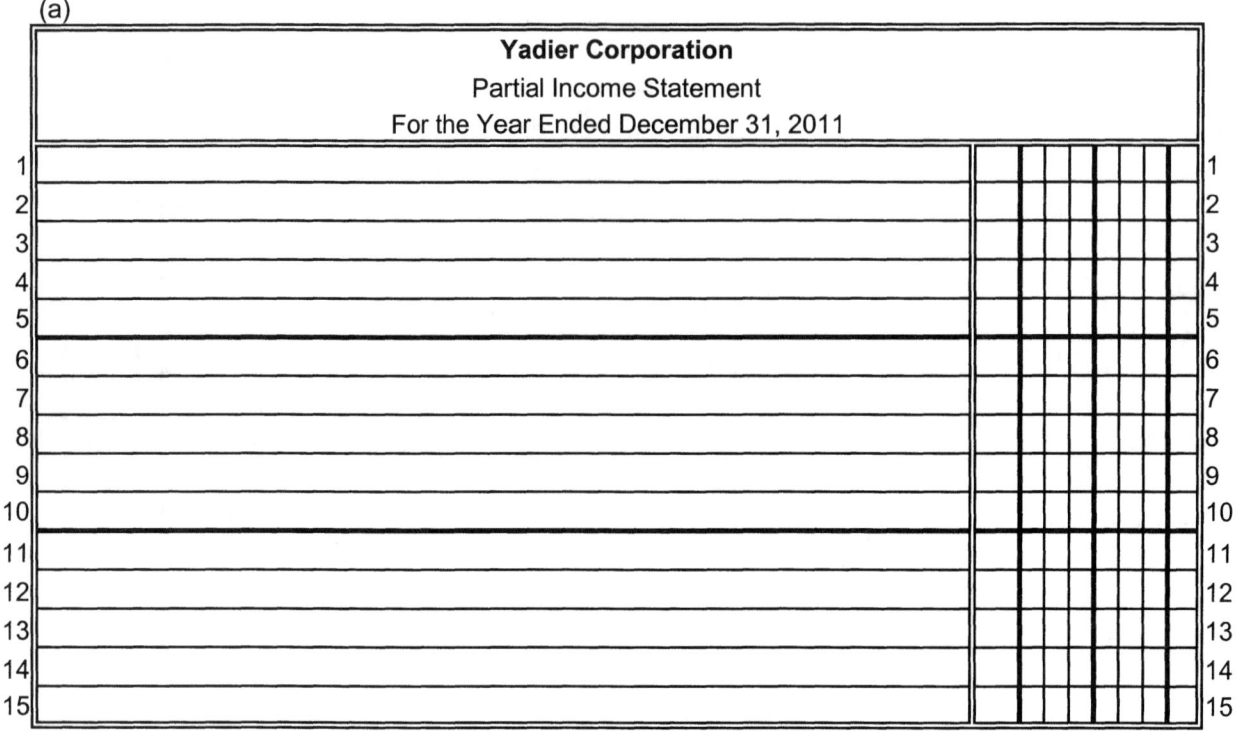

Yadier Corporation
Partial Income Statement
For the Year Ended December 31, 2011

(b)

(a)

	Condensed Income Statement For the Year Ended December 31, 2012	Douglas Company		Maulder Company		
		Dollars	Percent	Dollars	Percent	
1	Net sales	$1 549 035		339 038		1
2	Cost of goods sold	1 080 490		241 000		2
3	Gross profit					3
4	Operating expenses	302 275		79 000		4
5	Income from operations					5
6	Other expenses and losses					6
7	Interest expense	8 980		2 252		7
8	Income before income taxes					8
9	Income tax expense	54 500		6 650		9
10	Net income					10
11						11
12						12
13						13
14						14
15						15

(b)

1	1
2	2
3	3
4	4
5	5
6	6
7	7
8	8
9	9
10	10
11	11
12	12
13	13
14	14
15	15
16	16
17	17

(b) (Continued)

	1
1	1
2	2
3	3
4	4
5	5
6	6
7	7
8	8
9	9
10	10
11	11
12	12
13	13
14	14
15	15
16	16
17	17
18	18
19	19
20	20
21	21
22	22
23	23
24	24
25	25
26	26
27	27
28	28
29	29
30	30
31	31
32	32
33	33
34	34
35	35
36	36
37	37
38	38
39	39
40	40

Cheaney Corporation			
Condensed Income Statement			
For the Year Ended December 31, 2011			

	1																			1

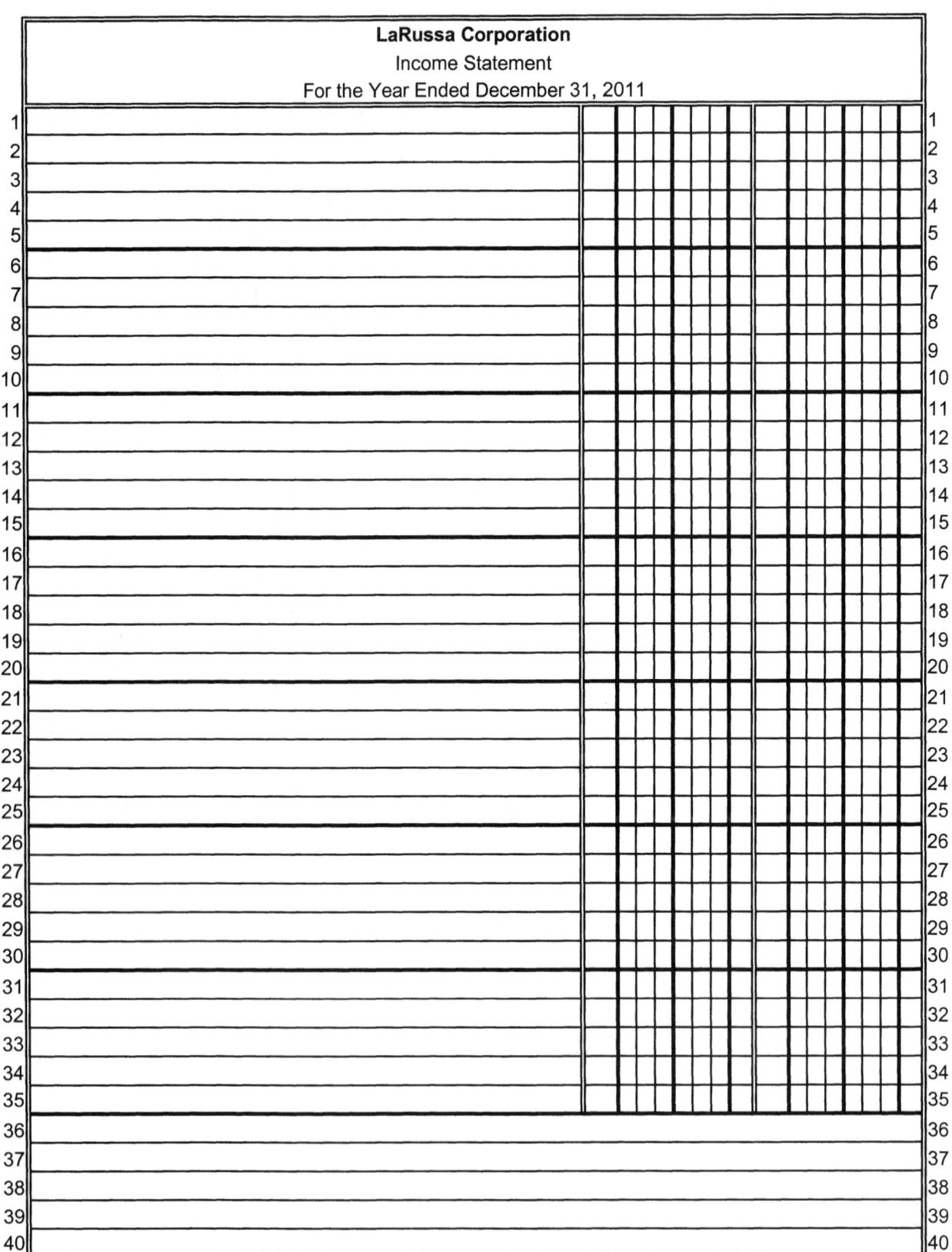

LaRussa Corporation

Income Statement

For the Year Ended December 31, 2011

(a)

PepsiCo, Inc.

Trend Analysis of Net Sales and Net Income

For the Five Years Ended 2008

Base Period 2004 - (in millions)	2008	2007	2006	2005	2004	
(1) Net sales						1
						2
Trend						3
						4
(2) Net income						5
						6
Trend						7
						8
Analysis:						9
						10
						11
						12

Name

Section

Date

PepsiCo, Inc.

(b)   (dollar amounts in millions)

PepsiCo, Inc.

2008 and 2007 Ratio Analysis: Profitability

	2008	2007
1 (1) Profit margin		
2		
3		
4		
5		
6 (2) Asset turnover		
7		
8		
9		
10		
11		
12 (3) Return on assets		
13		
14		
15		
16		
17		
18 (4) Return on common stockholders' equity		
19		
20		
21		
22		
23 Analysis:		
24		

(c)

(dollar amounts in millions)

PepsiCo, Inc.

2008 and 2007 Ratio Analysis: Solvency

	2008	2007
1 (1) Debt to total assets		
2		
5		
6		
7 (2) Times interest earned		
8		
9		
12		
13 Analysis:		
14		
15		

(d)

1	
2	
3	
4	
5	
6	
7	
8	

(a)

General Dynamics Corporation	
Income Statement	
For the Year Ended December 31, 2011	
	(In Millions of Dollars)
1	
2	
3	
4	
5	
6	
7	
8	
9	
10	
11	
12	
13	
14	
15	
16	
17	
18	
19	
20	
21	
22	
23	
24	
25	
26	
27	
28	
29	
30	

(b) (1)

(2)

BEA-1

	(a) Interest =				
	Accumulated amount =				
(b)		Invested Amount	6% PV Factor	Accumulated Amount	

BEA-3

		Deposit	FV Factor	Future Value

BEA-4

		Annual Deposit	FV Factor	Future Value

BEA-5

		Amount	FV Factor	Future Value
Initial deposit				
Annual deposit				
Total				

BEA-6

		Amount Borrowed	FV Factor	Future Value

BEA-8

		Amount	Discount Factor	Present Value	
1			Discount	Present	1
2	(a)	Amount	Factor	Value	2
3					3
4					4
5					5
6		Periodic	Discount	Present	6
7	(b)	Payments	Factor	Value	7
8					8
9					9
10					10

BEA-9

		Amount to be Received	Discount Factor	Present Value	
11		Amount to be	Discount	Present	11
12		Received	Factor	Value	12
13					13
14					14
15					15

BEA-10

		Amount to be Received	Discount Factor	Present Value	
16		Amount to be	Discount	Present	16
17		Received	Factor	Value	17
18					18
19					19
20					20

BEA-11

		Annual Return	Discount Factor	Present Value	
21		Annual	Discount	Present	21
22		Return	Factor	Value	22
23					23
24					24
25					25

BEA-12

		Annual Return	Discount Factor	Present Value	
26		Annual	Discount	Present	26
27		Return	Factor	Value	27
28					28
29					29
30					30
31					31
32					32
33					33
34					34
35					35
36					36
37					37
38					38
39					39
40					40

BEA-13

	Amount	Discount Factor	Present Value
1 Principal to be received at maturity			
2 Periodic interest			
3 Present value of bonds			
4			
5			

BEA-14

	Amount	Discount Factor	Present Value
8 Principal to be received at maturity			
9 Periodic interest			
10 Present value of bonds			
11			
12			

BEA-15

	Amount	Discount Factor	Present Value
15 Principal to be received at maturity			
16 Periodic interest			
17 Present value of note			
18			
19			

BEA-16

	Amount	Discount Factor	Present Value
22 Principal to be received at maturity			
23 Periodic interest			
24 Present value of bonds			
25			
26			

BEA-17

	Amount	Discount Factor	Present Value
29 Annual net cash flow			
30			
31			
32 Decision:			

BEA-18		Amount	Discount Factor	Present Value	
1 Semi-annual installment payments					1
2					2
3					3
4					4

BEA-19	Year	Cash Flows	Discount Factor	Present Value	
5					5
6					6
7	1				7
8	2				8
9	3				9
10	Total				10
11					11